Developing Trust: Online Privacy and Security

MATT CURTIN

Apress™

Developing Trust: Online Privacy and Security
Copyright ©2002 by Matt Curtin

ISBN (pbk): 1-893115-72-0

Printed and bound in the United States of America 12345678910

Trademarked names may appear in this book. Rather than use a trademark symbol with every occurrence of a trademarked name, we use the names only in an editorial fashion and to the benefit of the trademark owner, with no intention of infringement of the trademark.

Editorial Directors: Dan Appleman, Gary Cornell, Jason Gilmore, Karen Watterson

Technical Reviewer: Gary Ellison

Project Managers: Erin Mulligan, Alexa Stuart

Developmental Editor and Copyeditor: Kim Goodfriend

Compositor: David Kramer

Artist: Charles Bowen

Indexer: Ann Rogers

Marketing Manager: Stephanie Rodriguez

Cover Designer: Tom Debolski

Distributed to the book trade in the United States by Springer-Verlag New York, Inc.,175 Fifth Avenue, New York, NY, 10010 and outside the United States by Springer-Verlag GmbH & Co. KG, Tiergartenstr. 17, 69112 Heidelberg, Germany

In the United States, phone 1-800-SPRINGER; orders@springer-ny.com; http://www.springer-ny.com Outside the United States, contact orders@springer.de; http://www.springer.de; fax +49 6221 345229

For information on translations, please contact Apress directly at 901 Grayson Street, Suite 204, Berkeley, CA, 94710

Phone: 510-549-5930; Fax: 510-549-5939; info@apress.com; http://www.apress.com

The source code for this book is available to readers at http://www.apress.com in the Downloads section. You will need to answer questions pertaining to this book in order to download the code successfully.

To my family, for their love and support

Brief Contents

Contents

List of Figures

List of Tables

Foreword

THE PROBLEMS OF COMPUTER SECURITY are complex and inherently open-ended. There have been some significant advances in the research community, but many of these have been largely ignored in commercial systems that attempt to enforce security.

The problems of privacy are also inherently open-ended. They are seriously complicated by the limitations of the generally inadequate security of our information systems, but are also complicated by the realities of human behavior. Many privacy violations occur outside of the information systems in which data is stored. Those violations are in some cases catalyzed by misuse of data by trusted insiders, and in other cases arise as a result of system security inadequacies that allow system penetrations and information leakage. The intrinsic privacy problems can benefit significantly from system and network security, whereas the extrinsic privacy problems are much less tractably confronted by technological means.

Many people believe that they have nothing to hide, and that privacy is therefore less important to them. However, the burgeoning threat of identity theft is just one example of how the implications of privacy are rapidly changing. Ubiquitous monitoring and surveillance are other threats that must be recognized, as are large-scale data mining and aggregation. Anonymity presents further threats (such as bogus identities that create opportunities for character assassination and other affronts), although it also has important benefits.

Overall, providing adequate security and attaining sufficient privacy are both highly multidimensional problems, and are closely linked to each other. Security and privacy are both ultimately limited by people—designers, developers, users, system and database administrators, teachers, government employees, and so on. The educational needs are enormous.

Matt Curtin's book represents an important step in the process of helping system and application developers to understand the technological approaches and their limitations. This book is by no means the final answer, and must not be read with that expectation—because there are no easy answers. However, if you read and understand this book, you will have made a major step toward being able to design, implement, operate, maintain, and manage privacy-respectful enterprises with far fewer risks than would be the case otherwise.

Peter G. Neumann
Principal Scientist, Computer Science Lab
SRI International, Menlo Park CA 94025
Author of *Computer-Related Risks*, Moderator of the ACM Risks Forum
(http://www.csl.sri.com/neumann)
15 October 2001

Preface

IF YOU HAVE ANY ROLE in building, deploying, or operating computer systems, you need to understand privacy and security. Whether you're a programmer, a Web designer, a network engineer, or a technical manager, you need to concern yourself with the matter of trust, specifically, whether your customers can trust the systems you provide for them. Privacy and security aren't arcane areas of computer science anymore. If your users cannot trust your systems, your users will eventually stop using your systems.

This book was written to help you develop systems that people can trust. A subtle but important point can be found here: the problems that we address in this book aren't just technical problems. They're not about computers misbehaving. Our computer systems are used by people just like you and me. Users of these systems have families. They have concerns. They have plans. They have information that they consider private.

If people cannot trust systems we provide for their use, they'll tend not to use them to their full potential. If we want our systems to succeed—not just in terms of market penetration, but in terms of real and substantial changes in the way that people live, work, and play—we must encourage people to make the most of what we're offering. If we want our systems to succeed, we must make them worthy of trust.

As the 21st century gets underway, security in computer systems is all the rage. Computer security vendors offer every product and service imaginable. Each year, security-related purchases increase. Yet, every year we're seeing more failures, and the cost of such failures continues to rise.

We're clearly doing something wrong, but we need not abandon all hope.

Perhaps instead of increasing budgets to train our overworked systems developers in the latest products and techniques for providing security, we should step back to take a larger view of the big picture. When seeing the larger picture, we can view our problems from a different—wider—perspective.

This book was written with a specific goal of providing perspective. In identifying the target audience, I have also taken a wider view. The rise of the Web has dramatically changed the landscape of our system development staff. Rather than being made up of focused programmers with degrees in computer science or electrical engineering, trying to get software to behave on a particular system, our development teams now often include graphic designers, text markup folks, and many others with completely different backgrounds.

A problem that now faces us is a sometimes tremendous gap between the literature of computer science and the developers of our computer systems.

Our literature can help us to understand many of the problems that we're now facing and can provide us the insight we need to battle the problems of security and privacy successfully. Often, solutions are within our grasp, if we dare to see things from a broader perspective and to make applications of lessons learned in other contexts.

It is my hope that this book will serve to stimulate thinking, to encourage a greater interest in the research literature, and to promote the development of systems that we'll be proud to say we built, not just today, but decades from now.

Acknowledgments

I am deeply indebted to my predecessors in computer science, the many engineers and scientists who have developed systems and who have written about what they have learned. Their papers, books, and presentations have helped us to understand the problems we face in computing and how to find solutions. I hope this book is worthy of being counted in this tradition. The Usenet community welcomed me as a teenager, and many Usenet participants have helped stimulate the kind of critical thinking that would later help me formulate the basis of this book.

More specifically, I would like to thank everyone at Apress who helped make this book a reality. Without Jason Gilmore's initial query, I would not have had the privilege of working with a world class team of publishing professionals. Kim "How about a transition?" Goodfriend and Erin "IMPORTANT—Updated Curtin Schedule" Mulligan were especially helpful in making sure that the book actually got finished.

My colleague and friend Gary Ellison provided excellent technical review of this book. Gary and the rest of the posse—including Jim Hoburg, Brian Larkins, and Doug Monroe—have long kept me thinking about these problems and have provided much in the way of thoughtfood.

Cartoon illustrations were provided by my grandfather, Charles Bowen. I'm very happy to have worked with him on this project.

Finally, I wish to thank my wife Nicole for her tireless support, thoughtful remarks, and endless forbearance. I can only hope that I make life as interesting for her as she makes it for me.

Introduction

THIS TEXT IS A *HANDS-ON* discussion. It assumes that readers are looking for something that they'll be able to put into practice quickly.

Marginal notes will be used for asides and to highlight relevant quotes from others.

When we talk about *developers*, we're going to be using the term loosely, so that it can include anyone involved in any stage of design or implementation for these systems. When we talk about *operators*, we're talking about anyone with any role in the operation of a system. As for *systems*, well, that could mean a web site, a network-aware piece of software, or any type of device that uses a network to talk to other systems.

Issues that we discuss here will be relevant for all of these audiences.

Because privacy can be compromised quite by accident and can have ramifications that are so far-reaching into the business behind the technology, a strong case can be made against limiting one's view. Privacy—like all aspects of data security—is *everyone's* business and is only as good as the weakest link in the chain. As such, irrespective of what role you play in the organization, it's *your* job to understand what privacy is and what aspects fall under your responsibility.

We're not going to shrink back from jumping into the technology, but we're always going to do so without forgetting the big picture. Indeed, much of what we're discussing when it comes to privacy, particularly privacy problems, has to do with how things interact.

We'll open with a discussion of privacy and security theory, so we know just what we're talking about when we use terms like *anonymous*. This isn't just a book for pipe-smoking theorists, though. We'll move on from theory right into practice.

In the first discussion of practice, we'll talk about the problems that are present today, the problems that are hindering our ability to make the Internet everything we'd like it to be. We'll discuss secure design principles, particularly as they apply to Internet development, talk about the Internet as a deployment environment, and then take a look at several systems that were actually deployed on the Internet.

From there, we'll move to a discussion of solutions, The Cure for all of the trouble we caused in The Problem.

Whether you consider yourself security-savvy or not, whether you consider yourself technical or not, security (and particularly privacy) is now your concern. It doesn't necessarily follow that you're stuck behind the eight ball, however. With the right frame of mind and the right tools, you can arm yourself and bring the quagmire under your control.

Vernacular

*Never express
yourself more
clearly than
you think.*

—*Niels Bohr*

Our discussion is going to deal with some technical issues, so we're going to use some technical language. This isn't to introduce more abbreviations into the discussion, but is to improve clarity.

New terms will be explained as they're introduced.

A Few Friends

Discussions of computer security, especially cryptography, often enlist the help of a few friends to clarify explanations of protocols and scenarios. This book is no exception. I have drafted three of the usual suspects. If you're not familiar with our gang of actors, let me now introduce you.

The first actor in any system is *Alice*, which is much nicer than something like "person A." *Bob* is the second actor. Alice and Bob have a long history together. They'll go through quite a bit more together in this book. *Mallory* is our third actor, a malicious user.

About the Author

As the founder of Interhack Corporation, Matt Curtin is responsible for the technical leadership of Interhack's research, development, and consulting efforts. His present focus is to understand how complex systems interact "in the large" and how that affects security, privacy, and reliability. A frequent lecturer and author, Matt also tries to help developers understand how they can avoid the mistakes that undermine the trustworthiness of the systems on which we depend. His team at Interhack helps system managers and information technology directors make their systems trustworthy.

Matt also teaches Programming in Common Lisp and Operating Systems Laboratory at The Ohio State University's Department of Computer and Information Science, where he enjoys turning the brains of his students inside-out and helping them to find the path to Enlightenment. He is a member of the USENIX Association, IEEE Computer Society, and the Association for Computing Machinery.

When not working or writing about himself in the third person, he can be found reading just about any book he can get his hands on, studying the Russian language, music, literature, physics, mathematics, or history. Matt is both a student and a teacher of Life.

About the Technical Reviewer

As a Visiting Fellow at Interhack, Gary Ellison is a key member of Interhack's Internet Privacy Project, studying data security and privacy issues on the Internet and in Internet-connected applications. Numerous technical reports have been issued on various findings from the project, ranging from failure of opt-out systems to discussion of the privacy implications of myopic design in the large.

Within the Java Software Division of Sun Microsystems, Gary is the Java Security Architect for Java 2 Standard Edition (J2SE). Gary is also responsible for the architecture and design of the other security components of J2SE, including Java Authorization and Authentication (JAAS), Java Cryptography Extension (JCE), and Java Secure Socket Extension (JSSE). Due to the interdependencies of security and networking. Gary participates in the architecture of the networking infrastructure within J2SE.

Prior to joining Sun, Gary was in the Internet Services Group at AT&T Laboratories and Bell Laboratories. He was the lead engineer responsible for security, architecture, deployment, and implementation of AT&T's corporate web server and extranet services.

Part I

Understanding
Security and Privacy

CHAPTER 1

Why Privacy,
Why This Book

AS THE WORLD BECOMES INCREASINGLY wired, the issue of privacy becomes more and more important. Privacy has been hotly debated from all sides in the past few years and there is no indication as of this writing that the privacy debate will subside. How and if it will be resolved is anyone's guess.

What is clear, however, is that the topic is hot and that you, as a designer, implementor, or operator of any network-aware technology, must address it. Is posting a "privacy policy" sufficient to keep you out of the hot seat? What if the policy is violated? How could a violation of your privacy policy occur? What can you do to prevent violations from happening in the first place?

And while we're at it, what is privacy, anyway? What is a violation of privacy? Ask an online marketer and you'll get a definition that's very different from the answer you get from a civil libertarian. Why is that? What definitions for privacy have been used? What does privacy mean in the context of information science?

Our discussion of privacy will consider these questions and will help us to understand why privacy is a necessary first step in the quest to achieve security in computer systems.

Privacy as an Aspect of Data Security

Computer and information science literature is fairly rich with security theory and practice. Sadly, there's a wide gulf between theory and practice. There are many reasons for this, not the least of which being that there's a widespread feeling that security "gets in the way" of productive work, that money spent on security could be better spent on adding more features, and that security is just "too hard." Every year, thousands of new computing professionals are released from universities and unleashed on the workforce without having had any serious consideration of security in their studies.

The history of our increasing dependence on technology, particularly in the Internet context, tells an ironic tale of "progress at any cost," where the price we pay for progress is often *regression* in such basic areas as reliability and security. Before you laugh, consider for example whether the operating system that's running your computer implements half of the safety features found in the Multics operating system from 1965 [97, 195]. Virtually no modern operating systems support many useful security and privacy features first implemented three and a half decades ago.

Consider also the kinds of mistakes that we're making. The 1988 Internet worm propagated itself largely by overflowing an input buffer on remote machines. Taking advantage of the buffer overrun, the worm would exploit the ability to execute instructions on the remote machine and copy itself to the new target [56, 174, 180].

Up to this point, hardly anyone had heard of the Internet; it was still the playground of scientists. Everyone on the network pretty much trusted everyone else on the network. Security was something that people thought out, but security wasn't exactly the highest priority in the Internet community, which was all about building connections and enabling communication rather than placing limits on it. The Internet worm was not intended to be destructive; its only purpose was to propagate itself. However, a critical mistake in its design caused it to crash systems some time after the infection. So widespread was the worm that it effectively shut down the Internet, demonstrating the network's vulnerability to attack. Almost immediately thereafter, the Computer Emergency Response Center (CERT) was formed as a means of providing a central point for addressing security issues and for collecting information about Internet security incidents [31].[1]

In 1999, more than half of the CERT advisories issued were about buffer overflow problems. After 11 years, hundreds of papers and advisories, thousands of vulnerabilities exploited, and millions of dollars lost, we're making the same mistakes. Because of increased dependency on and greater acceptance of these systems, the effects of these mistakes are more far-reaching and their costs are much greater.

Even standing still—neither progressing nor regressing—in a society where we give more responsibilities to these systems is effectively a step backwards.

Anatomy of an Attack

Understanding how to protect against attacks necessarily involves understanding how attacks work. That is, we need to know how attackers see our systems if we're going to be able to build them in such a way that they will be able to resist attacks.

Attacks—whether computer-based or in the real world—generally have four main states. Naturally, the specifics of what happens in these states will vary depending on the technology involved, but the principles here are applicable across technologies.

Reconnaissance is the collection of information about the target. Learning as much as possible about the target is important because it might reveal something obvious, something relatively easy. At the very least, it will give an indication of where the system designers have paid attention to security, thus showing the attacker where not to start poking around. An attacker will never want to spend more time or effort than necessary to compromise a system, so reconnaissance data will help the attacker narrow his scope.

Analysis of the data gathered will make the reconnaissance data usable for the next stages of the attack. This involves sifting through potentially huge numbers of facts, rumors, or tips, and categorizing the data. It is this stage where potential weaknesses and vulnerabilities will be identified.

Planning involves the formulation of the attack itself. Armed with the knowledge of what classifications of attack are most likely, a detailed plan can be constructed involving which attacks will be tried, how the attacks should affect the target, and what new avenues of attack might be enabled if the attack is successful.

---

[1] The center is now known simply as CERT, which is no longer an abbreviation for anything, just as companies like AT&T and SGI have adopted their initials in favor of their full names.

Execution is simply following the plan. The best attacks are swift and efficient, taking little time and leaving few tracks. In general, if the plan is good, the execution phase should be a simple case of following a decision tree until all of the options are exhausted or until the objective has been accomplished, and then getting out of the system before anyone notices.

An Example Attack

To see what it's like to look at a system "from the other side," we're going to assume the perspective of an attacker. So take off your tie, pretend it's 12 hours later than it is,[2] and check to see that you're wearing your black hat. Time to be the bad guy.

Your assignment is to attack Example Systems, Inc.[3] It's rumored that Example Systems has a large credit card database. Because Example Systems advertises a payment processing service for electronic commerce sites, the rumor seems plausible.

Credit card databases are good targets, because there are so many options available to you once you have them. They can be sold in groups on the black market and they can even be used to blackmail the vendor. If you're creative or don't mind doing a little more work, you can make the databases even more valuable, perhaps by combining the credit card data with information from other sources that would make the cardholders good targets for identity theft. At the very least, you can publish the list or a part of it and get your handle splattered all over the newspapers of the world while they report the break-in, which will give you status among your peers in the black hat community.

We're going to gloss over some details of the attack in this section so that we can focus on the *process* of moving from state to state through the attack and how each step will build on the previous one.

Recon

The first order of business is to find out exactly what we have and to assess what kinds of weaknesses might be present. By searching accessible directories like DNS and WHOIS, we discover that a particular network belongs to Example Systems. They (hopefully) won't just give us their credit card database because we want it; we're going to need to find out in what ways we might be able to fool them.

---

[2]   Of course, this admonition doesn't apply if you're reading this after midnight.
[3]   This section is a work of fiction; any similarities to entities whether living or dead are merely a coincidence.

Let's first take a look at the Example Systems network. Let's see how many machines are running, what software is running on those machines, and whatever else we can find in the process.

With the use of a scanning tool like nmap [72], we can find out what's out there. Table 1-1 shows the results of our probes.

Table 1-1. Example Systems Network Scan Results

Address	Available Ports
192.168.1.65	23/tcp
192.168.1.66	7/tcp, 9/tcp, 13/tcp, 19/tcp, 21/tcp, 22/tcp, 23/tcp, 25/tcp, 26/tcp, 37/tcp, 53/tcp, 79/tcp, 80/tcp, 110/tcp, 111/tcp, 119/tcp, 194/tcp, 512/tcp, 513/tcp, 514/tcp, 515/tcp, 540/tcp, 2000/tcp, 8080/tcp, 8888/tcp
192.168.1.67	7/tcp, 9/tcp, 13/tcp, 19/tcp, 21/tcp, 23/tcp, 37/tcp, 79/tcp, 111/tcp, 512/tcp, 513/tcp, 514/tcp, 515/tcp, 2049/tcp, 2766/tcp, 4045/tcp, 6000/tcp, 6112/tcp, 7100/tcp, 10005/tcp, 32771/tcp, 32772/tcp, 32773/tcp, 32774/tcp, 32775/tcp, 32776/tcp, 32777/tcp
192.168.1.84	139/tcp
192.168.1.85	80/tcp

Scanners can vary widely in implementation, but all basically have the same goal: to find out how many hosts are on the network and to see what those hosts are running. This is basically the electronic equivalent of running up to every house you can find, twisting the doorknob, and keeping track of the ones that aren't locked.

Analysis

So now we have a little bit of information that might help us to understand what the network looks like and what kinds of target options we might have available. In addition to being able to report which ports are available, nmap performs a few other tests, including how difficult it is to predict the target's TCP sequence numbers and what operating system the host is most likely running [73].

When we move beyond the collection of raw data and into the use of those data, we move out of collection and into analysis. Thus, nmap doesn't just perform raw data collection, it also performs some analysis for us. The results of nmap's automated analysis can be seen in Table 1-2.

Looking at the automated analysis of the data on the level of each host, we can begin to analyze the network. If we step back, we will start to see a picture of the network emerging. We see a switch or a router, and several hosts, running a variety of operating systems. Now we can begin to infer things about what roles are played by different machines. For example, the Mac is probably a client, likely one used for content creation and/or browser testing. The Windows machine is probably in the same general classification as the Mac: a client machine. FreeBSD could be used either as a desktop or as a server. The Solaris machine here is very likely the largest, most reliable system, and probably where the most important work is done.

Table 1-2. Analysis of Host Network Traffic Responses

Address	TCP Sequence Prediction	Operating System
192.168.1.65	Class = trivial time dependency Difficulty = 0 (Trivial joke)	Cisco Catalyst 1900 switch or Netopia DSL/ISDN router or Bay 450
192.168.1.66	Class = 64K rule Difficulty = 1 (Trivial joke)	FreeBSD 2.1.0–2.1.5
192.168.1.67	Class = random positive increments Difficulty = 21167 (Worthy challenge)	Solaris 2.5, 2.5.1
192.168.1.84	Class = trivial time dependency Difficulty = 0 (Trivial joke)	Windows NT4 / Win95 / Win98
192.168.1.85	Class = random positive increments Difficulty = 4167 (Formidable)	MacOS 9 on a Power Macintosh 7200/75

Let's return to the scan results in Table 1-1. In the Available Ports column, we can see what ports the machine offers to the network. Because these ports are typically indicative of what services are being offered, we can guess with pretty high accuracy when a machine is a web server, a file server, a desktop machine, or something else. Now we can correlate what we know about the operating system with the list of services offered in order to adjust the certainty of each of our guesses. Table 1-3 shows what we've managed to learn so far.

We're throwing a lot of pretty technical terminology around here, so let's be sure that we understand exactly what we're talking about and why these things are even relevant.

Recon has shown us which systems are available, what each system's operational environment is, and which services each host is offering. Each

Table 1-3. Initial Map of Example Network

Host	What We Know About It
192.168.1.65	Switch or a router, accessible by Telnet.
192.168.1.66	A really old FreeBSD machine running lots of things including mail, Telnet, FTP, HTTP, and something at 8080.
192.168.1.67	Solaris, with many ports open, but not mail or web.
192.168.1.84	Windows, only running a NetBIOS service.
192.168.1.85	MacOS, only running a web server.

combination of environment and service has the potential to fail. Failure is important to security.

Our analysis is focusing specifically on security, so we need to give special consideration to failures. As we walk through each of the available services for each host, we need to consider what risks there are and what problems might be exploitable. The very first thing to do is to see if someone else has found an answer to the question.

- Vendor bulletins and their security patches. Sources for this kind of security information are myriad.

- Security advisories from groups like CERT [30], CIAC [34], SANS [169], and NIPC [141].

- Vulnerability databases—both commercial and free-access databases—can be found online.

- Security mailing lists, including perhaps the best known of all, Bugtraq [29].

- Other sources, such as Usenet, IRC, or anywhere else that people can be found talking about security.

Forgetting about vendors' bulletins is easy. I even forgot to include it in the list in the first draft.

Obviously, some sources are better than others. There is no substitute for spending some time in the field and learning directly which sources work best for your particular interests.

What we're describing here isn't rocket science. This relatively simple comparison of environment and service with known vulnerabilities often reaps a large harvest, simply because people do not keep their systems up to date. Failure to keep systems up to date is also a problem that can affect vendors who use their own software. Microsoft's own Windows Update site was compromised with the 2001 Code Red Internet worm [117].

Even when we're looking at a network without vulnerabilities to known problems, this view is important. Our knowledge of things like the environment or the service will help us to understand quickly which avenues of attack are more feasible than others, allowing us to spend our time "productively," looking for vulnerabilities where they're most likely found.

Services that aren't available simply can't be attacked.

The services that are available also tend to suggest things about the network architecture, which hosts are clients, which are servers, and which roles various server machines play. From these points, we can begin to build hypotheses about where trust relationships might exist, so that if we can't break the target, we might be able to attack a weaker host that is trusted by the target. If we can compromise a host that our target trusts, we can typically get to the same result with only one additional layer of indirection.

Why should we care what operating systems various hosts on the target network are running? This will provide hints about what roles are played by various machines (e.g., if you have a Windows machine and a Solaris machine on the network, it's probably pretty safe to work with the assumption that Solaris is the server).

Knowing the operating system will also help us to understand what classes of attacks will be most likely to be successful against the target host. Rather than running through thousands of attacks, trying each one until we find something that works, we can throw out entire groups of attack that will obviously not work on the target. Additionally, this will help us to understand what we're likely to be able to get the machine to do if we are able to compromise it. If, for example, it's an NT machine that we're attacking, we're not going to want to try to use some trick for running commands that will only work in *bash* for Unix systems.

Planning

Now that we have an idea of what we're dealing with, we can put together some kind of plan. What we've done is performed the recon and analysis work against a specific target: Example Systems. Now we need to turn that into the plan of action.

Here's what we know so far:

- We know our target hosts.

- Attacks against Windows, MacOS, FreeBSD, and Solaris will work on various hosts.

- There's a machine that seems to be the web and mail server.

- Another machine—a larger one—is probably something like a database server and might be where we really want to focus our attack.

- There are client machines on the network as well, and they might make good stepping stones for us if we can't break directly into the larger machine that we think is the database server.

Also, note what has happened during the course of finding and analyzing the data we have gathered:

- We have narrowed the number of possible machines involved from over four billion[4] to about a half-dozen.

- We have narrowed the number of avenues of attack against services on each host from over 130,000 per host (65,535 TCP ports and just as many UDP ports, plus additional protocols that don't use ports, such as ICMP) to one or two on some hosts, and perhaps two dozen on others.

- We can eliminate literally thousands and thousands of known attacks from our list of possibilities based on the combination of operating systems and available ports. We're not going to try every known Windows exploit against the FreeBSD machine, for example.

Put another way, we've been able to make an impossible-to-manage number of possibilities turn into a comparatively tiny number of possibilities. Instead of trying millions of attacks against billions of hosts, we're dealing with dozens of attacks against a half-dozen hosts. Directing a few dozen attacks against a half-dozen hosts isn't difficult to turn into a real plan of action. Following such a plan is quick and easy. We can even script it.

Execution

In general, the process of execution will vary for different classifications of attackers. Script kiddies are just going to run a program that will run through the known exploits, trying them and moving on if one wasn't found. Script kiddies are the idiots trying to *winnuke* your BSD Unix machines.

At the other end of the spectrum of attackers we find dedicated, knowledge-able attackers, the types who will work for intelligence agencies or be funded to perpetrate corporate espionage. These attackers will tend to use the execution process to gather still more information, which will naturally lead to more analysis, more plans, and more attacks. They are also the ones that get more dangerous with every minute they're on your system.

For the purpose of our discussion, this is all we really need to know about execution.

---

[4] IPv4 has a 32-bit address space. Theoretically, then, the number of hosts on the Internet would be 2^{32}, or over four billion. In practice, it isn't quite so high, because of large blocks of network space that have been reserved for each host's loopback network (127.0.0.0/8) and "private" networks [165]. Even so, we're still talking about roughly four billion hosts.

Wondering When We'll Talk Privacy?

The example attack we just considered is significant in the discussion of privacy because the attack would have been ridiculously difficult to execute by brute force. With some knowledge of the target, however, we were able to turn the plan of attack into a straightforward proposition.

Most system managers will not tell the world what systems they're running, what versions they're running, when the last time they patched their systems was, etc. Why not? It's a matter of privacy—why give a potential attacker more information about your infrastructure? After all, he's probably just going to use it against you.

Nevertheless, in our example, we were able to take an unknown network and to construct an easy-to-manage, efficient plan of attack. How? By collecting and analyzing information about the target, whether the system's managers wanted such data to be broadcast or not.

By looking at privacy in the context of security, we have seen how privacy isn't just a "consumer" issue, something that deals only with individuals. Privacy is an important topic for anyone—or any organization—with information that shouldn't be published and shouted from the proverbial rooftops. We've also seen how the failure to maintain control over the flow of information had turned an attacker's job into something easy enough to be scripted into an automated process from what would have otherwise been an impossibly huge task.

So was the victim's privacy compromised? At what point did compromise happen? To find the answers to these questions, let's look more at the issue of privacy itself: what it is, how it's important, and how it works.

CHAPTER 2
Privacy Theory

WHAT IS PRIVACY? DICTIONARY DEFINITIONS convey such notions as a quality of being apart from observation, freedom from unauthorized access, and secrecy. Marketers often define various levels of sensitivity, ranging from "sensitive personal information" to "non-personally-identifiable information" and define what they may and may not do with various types of information [144].

What is privacy? After a one-paragraph discussion, we don't seem to be any closer to understanding what privacy is, even though we've kicked around a few ideas that everyone will agree are somehow related to privacy.

A useful definition of privacy found in computer science literature is "the ability of an individual (or organization) to decide whether, when, and to whom personal (or organizational) information is released" [168].

Even more succinctly, privacy is *informational self-determination* [76].

With a succinct definition of privacy, we can begin to formulate ideas about what privacy means and what it implies. Before we can understand the problem in all its intricacies, however, we need to give more thorough consideration of what privacy means in the real world. We will consider the properties of data, mechanisms for controlling access to data. After we consider real-world privacy issues, we'll discuss what properties data have and access control mechanisms.

Real-World Privacy

Privacy is so common, so fundamental, that we often don't give it much consideration until long after it's gone. Then we start to wonder what happened to it. Even now, after decades of privacy erosion, there are still many examples of privacy in the real world, with legitimate and important uses.

Consider the keys to your home and to your car. Why do you use them? Locks provide a very basic level of protection against unauthorized access. Why do your locks work only with your keys? *Privacy.* Specifically, the exact shape and size of each key is private. Only the holder of the key knows its exact dimensions, and only its exact dimensions will open the door.

When you go to an automated teller machine, you put your bank card in the slot; but that's not enough for you to get your hands on a big wad of cash. You need to enter some digits—a personal identification number (PIN)—a code that only you know. Why is there a PIN? If a thief steals your card, he won't be able to engage in transactions immediately. The privacy of your PIN provides you a level of security from criminals.

We deal with these issues, and we often think of them as *security* or *safety* features, but we rarely stop to consider that the success of these schemes depends entirely on the privacy of some datum.

Clearly, when seen in this context, persons who claim that they have no need for privacy because they have "nothing to hide" are merely fooling themselves. Burying one's head in the sand doesn't reduce one's exposure to vulnerability.

What Does Privacy Mean?

We see that privacy is both legitimate and important for providing safety and security. Let's consider some more specific examples of privacy concerns that are present to individuals, organizations, and societies.

Individual Privacy

Commonly, when we hear about privacy, we immediately think about individual privacy. Some might think of what Justice Brandeis called a person's "right to be left alone" [26, 190]. Others might consider a less abstract humanitarian case: the relationship that individuals had with totalitarian societies like Nazi Germany, the Soviet Union, and even through certain periods of American history like the Salem Witch Trials or the McCarthy era. Still others might think about more immediate examples: video cameras, personal identification systems, and other technologies employed for the specific purpose of watching what people do.

Many studies have shown that individuals—at least persons in the U.S.— are generally concerned about privacy [152]. Although these persons might disagree on exactly where the line of privacy invasion might lie, there are some specific types of information that are generally recognized as being sensitive and especially good examples of a person's need to control information about himself.

Medical privacy

The relationship between a patient and a physician is perhaps the most brutally honest and direct relationship that two people can have. There are no secrets, no limits on the depth of information shared. At least since the days of Hippocrates in the fifth century BCE, physicians have been aware of the need to engender their patients' trust. Few things will undermine a physician's image of trustworthiness faster than a failure to keep secret the details of a patient's medical history. Imagine hesitating to tell your doctor about a particular ache or pain because you fear whom else your doctor will tell!

Interestingly, as widely recognized as the need for medical privacy is, there are many competing interests involved in the debate on the use of medical records. Doctors need access to the information in order to make fully-informed decisions. Insurance companies want access to the information so they can manage their risks and keep the provision of medical coverage financially viable. Marketers want access to the information so they may offer their goods and services to people who might be interested in them.

In many places, legal protections are granted for medical records. Many such regulations have various loopholes that patients might be surprised to discover. Of course, there's also the risk of exposure of the information accidentally, as happened in 1999 with the University of Michigan health system [185]. A student trying to find information about a doctor followed a link and found files with thousands of private patient records, including names, addresses, phone numbers, Social Security numbers, job status, and treatments. All of these data were available on the public web.

You can't accidentally expose what you don't have.

Rental record privacy

Making a convincing case that what we read isn't anyone else's business isn't generally difficult. Taking this a step further, it isn't difficult to show that people can have vested interest in keeping such information private. Namely, the publication of library rental records could have serious consequences for those who are reading things which might be considered politically unpopular. Even in the United States, whose legal system theoretically guarantees due process, various types of persecution by government agents and private individuals can have serious and negative effects on those who hold unpopular views. Thus we see the need for legal protection of library rental record privacy.

Closely related to library rental records is the case of video rental records. In the United States, previous to the enactment of The Video Privacy Protection Act of 1988, anyone could obtain the video rental records of anyone else. Congress enacted this legislation after a Washington newspaper published the video rental records of Judge Robert Bork after his nomination to the U.S. Supreme Court.

Judge Bork was not confirmed for the appointment.

Financial records

Another sensitive issue is the matter of financial records. Again, protection of these records from publication is a simple matter of safety. Present systems of authentication—proving who you are—are weak and are often based largely on whether you know enough details about the accounts in question. Identity theft—taking on another's identity—is often perpetrated for the specific purpose of conducting financial transactions in the name (and therefore against the accounts) of the victim. General publication of this information is therefore a serious risk to the safety of the published accounts.

Personal safety

To a certain degree, an individual's personal safety is connected to certain privacy matters. Knowing someone's else's schedule provides an attacker with important information about when an attack would most likely be successful.

What's interesting is that, in this context, we often hear the case against privacy. Sun Microsystems CEO Scott McNealy, for example, argued against absolute privacy, citing examples of systems that use "personal" information to benefit people, including such examples as providing medical information to medics and automobile location data to authorities in the event of an airbag deployment [125]. McNealy seems to believe that in this, he's a privacy pragmatist, willing to surrender privacy of mundane matters to achieve certain benefits.

Many of the points often made by the privacy pragmatists are valid: yes, these systems that collect everything about what we're doing online can be of use. The question, however, is raised: Is sacrificing our privacy the only way for us to achieve these benefits?

We return to this question in Chapter 6.

Organizational Privacy

People aren't interested in privacy at only an individual level, however. Because organizations are groups of people, such organizations will, to some degree, reflect the concerns of the people of whom they're made.

If we accept that privacy is informational self-determination, we also accept that any information owner has an interest in privacy. Consequently, companies, governments, and other organizations have an interest in the privacy of information they consider proprietary or otherwise not fit for public consumption.

Given this view of privacy, it's now easy to see how privacy is not merely the concern of consumers, but of anyone with information that's not appropriate to shout from the proverbial rooftops.

Clearly, corporations value their privacy. If they did not, they wouldn't spend the money on products, staff, and consultants to help them build an information infrastructure that's safe from prying eyes. There's hardly a company that doesn't employ firewalls, virtual private networks, or cryptography—likely even all of these technologies—to keep its information private.

Whether this is pure paranoia or the manifestation of a legitimate need is largely a matter of perspective. Briefly consider some specific examples of corporate data that in the hands of competitors—perhaps foreign competitors with different standards for what is "ethical" behavior—could be harmful.

Organization charts

People are the weakest links in organizations. Organizations depend on them. If too many with a particular skill leave a project or organization in too little time, there is a greater risk of failure. Having a detailed understanding of an organization's structure and its key players would be important for someone who wants to undermine the organization.

Some persons find it somewhat difficult to believe that this sort of information is valuable. It's noteworthy that recruiters have offered to hire me to obtain organization charts and employee directories in various companies. Naturally, I refused, but the fact that recruiters—I can remember two separate occasions in the past year—would contact me specifically to ask whether I would attack an unsuspecting target without authorization and turn over proprietary information learned in the attack shows that there is value in the information.

Documentation

Consider the value of documentation in the form of email, memoranda, meeting minutes, and the like to competitors. Business plans, marketing strategies, and product designs often represent many thousands of hours of work on the part of the company's employees. Such documentation therefore carries with it a certain value—at least what the company paid the people to write it—even if not directly connected with an extant or planned revenue stream.

Databases

Databases typically contain some of the most highly prized information that an organization possesses. Everything from customer lists to employee salary data can be found in databases. In fact, databases are often the target of attacks against systems. Credit card numbers, customer lists, employee lists, and the like are often the "prizes" sought by system crackers.

Societal Privacy

Stepping back even further to get a view of privacy as it relates to an even larger group of people, we can start to look at societies.

Individuals are concerned about privacy because it places them at a disadvantage, perhaps exposing their vulnerabilities to other individuals and organizations. Similarly, organizations are concerned about privacy because of how it places them at a competitive or strategic disadvantage. Competitors, clients, and others could use such knowledge to exploit the organization's vulnerabilities.

Irrespective of our context, the issues at hand remain the same. As the number of people involved increases, however, the stakes get higher. This is why organizations spend so much more on privacy-enhancing and policy-enforcing tools than can individuals. Simply stated, they have more to lose. This becomes even more obvious when we we zoom out far enough to look at a society.

Although many in North America seem to have forgotten that the world is a dangerous place, this is not random paranoia. With the terrorist attacks on New York and Washington on September 11, 2001, we were reminded that the United States is an attractive target for various political movements, terrorist organizations, and others whose activity the U.S. opposes.

Such organizations are going to be able to use technology to gather intelligence data, to sort through it, and to coordinate their attacks. Instead of blowing up buildings, it's possible to implant logic bombs into computers, and to diddle data that others rely upon. An organization that wants to launch an attack against a society doesn't need to deploy its people and its equipment in the target country. Attacks designed to cripple the U.S. infrastructure can be launched completely from remote locations.

As we saw in the previous chapter, the first step of an attack is recon—the collection of intelligence in order to plan an attack that is more likely to achieve its objectives. Knowing what to attack and how to attack it are, of course, critical issues in planning a successful attack. If we give out a great deal of information about our infrastructures and we build our systems in such a way that they do nothing to deter these attempts to collect such information—or worse yet, advertise what to attack—we're inviting an attack, one that will succeed. Our best weapon to foil an attacker's recon attempts is to maintain our privacy, to stay in control of who may know what about our systems.

Concern over directing the U.S. infrastructure against itself prompted the formation of Infragard [90], made up of law enforcement, academia, and industry.

We've seen what privacy means to individuals and groups of people. The lesson that we can take away from this consideration is very general: everyone has a vested interest in privacy. What we're facing now is the need for privacy at a very high and very general level, one that is true for all systems. We could raise the question, though: why do we need to give this consideration when we're talking about the Internet, especially systems intended for public use?

During the 1990s, we saw tremendous growth in Internet connectivity and we were fascinated with the idea of exchanging email with others. After the rise of the graphical Web, use exploded into the daily life of mainstream users. The need for Internet connectivity became greater than ever, was served, and left us with this ubiquitous infrastructure that now supports the services that we use every day.

All of this connectivity, of course, made it possible to do even more than we originally imagined. Everyone in the world is connected to everyone else through the Internet. Thus, our personal computers, our companies, and our governments are all on the same networks as people who would like nothing more than to attack us, our companies, and our governments.

When we're building a system, we think about our intended users. When we build systems for the Internet, we also need to think about how others—even hostile persons—will use it. Building a system in a closed, friendly environment is a very different problem from looking at building a system in an untrusted, potentially hostile environment. The Internet is the latter. The more quickly we realize that and reflect that in our designs, the better off we're going to be.

Before we're ready to make such tremendous changes in the way that we think about building these systems, we're going to need to be sure we understand what our systems support and what they do. When we have everything digitized and living as data in the computer, what, really, do we have?

Let's consider data, the building blocks of information. We'll then move on to discussion of access control.

Relevant Properties of Data

In common usage, the words *information* and *data* are almost interchangeable. Throughout much of this discussion, we have not been careful to distinguish between them. In this particular section, however, it is important to distinguish between them. Data[1] might be thought of as facts (whether true or not), perhaps things like log file entries, transaction logs, etc. Information refers to data that have been used in a particular way, i.e., data that have been interpreted become information.

The reason we make this distinction here is because the properties we now discuss apply specifically to data; they need not be interpreted before these properties become active.

Ownership

Despite the debates over the ownership of data and information that continue to rage, it is generally acknowledged that at least certain data are owned. For example, you own your thoughts and memories. If you wish, you may share them with others freely. If you prefer, you may share them in a more controlled fashion, perhaps by giving a talk at a limited-invitation affair. You might prefer not to share them at all.

If we consider legal definitions of ownership, we can see the whole body of law regarding intellectual property addresses this issue of "ownership." Tremendous damage can come to a brand, for example, if someone else engages in commercial activity under the name of a brand, particularly if it's in a similar type of market, such that consumers would be fooled into confusing the two brands. We use trademarks to protect our companies and our brands against these problems.

Another example would be in writing. Consider this book, for example. If you were to duplicate this book in its entirety and to sell it, you would be causing me direct harm. First of all, you didn't have the ideas needed to put this book together. You didn't spend the time to put these ideas into words. You didn't create diagrams and pictures. You didn't spend time talking to technical editors, developmental editors, and copy editors, trying to make sure that everything

---

[1]   Data is the plural of datum. In common usage, the word "data" is often used for both singular and plural. However, there is good reason for us to preserve the distinction in our discussion. I'll therefore risk being labeled a pedant—it wouldn't be the first time—and preserve the distinctions between information and data and between data and a datum.

comes together just right. I did, and as a result, the diagrams, the words, and the presentation are mine—few will seriously debate this point. If you duplicate my work, selling it through your own channels and people buy "your" book instead of mine, you are causing me material damage, depriving me of compensation that's due for my work. People don't generally buy books because they're so enamored with the production details. People usually buy books because of the information contained in them. Copyright law protects these kinds of creative works.

What does this have to do with privacy? Privacy is informational self-determination. I, the owner of this specific compilation of my thoughts, have determined to distribute this information to readers of my book. If my words are separated from the channel I have chosen for distribution, I have lost control of where my thoughts and ideas have gone.

Of course, in writing a book for public consumption, this is part of the point: to be financially compensated for providing insight, for helping others to think in different ways, which will hopefully lead to new ideas, that will in turn be presented for public consumption. The level of control that we're able to maintain over information printed on the pages of a book is therefore fairly low, but it satisfies our requirements.

The level of control needed over other types of information is much higher. Private communiqués, confidential reports, and state secrets are by definition intended to inform and to influence much smaller and more select audiences. Losing the ability to control who may know a datum that you own is a violation of privacy. Whether it's your Social Security number, your company's financials, or the list of your government's spies operating abroad, the issue is the same: loss of informational self-determination is a violation of privacy.

Nymity

At the center of the debate is an issue that few know even exists.

Nymity refers to the level of identifiability that any datum has. Three types of nymity we'll consider are the following:

Anonymity: having no name.

Pseudonymity: having an assumed name.

Verinymity: having a true name.

As we shall soon see, the lines among these types of nymity are blurry and confusion about these terms is especially exacerbated by online marketers trying to relieve the public's concern about online data collection and analysis practices. Marketers claim that they're profiling users anonymously, when in fact, the risks that are being foisted upon the public are not the risks of anonymity, but are instead the risks of pseudonymity.

*We all know
what hap-
pens when you
assume.*

One of the metrics that marketers use for determining what may and may not be done with data collected is whether a datum is *personally identifiable* [144], assuming that anything which fails that test qualifies as anonymous. This is a dangerous mistake, however, because it fails to recognize the nature of identifiability. As Figure 2-1 shows, we don't have clear distinctions between points along a scale; we're dealing with a subtle issue where poles of black and white are separated by many, sometimes indiscernible, shades of gray.

*Strong
Verinymity*

*Strong
Anonymity*

Figure 2-1. The Nymity Spectrum

Anonymity

Anonymity is simply the state or property of having no name. From time to time, we see books published by "Anonymous," quotations attributed "anonymously," and the like. When we see ten books published by anonymous authors, we don't know how many authors there are; there might be ten authors. It's also possible that all ten books were written by the same author. Two authors could have written five books apiece; five authors could have written two books apiece; three authors could have written three books each, with another being written by a fourth author. This is one of the features of anonymity: there is no *linkability* between one anonymous action and another. Anonymous systems simply cannot support the notion of reputation.

This is why anonymity is desirable in some systems that have become institutionalized, including suicide hotlines, Alcoholics Anonymous, and voting by secret ballot.

It is this very same property that also comes under fire from critics. People who speak anonymously do not have the same consequences for libel as speakers known by name. Even setting aside the legal ramifications, there's no way to identify an anonymous speaker to determine if it's the same anonymous speaker who has given good information in the past, the same anonymous speaker who has given bad information in the past, or someone who has never spoken anonymously at all.

Pseudonymity

In some contexts, anonymity is not an optimal property. A technique that has been in longstanding use for protecting one's identity while enjoying the benefits of reputation has been the use of an assumed name, a *pseudonym*. Pseudonymity is fundamentally different from anonymity in the issue of linkability. One action can be linked to another action performed under the same pseudonym. With linkability established, reputations can be had.

Pseudonyms are generally well-understood. Examples are not difficult to find: Mark Twain and Bob Dylan are both popular examples of pseudonyms.

An important pseudonym in the history of the United States is Publius. In New York State newspapers, a series of 85 essays were published in the name of Publius between October 1787 and May 1788, urging ratification of the proposed United States Constitution. The essays were written by Alexander Hamilton, John Jay, and James Madison. In publishing under a consistent name—one that could build up a reputation but wasn't necessarily tied to themselves—they showed how pseudonyms could be effectively used to balance the features of reputation against privacy.

Verinymity

The term *verinymity* is a neologism from the parts "veri" (meaning "true") and "nym" (meaning "name"). Thus, *verinymity* is the property of having a real name. That name needn't be your legal name, but it must be something that can be linked back to you individually.

Examples of verinyms include such things as your legal name and government-issued identifiers like Social Security and driver's license numbers. Other, perhaps less obvious, examples of verinyms would include address and telephone numbers, especially when there's an additional datum to qualify the individual, such as a first name.

Even stronger verinyms include biometric data, including fingerprints, retina scans, and voiceprints.

Nymity in practice

An important difference between pseudonymity and verinymity is that pseudonyms can be assumed and then abandoned by their users. That is, if you decide that you're going to be known as "Zaphenath-paneah," you can easily assume that name. Simply start telling people that's what your name is. Publish things in that name. Establish a new email address with that name. Get yourself a phone number in that name.

You get bonus points for identifying Zaphenath-paneah's more widely recognized name.

To leave the pseudonym behind, you do the same thing as if the holder of the name has died. Phone and email service would be terminated, no new transactions would be performed with that name. Now (theoretically speaking) there is no connection between the user of the name and the name itself.

Another important property of pseudonyms is that the name doesn't need to be used in all contexts. Being known as Zaphenath-paneah to your grocery store doesn't mean that you can't be Elvis at the bookstore. And you can be R.U. Thayer to the telephone company. You decide which identity you use. Doing this would prevent correlation of activity in one space with activity in another space. Analysis of detailed marketing data wouldn't allow anyone to determine that R.U. Thayer, who has 14 telephone lines coming into his house, is the same person who bought all of those books about Graceland. There's no reliable way to tell that Elvis and R.U. Thayer are the same person.

Because verinymity means the ability to point back to the individual, the name—recall that this is whatever identifier is in use, so although the legal names might be the same, they have different Social Security numbers, or ZIP codes, or something else that can be used to identify which one we mean—used to identify someone in one space necessarily refers to the same person in another space.

Furthermore, each pseudonym can have a different lifespan; they can be created and left behind as needed. Leaving one behind doesn't require leaving behind another. So, Zaphenath-paneah can keep buying groceries well after Elvis quit buying books about Graceland.

Thus, the key difference between pseudonyms and verinyms is *disposability*. Pseudonyms can be easily adopted and just as easily abandoned. Verinyms are extremely difficult to change (think witness protection program). That's difficult enough when you need to change someone's verinymous name. Recall our mention of biometrics above. That's an even stronger verinym than a legal name or government-issued identifier. Just try changing your DNA.

The fuzz betwixt them

Look back at Figure 2-1. Notice that you don't see three standalone areas, anonymity, pseudonymity, and verinymity. It's a spectrum, with smooth gradation that takes us from one extreme to the other in steps so small that they're nearly indistinguishable. Ian Goldberg calls this "The Nymity Slider" [77].

We now understand the elements of anonymity, pseudonymity, and verinymity. We can see how these are different points in the spectrum of nymity. But what about all of the stuff in the middle?

Strong anonymity is very difficult to achieve online. Even in systems where there are lots of protocols to push the data around, to hide them in various ways, the basic fact of the matter is that to have an interactive transaction, discussion, or anything else, traffic is going to have to flow from one computer to another. Internet-connected computers have *IP addresses*—the numeric identifier that represents that host uniquely on the global Internet. An "anonymous" conversation between two hosts is difficult, because in the short term, you can link the traffic of that host with other traffic from that host. Depending on details of the system, like whether it is a single-user machine or multiuser, whether it has a constant IP address or one that changes every time it joins the network, etc., the window of linkability might be very short or very long. IP addresses—the fundamental underpinnings of the Internet—therefore are pseudonyms.[2] When you use a particular computer or a particular IP address, you're assuming that name. When you stop using the computer or the IP address changes, you stop using that name.

Several approaches to decreasing linkability on internets have been developed and explored over the past few years. These include Onion Routing [78], anonymizing proxies, mix networks, and posting to public newsgroups.

Access Control

Another critical aspect of security, particularly in its privacy aspect is *access control*. Is the question of access as simple as a "yes" or "no"? What kinds of access exist to data?

In the context of access control, sometimes more technically-minded users will think of access control policies that are enforced by their tools, specifically operating systems. Although these are useful for demonstrating the basic principle of granularity of access, it's important not to be constrained by what kinds of options have been available in the past.

> *Control! Control! You must learn control!*
>
> *–Yoda*

Unix-based operating systems, for example, are well-known for providing *read*, *write*, and *execute* access to files. Most modern Unix implementations also provide for a means of more sophisticated access control, where additional privileges can be specified and where such privileges can be managed with more granularity than the basic *user*, *group*, and *other* distinctions provided by the base operating system.

More generally, it's worth considering the types of access controls available and when they would be used.

---

[2] IP addresses are verinyms for computers. The users behind them, however, have the property of pseudonymity to other computers on the network unless those computers can get user identifiers from the host.

Access Control Types

There are two types of access controls: mandatory access control (MAC) and discretionary access control (DAC). DAC leaves access up to the discretion of the datum's owner. This is highly flexible, allowing a very granular level of control over who may and may not know a particular datum. MAC basically works by having some kind of administration that sets up rules for the system, to which all of the system's data creators, users, and maintainers must adhere.

DAC basically means that nobody tells anyone anything. If you want to learn something, you're going to have to get it straight from the horse's mouth. MAC systems are common in corporate and government settings where labels like CONFIDENTIAL, SECRET, and TOP SECRET are used. The rules of the system define who may access information at various levels of classification. In such systems, if you need to access a datum, its classification will be checked, as will yours. If your classification is high enough, you'll be granted access.

Another type of MAC is Role Based Access Control (RBAC) [63]. Rather than providing labels for all types of data and users, users' roles are defined, and access to data is specified per role. For example, if we have a system where we have a researcher, an administrative assistant, and a system administrator, we might classify the data such that the researcher can do anything, the administrative assistant has the ability to create copies of finished reports, and the system administrator has the ability to move the data to various other parts of the filesystems. RBAC is potentially a very flexible mechanism for access control, able to be defined at a very high level or at a very granular level, to meet the needs of the system.

Implementing Access Controls

We'll need to start by defining what kinds of access to the data are possible. When working with data and defining what can be done with them, it's best to start out in general, with high-level definitions and requirements. How many types of access we'll design and implement will depend on such things as system requirements, budget, and available technology. Some examples follow.

Read: The ability to see a datum, to know it.

Copy: The ability to duplicate a datum.

Create: The ability to create a datum.

Write: The ability to write data.

Modify: The ability to change data that are already present.

Delete: The ability to remove a datum.

In the most general case—with stock operating systems and basic applications—we're doing very well to have even this level of granularity in access. In fact, it's rare that we can get this kind of granularity. When, for example, would it be permissible for someone to have access *to copy* but not *to read* a datum?

If you're thinking at the level of the filesystem, you probably reason that copy access relies on read access. Copying goes something like this: you need to read it, to open a new file descriptor for the copy, and then to loop through the source, writing a copy of the stream to the target.

This is a good way to demonstrate how we technical people tend to think in circles that are small: we drill down into things in order to figure out what's happening and how to find a way around a problem. It's also a good way to demonstrate how thinking that way—at too low a level—can actually lead us astray when we're dealing with conceptual issues.

Imagine providing a level of distinction between read and copy access now. The most obvious way to do this would be to encrypt the data. Now, the process of copying the file, as described above, still applies. However, in the process of copying the file, the user performing the copy had no ability to ascertain the "real" contents of the file: it just looks like a stream of garbage. If a digital signature is present on the file itself, another user with legitimate read access will also be able to tell if the copying user made an unauthorized modification to the data.

The idea that the technical administrator of a system doesn't necessarily have authorization to read the data on the system might be somewhat foreign. In military and other government installations, administrative personnel need to be cleared to handle the information that will cross their desks. A similar notion exists in the commercial world among executive assistants.

Typically, this means that the assistants' levels of clearance depend on what levels of clearance their bosses have. With the rise of computers and other automation, we have dramatically increased the level of productivity to the point that instead of having several administrative assistants for each executive, we're now seeing much leaner administrative staff, often a single assistant can suffice for several executives.

What this means is that instead of an executive dictating a letter to someone who will actually type the letter, then review it, and rework parts of it, we now have the executive banging away on his own keyboard, writing the letter without any review from the outside, and sending it directly to the recipient. Suddenly, the need to have assistants who are "cleared" to the same level as their bosses seems antiquated.[3] Although we're providing users with *more* direct access to the data, it's still not exactly direct access. Instead of working through layers of people,

---

[3]   On the other hand, with the kind of spelling, grammar, and other usage gaffes that are now finding their way into final form, one could argue that all of this productivity comes at a high price. I digress.

we're working through layers of software. We get more into the sorts of problems that can arise in this sort of situation in Chapter 3.

System administrators are the executive assistants of the computer age. Does the system administrator have read access to the entire employee directory, including employment history and salary data? Does the system administrator have read access to the customer database?

If the system administrator doesn't logically have access to the information itself, why does the system administrator so often have the technical means to read it? Sure, administrators need to copy it, to be able to restore it from offline media, to move it from one system to another, but why should a system administrator, in the course of performing some sort of technical function for the organization, be granted access to the keys to the proverbial kingdom? Considering how many organizations outsource their information technology staff, how often contractors and temporary employees are used in these functions, and how valuable this kind of information is not only to the organization that holds it, but to competitors, it seems like we're creating a potentially dangerous situation where we're badly mismatching what's needed with what's provided.

In fact, it is precisely this mismatch between requirement and provision that is often the basis of unmanaged risk. It's often the risks that are unevaluated or unaddressed that are exploited.

When we're designing our systems, therefore, we need to give serious consideration to the issue of access control. Whether we use MAC, DAC, or RBAC will depend on what we're trying to do and what we need to use. Recognizing the properties of the data we're handling, understanding what privacy is, and having privacy as a requirement are all important if we're going to succeed in building trustworthy systems.

Our systems' designs should address our requirements closely, being sure to provide not only the functionality, but the means to enforce policy we need. Policy enforcement turns out to be a more complicated matter than many people initially realize. We'll consider it now in more detail.

CHAPTER 3
Policy Enforcement

COMPUTER SECURITY, LIKE ANY SORT of security, is basically the business of enforcing policy. Some security policies require armed guards. Others require firewalls. Despite the fact that we're dealing with technology like networks and computer systems, the basic issues remain the same irrespective of our context, so we can look in the Real World for many examples that can be useful to us in determining what kinds of things are important in computer security and what we can do to deal with the risks that present themselves.

Policy enforcement can be complicated, because we're dealing with so many issues that are so interdependent. Technology, policy, and management issues all play into the others, defining what we can do, what we want to do, and how we can form a cohesive means of addressing the policy enforcement problem.

To a large degree, our policy enforcement mechanisms are about the prevention of unauthorized activity. We'll conclude our discussion with prevention. Before that, we'll talk about threat models, where we identify our attackers and their attacks and figure out how to address those risks. Before we can build threat models, we need to understand the guts of policies, what they can do for us, what we need from them, and how we can get policies that meet our requirements. Building policies is tricky, though. We need to be able to recognize the technology that we're dealing with—a world of agents—and the kinds of issues that face our systems before we can define our policy. Finally, we cannot really understand the world of agents from the perspective of policy enforcement if we don't understand what policy enforcement means and exactly we can accomplish.

Having seen where we're going to end up—effective prevention—and how we're going to get there, let's get started with the concepts of policy enforcement.

Concepts

Policy enforcement is really an operational and management problem. The tools used for policy enforcement, however, are often going to be technical in nature, and what support we can provide to the operational folks will depend on the state of the technology. Having all of the security technology in the world—digital signatures, zero-knowledge proofs, tamper-resistant hardware, and long lists of other toys we love—is completely useless to us if we don't understand what it is that we're trying to accomplish.

The concepts that underlie all of these systems are high-level and should be well understood by everyone involved in the operation of any system with security requirements. By now, I hope that we've successfully established that "systems with security requirements" should mean all systems.

All security problems that we're trying to solve should fall into one or more of the following categories. Think about these concepts when trying to break down the problem of "securing" a particular target. These are the pieces from which you'll need to assemble a comprehensive answer to the question of how to secure a system.

Identification

Identity is simply who you are. The process of announcing or revealing identity is *identification*. When you meet someone, you typically give your name (or perhaps a pseudonym). This is nothing more than a statement of the name to which you will answer.

In computer systems, identity refers not only to people, but to any kind of entity. Users are certainly included, but so can other computers, other processes, other programs. It's noteworthy that identification can be anonymous—one could simply announce oneself with some useful datum like the ability to speak a particular language—or named. Identification is the process of giving another entity your nym.

Of course, anyone can say anything. Identification is limited to the exchange of a nym.

Authentication

Authentication is something that's often confused with identification. That is, when someone announces who he is, we tend to believe it. There are some cases where this is clearly not enough.

If Mallory shows up at a restaurant or grocery store and tells the people in the cash office that she's from the armored truck company and is there to pick up their money, there might be some reason for skepticism. In particular, if the cash office employees believe her, they're going to hand over a *lot* of money. Thus, there's some impetus for an attacker to impersonate an armored truck company guard. If you only need to say that you're from the armored truck company and you can get your hands on $10,000 cash, you could make a pretty lucrative—albeit dishonest—living stealing all of the money that grocery stores think they're depositing in their bank accounts.

In a case like this, there's an additional need to prove that you are who you say you are. Identification is when you announce who you are. Authentication is the process of proving your identity.

Authorization

Once we have determined identity and it has been proved, the next question is what is the authenticated user is allowed to do.

Authorization is determining whether someone has permission to take the requested course of action. Someone can identify himself as a random person who lives in the neighborhood and can thus authenticate himself by showing his government-issued driver's license that has his address printed on it. That doesn't mean, though, that he is allowed to enter your house and to take all of your valuables.

It's clear that the first three issues build on each other. Someone needs to announce who he is to begin the "transaction;" we can't authenticate someone if we don't know whose credentials we're supposed to examine. Once a user identifies herself—by telling us she's Alice—we then know what to look for in response to our challenge to prove that she's Alice. Once she has proved that she is Alice—perhaps by presenting some kind of credential like a signature or a password—she's authenticated. Now when we look at what Alice wants to do, we can see whether she has the authorization to take the requested action.

Authorization tends not to be useful without identification and authentication, unless the requested action is something that's allowed by absolutely everyone.

Confidentiality

The principle of *confidentiality* deals with keeping a datum secret. It's important to note that there are two distinct issues when it comes to confidentiality: transactional data (needed to support the session) and session contents. In the example of a telephone call, transactional data would include things normally used for billing records (e.g., who called whom, call duration, time of day), and additional data that could be gathered by watching for a period of time (e.g., call frequency). The contents would include the conversations themselves [51].

Confidentiality, like many security principles, is a spectrum. At one end of the spectrum is high confidentiality. If only the participants in a conversation know of it, the conversation is highly confidential. At the other end of the spectrum is public information or common knowledge.

Integrity

Seeing each of these elements at work in a single example can be helpful.

If Alice tells her stock broker Bob that she wants to sell all of her high tech holdings, Bob needs to establish several things. The first issues are knowing *who* placed the order (identification), ensuring that it was *actually Alice* (authentication), and verifying that she has *authority* to place the order (authorization). It's also helpful that Alice's request not be public knowledge (confidentiality).[1] The next step is for Bob to ensure that the order he got is the same that Alice placed.

Even in face-to-face conversations, it's possible for a listener not to understand what a speaker says. The children's game of "telephone," where one person whispers a word or phrase into another's ear, who whispers it on to the next, etc., until reaching the last person in the room, demonstrates that as information is passed from person to person, it has greater and greater potential to be mangled.

There are many ways such mangling can happen accidentally. Everything from human error to an equipment failure can cause this.

Things get even more complicated when introducing third parties who might be able to profit by altering the contents of a message. Imagine Alice and Bob going on a blind date. If Mallory is able to change the message while it's in transit, she can direct Bob to a different meeting place, making Alice think he stood her up. She can even impersonate Alice by meeting Bob where he's expecting to find Alice. Now imagine that instead of a social date, it's a business meeting between

---

[1] She is, after all, a famous character in cryptography and the orders she makes might move markets.

two people who haven't met face-to-face. If the imposter is a competitor, who knows what secrets might be revealed during the course of the meeting.

Integrity is being sure the message we got was the same that was sent.

Nonrepudiation

Nonrepudiation is the opposite of deniability; it's the ability to prove that someone was a party to a transaction or event. That is, if a transaction includes some nonrepudiation feature, none of the participants can later claim that they were not a party to the transaction.

A common real-world example of nonrepudiation is signing the receipt on credit-card transactions. Anyone can put a charge your card, but you can contest the charges and claim that they're unauthorized. In such a case, it's up to the merchant to prove that you were a party to the transaction. Producing a copy of a receipt bearing your signature is the standard way to prove that you were part of the transaction.

Administration

Administration describes how well a system—whether a piece of software, a service, a network host, or a policy—can be managed. The greatest technology in the world isn't much use if it cannot be managed. Of particular concern to businesses is whether the technology that they deploy will actually help them increase their business' productivity. Imagine if, instead of using your computer directly, you had to tell a computer operator what you wanted the computer to do. That operator would then type some commands to the computer, have it do its thing, and return the results to you. Administratively, that sort of system would be extremely expensive.

Imagine a firewall that, instead of having a policy configuration that would be used to determine whether a given packet is allowed to pass from one network to another, would require the system administrator to be logged in to the computer to answer a dialog box for each packet, whether to pass it or to deny it. Again, such a system would have such a high administration cost that it would be unusable.

Issues like how much attention systems need and what they cost to operate are all matters that fall into the general area of administration.

Administration is important for us in policy enforcement because systems that are difficult to manage can be difficult to keep secure. It doesn't always follow that "bigger is better" when it comes to security. So when we're looking at our systems and our policies, we need to think about what it takes to keep the system itself running. If we're deploying a system into a lean environment and there aren't going to be folks sitting around watching our stuff, but it has a high administration cost, we could be building a system that's doomed to fail because it's going to depend on the reaction of someone who isn't there to see the blinky red light.

Agents

All of this business of user authentication, authorization, access control, and the like sounds very impressive. Most people don't even consider the nature of data in this level of detail. This is, of course, why we often hear things like "identification" and "authentication" being confused. Some might therefore conclude that the view we've been building thus far is fairly complete.

Perhaps if we were working with the Real World, that would be true; however, we're discussing the management of risk online. Although the concept of *agents* does arise in the real world, through such mechanisms as power of attorney, it's not the most common case. In the real world, people tend to do things themselves. Simply put, an agent is someone or something that acts in another's behalf.

In the world online, however, we *can't* do things directly ourselves. The world online *is* a world of agents. Our computers only do what we tell them. But in order for us to tell them, we need to run some kind of software on top of them, software that will (hopefully) present us some means of communicating what we want and turning that into instructions for the computer to perform. Until such a time when you can plug your brain directly into IP networks, everything we do online will be done through agents, typically layers of agents.

Technically speaking, even when "doing something yourself," you're probably still employing agents. For example, although the ideas for this discussion are in my brain, my brain needs to rely on its agents to communicate what's happening in the outside world. To get my thoughts into printed words, my brain needs to send signals to my fingers to type the words I'm thinking. My brain relies on my eyes to see what text is appearing on my screen so that it can be reviewed, rearranged, and finalized. These are all things that we often take for granted, yet when we stop to think about them, they're obvious. Medical research is able to help people with various types of disabilities, recognizing that the functions of their own agents can sometimes be managed by artificial replacements.

The issue of agents online is therefore not unlike the issue of agents offline. In some sense, anytime that my consciousness tries to communicate with another consciousness, it will have to employ layers of agents.

Granted, these notions of agents aren't nearly as interesting as the romantic picture of intelligent agents painted by some, where intelligent agents will float around in cyberspace doing things that we'd want them to do on our behalf. However, it is important to recognize today's systems are, in fact, layers of stupid agents, programs without any significant reasoning ability or common sense.

When we design our policies, we talk in terms of who may do what. The reality of our environment, however, is that enforcement of that policy is really a question of *whose agents may do what.* So we need to give consideration to things like who has access, malicious software, and malicious software in a world of software agents. Finally, we must return to the question of whom we've authenticated and what difference it makes.

Who Has Access?

The question of "Who has access?" is a good one. We grant access to computer *accounts,* because that's the closest we can come to granting access to *people* in computer systems.

The point of this question in the context of agents is to show that we need to grant access to our agents to do things for us online. Our agents online—stupid systems that they are—do not have the ability to think about things the way we do. There's no way to show our systems the company's security policy and have those systems reason on each requested action to determine whether it violates the policy.

We communicate issues of policy to our systems by way of configuration. No smarts live in the configurations—the intelligence lies in the human who configures the system. It's the user's job to translate policy in the real world into configuration for systems to enforce that policy.

This is an extremely important point.

One might argue that with widespread adoption of biometric authentication systems, we'll see a significant difference in the kinds of risks that we're dealing with in the case of who has access. I'm not sure that this is true; the fact of the matter is that even with biometric authentication mechanisms, we're probably just shifting the set of attacks that will likely work from one to another. More importantly, even if we connect the authentication to the individual, the manipulation of the bits will still be done via some agent. I know of no technology in the foreseeable future that will create much opportunity for a person to communicate directly with his recipient's mail server, which is to say, without any computer at all. And even if we do get to that point, the mail server is still an agent, a mail transport agent.

Malware

Malware is a term meaning "malicious software," irrespective of how it actually does its nefarious deeds. This term is useful because it focuses on the *effects* of the software, as opposed to other terms, such as viruses, worms, and trojan horses, which refer to *behavior.* Misuse of these terms is rampant, generally only confusing the issue.

Viruses

Viruses[2] are thus named because they work as do their biological namesakes. Viruses are thus not *programs,* but rather *code segments* that attach themselves to programs so that when the program is executed, it will also run some additional code. The important issue needed to identify a virus is that it requires a "host," a working program to which it can attach itself to do its work.

Worms

The term *tapeworm* was originally used in the context of computers in John Brunner's 1975 novel, *The Shockwave Rider* [28].

Of course, the name that stuck to the implementations was a shortened form of what Brunner imagined. *Worms* are thus named because they are programs whose job is to spread (or "to worm") their way through a network. When initially run, a worm will begin its work on that machine. It will then look to see what kinds of connections that machine has. Trust relationships are especially good for this purpose, because it often means that the client machine's connections to the others will be made with comparatively little in the way of additional layers of security that would inhibit the spread of the worm.

There is no inherently evil purpose to worms. Some worms are completely benign, authorized to run on networks, seeking out idle computing cycles that could be devoted to some processing jobs. The first implementations of computer worms at Xerox PARC in the early 1980s did just this [175].

The aforementioned 1988 Internet Worm incident that led to the formation of CERT changed forever the way that we look at worms. Malicious worms were generally believed to be theoretical up to that point. That showed us that it was possible to create a worm "in the wild," to release it on a large unsuspecting population (Internet users), and then to have it infect a significant portion of the Internet.

Trojan Horses

Trojan Horse programs are named after the large wooden horse full of hidden soldiers used by the Greeks to capture the city of Troy during the Trojan War.

Simply stated, Trojan Horses are programs that appear (or advertise) to do one thing, while having the ability to do something else. A trivial example would

---

[2] There is no other workable plural construction of "virus" in English. Various nonstandard plural forms are floating around on the Net, but "virii" and friends just don't cut it. Tom Christiansen put this matter to rest, hopefully for good [32].

be a program that is a game that secretly deletes your files while you play it. By the time you notice what's happening, it's too late.

Other examples would include programs that are attached to email in a way that makes them appear to be harmless data, but that are really executable programs. Some of these take advantages in weaknesses in programs like Microsoft's Internet Explorer that will cause these to be executed automatically [5]. Others take advantage of weaknesses in the client software that fool the user into doing something more than what he thinks [186]. Still others take advantage of user ignorance and gullibility. One hoax that recently floated around the Internet advised people to delete a Windows DLL and to spread the word. This was a virus, but completely user-based.

MSIE: Microsoft Indecent Exposure

—Doug Monroe

The key element of Trojan Horses is that something other than the user's expectations is being followed. Whether the user knows he's running a program or thinks he's reading non-executable data in a "safe" viewer program, something beyond the expected functionality takes place. The Trojan Horse isn't just a work of art, it also contains Greek soldiers.

Stupid Agents and Malware

Starting in the early 90s, there was a message that went around on Usenet about every six months warning people not to open an email message with a subject of "GOOD TIMES" because it would delete all of their files. At the time, this was completely absurd, because email was just plain text, clients didn't have the ability to execute programs, and even with the ability to attach files, they weren't executed by the simple action of reading the message. Email was safe! "Stop sending us these bogus alerts already!" we cried to the new users who insisted on forwarding them to everyone they knew.

Right about the time we got this through our users' thick skulls, Microsoft decided that it needed to be in the Internet mail client business and proceeded to implement tools that would allow malware like "GOOD TIMES" to be realized. Although "GOOD TIMES" was a hoax [96], ExploreZip [61], Happy99 [81], and Melissa [126] were not.

As long as we cannot get bits from our brains directly on to the Internet, agents are a necessity. Even so-called "smart" agents are incredibly stupid, able to be fooled by just about any kind of attempt that arises. Malware has historically been difficult to distribute widely for many reasons, but that's not necessarily the case now. With so many people using stupid agents that can be easily fooled into doing unsafe things, attackers can take advantage of agents' stupidity to distribute their malware and to have it run on others' machines.

That boy is about as sharp as a bowling ball.

—Foghorn Leghorn

A large part of the problem is that we treat agents exactly as we would treat the users themselves, assuming that there is a direct one-to-one relationship between the agent and the user.

Who Is Authenticated?

The idea of authentication is especially interesting because it's predicated on the idea of authenticating users: "You need to authenticate!"

Many authentication methods are available. The most common example of user authentication that we see today is the password. Users set passwords so that systems can be sure that the person who is attempting to use the system now is the same person who set the password in a previous session. The process is usually started by a system administrator creating a new account and an initial password. The big problem with passwords is that they're horribly obsolete technology. Users choose bad passwords. Passwords are short enough and computers powerful enough now that passwords can be broken by brute force without much difficulty.

Another common authentication system is based on *public-key* (or *asymmetric*) cryptography. These systems are based on an algorithm whereby two "keys" can be created, such that they're mathematically related. One is published, and the other is kept private. Using these systems, Alice can prove that she has access to Alice's private key, which should also mean that she proves she's Alice.

Of course, access to the private key is usually protected by a passphrase of some sort—basically a longer version of the same obsolete technology that we're trying to avoid using in the first place—so there are practical problems with this model as well, at least in terms of the attacks that local users can carry out against each other.

Another authentication mechanism combines hardware and software, where a *challenge* can be presented to a user, typed into a tamper resistant device—they usually look like small pocket calculators—and a *response* will be displayed on the device's screen. The user then enters the device-computed response and the system grants access if the response matches the challenger's expectations. These systems require that the user has the device itself. To prevent someone from being able to use a device that's been randomly found, we often deploy them with some kind of password needed to turn them on.

Passwords seem to pop up again and again even in "passwordless" authentication systems. Go figure.

Specific mechanisms of authentication and related problems are covered in various books including Bruce Schneier's *Applied Cryptography* [170].

But once authentication has taken place, to whom has access been granted? The user or the user's *agent*?

Once again, we're dealing with the world online, a world of agents. We use programs to manipulate bits for us. As long as that's the case, even in systems that tie back to the user specifically (e.g., retina scans, palm-print readings, and DNA matching), once the authentication has taken place, access has been granted to the user's agent, some piece of software.

Returning to the discussion of agents, we can see that there are numerous risks that now confront us. Our agents are generally stupid, simply interpreting events like mouse clicks and keystrokes and turning them into bits that get written to some device that eventually spews them on to the network. Many agents developed with the popularization of the Web are getting "smarter," but in all of the wrong ways. They know how to execute scripts, they know how to launch programs, they know how to present things such that users can be fooled into running executable programs, but they typically fail to recognize the environment they're working in. Rather than seeing the world as full of untrustworthy data that's waiting to exploit it, most agents see the world as full of data that it needs to figure out how to interpret in behalf of the user.

So we have email-based malware that floods mail servers with hundreds of thousands of copies of messages, viruses that attack machines and their data, and all manner of security problems that arise from doing the Wrong Thing with the available data.

Because the *agents* have the authority to modify data, once their stupidity is exploited and they do the Wrong Thing, they do so not with the authority normally granted to a stupid program, but with the authority of the user on whose behalf the program normally operates. My programs do not have permission to mangle my data. But if I run my programs, and they're fooled into believing that I want them to mangle my data, they'll happily do so.

If this doesn't sound frightening, let's put this in slightly different terms.

Imagine a child given signing authority on his parents' checking account. The child is told "When the phone bill comes, see how much it is, and write a check for that amount. Then send it in the envelope they include with it." The child's directions are clear. Everything will probably be fine.

Now imagine the child being sent a bogus phone bill from a malicious source. The bill will *look* genuine. Would a child notice that two bills arrived in one month? Would a child notice that one went to a different address? Or would a child just go about the process like always, and dutifully sign away his parents' money to the attacker?

The situation with today's software is, in fact, worse than this. Our most sophisticated computer systems have no common sense—even compared to young children—yet some of the worst software available today (web browsers) can act as a signing agent for users, creating digital signatures. Digital signatures are the cryptographic version of signing something in real life: it can be taken as proof that you originated a message, that you've seen a message, or even that you agree to it. Not everyone is pleased about the prospects of digital signatures being legally binding [172].

Have you crashed your browser today?

Historically, our consideration of software and building systems have included some discussion of problems with design and implementation. In some cases, we've even been advised to program defensively, to reduce the impact of such software defects on our own systems. With malware alive and well on today's networks, we need to expand our consideration of how systems interact. No longer can we just think about best case scenarios being interrupted by accidental problems. If we're to build systems worthy of trust, we need to consider cases where our systems are being actively attacked by programs.

Policy

Policy is perhaps best defined as the statement of what an organization or individual will and won't do. Online, we often see privacy policies which are usually little more than a legal description of what the organization has chosen to do with information about its users so that when a risk turns into an exploit, users will not have legal recourse.

Despite the ability to represent them as something they're not, policies do have a very important role.

First of all, before decisions can be made about particular technology, what it will and won't do in the deployment, the organization needs to decide what it's trying to accomplish. Businesses typically start with high-level objectives, with vision and mission statements that define what they're trying to achieve. Beyond that, they build policies that define how the work will get accomplished, how the standard case will be managed, how to deal with anomalies, and where responsibility for various pieces of the puzzle lie.

There is little difference between a corporate policy that describes how the corporation gets its work done, and policies that are more specific in purpose, such as a security or privacy policy. In our case, we're going to be considering privacy as an aspect of data security. That translates into defining what our systems will do, not only for our own use, but to prevent them from being useful to attackers. Policies and their roles are covered in more detail in Schneier's book *Secrets and Lies* [171] but three critial policy issues are worth considering here: inventory (what's being managed with the policy), value (what the system that's being managed is worth to its users), and practice (what will be done day-to-day).

Inventory

Before being able to protect any asset, we need to know what assets we are protecting.

Building an inventory of technology assets might seem strange, particularly when we look at it from a perspective of network-based attackers. Network-based attackers don't necessarily care about the monetary value of the physical machines. They want to know things like how much bandwidth the network has, how much disk space is available, and what utilities (like compilers) the system has installed. They also care about how closely the systems are monitored, how clueful the administrators are, and whether the systems are current with security fixes. Strange or not, these are the assets that you need to protect.

Of course, all of this is in addition to the more obvious things, like your customer databases and all of the good stuff that would be of extreme interest to your competition.

Value

Once we have identified our assets, we'll need to identify their value. This will help us to know just how much time and effort we should put into protecting the asset. Never would we want to build a million-dollar safe to protect $1,000. This is an important point to keep in mind, because as we get into the issue of threat models later in this chapter, we're going to see how spending money can get an attacker closer to the target much more quickly (and maybe even effectively) than banging on the front door from the outside.

Identifying value is a deceptively difficult problem in many cases. On one hand, value might be measured in terms of how much the organization spent on it. On the other hand, value is best represented in some systems when discussed in terms of its value to the organization, how much it costs the organization to be without it. In critical systems, we should know what that value is, perhaps per minute or per hour.

Practice

The processes that people follow when going about their daily work are going to be at least as important as defining the organization's policies. If everything is officially deemed confidential, but people are making lots of printouts of things, without giving much thought to how many copies exist or where the copies are, there's a pretty significant mismatch between the official policy and how well the policy can be enforced.

Where there is mismatch in policy and enforceability, there's a risk to be addressed.

Comprehensive policies, therefore, will need to include practices that will help to ensure the workability of the policy. *Best current practice* (BCP) is a phrase that's tossed around quite a bit in certain circles, and it's a useful phrase for spelling out exactly how people are expected to make the policy work. Even the Internet Engineering Task Force (IETF), which specifies standards for the Internet community, specifies BCP documents. BCP documents often define policy decisions that lead to enhancing the value of Internet systems, effectively recommending policy that's compatible with the overall goals of the Internet community.

Building Effective Policy

Effective policies will need to include these three elements: inventory, value, and practice. They'll also need to consider these elements from various sources. Watching how legal, management, and technical groups will address the very same assignment to identify how these three issues apply to their organizations is very telling of why we have so much difficulty understanding each other. We're almost from different planets. Things that management considers important might be almost irrelevant to legal types, and what lawyers think is a good idea might be completely impossible to implement. It'll take a few rounds of everyone providing constructive criticism to get policy right.

When weighing the risks that are posed to a system and trying to determine just how to address them, we find that standard policy definitions just aren't up to the task. It's often worth the additional effort to specify a completely different document, one whose sole purpose is to identify the threats against the system and to specify how those threats are to be addressed.

Threat Models

Whether a part of a larger policy definition or a standalone document, a *threat model* is a definition of what kinds of threats there are to the organization. Comprehensive threat models can be gargantuan if they go into painstaking detail, articulating every single threat that there is and every single source that there is. Useful threat models don't need to be huge, but it is often surprising just how large they can become in a relatively short period of time.

The basic issues that you have with threat models are the threat sources and the threats themselves.

Threat Sources

Threat sources are important to consider because they're going to help us to understand what kinds of resources are available to the attacker and how much he'll know about the target and its weaknesses. In some cases, it's worthwhile to split threat sources into two: threat sources and attacker resources. For the time being, however, we'll deal with this simpler case.

Depending on the target, models for threat sources will vary. The basic issue in question is "Is the attack coming from a government intelligence agency or from a six-year-old kid with an Ovaltine secret decoder ring?" Of course, most attackers fall somewhere in the middle of those extremes. Therefore, it's worthwhile to define a model that includes not only the extreme cases, but points along the line between the extremes. Table 3-1 shows an example of some attackers that would be worth considering along with a brief description of each.

Table 3-1. Sample Attackers

Attacker	Description
Outsider	No knowledge of the organization
Customer	No knowledge of the organization beyond that which is given to customers
Partner	Non-employees, but there is some knowledge of the organization through business relationships
Insider	Employee of the organization, but unassociated with the target itself or its management
Key insider	Employee of the organization, associated with the target or its management

I call this a simple model, because it does not take into account the ability for the attacker to spend some resource—usually time or money—to get the information he needs to act as an attacker closer to the target. Some examples of how this would work would include a dedicated random attacker who would take the time to read the target organization's web site content to determine what the offerings are, whom he can contact for various things, and the like. Other possibilities include spending money instead of time, perhaps in bribes to insiders—maybe someone like a janitor, who would have physical access to the target or things like backup tapes—that would allow the attacker to get his hands on information that would effectively make him as formidable an attacker as an insider or key insider.

This is what we need to keep in mind when talking about the value of the target. A $1,000 bribe wouldn't make much sense against a target worth less than that. So, if an organization has information that's worth one million dollars, figure that spending close to close to one million dollars is a worthwhile "investment" for an attacker able to move that kind of money.

Threat Types

Threat types are how we identify the nature of the threat. By identifying several relatively high-level types of threats, we can look at our design and implementation to ensure that we're taking reasonable precautions, treating risk types comparably, and not putting all of our eggs in one proverbial basket.

We'll consider some examples.

Known vulnerabilities

Despite being straightforward—note that I didn't write *easy*—to address, *known vulnerabilities* is a very common threat type. The reason why I didn't assert that this is easy to address is because in practice, many system administration teams are overworked, understaffed, and underappreciated. It's difficult to stay on top of the daily stream of bugs and their fixes. Getting the fixes installed before someone attempts to use the vulnerabilities to compromise the target is even trickier. Attackers are relatively well-coordinated, agile, and able to run exploit scripts quickly.

Defenders tend not to be on-site around the clock, watching their systems for strange activity, checking every report from every vendor to see whether the newly-reported problem applies, and applying the fixes on the ones that do.

Of course, the known vulnerabilities problem is tricky, because it's a race where attackers have a head start. Once a vulnerability is known, we can configure virus detection software, intrusion detection systems, and the like to look for them.

What we're talking about here primarily, however, is not the type of race where we want to see whether the attacker or the defender will be the first to address the problem on a given machine. What we're primarily talking about is the undermanagement of Internet-connected systems that is so common now. This undermanagement causes bugs that are known to have security implications to go unpatched for months or even years before an exploit occurs.

Configuration errors

Policy is just a definition of what you do and don't want to happen, typically in a human language like English. *Configuration* is an articulation of policy in the language of the device you're configuring. That is, you're telling the device what you do and don't want to happen. Ideally, we should be able to configure devices, specifying what we will allow, and denying everything else. This is an important concept we'll return to in Chapter 6's discussion entitled Fail-Safe Defaults.

Because security devices (and devices configured with security and privacy in mind) are systems that enable technology to enforce policy, there isn't anything inherently "safer" about these things. There really isn't anything particularly special about firewalls, intrusion detection systems, or anti-virus software. These devices merely recognize what kinds of traffic or data they're handling, and consult their configurations to determine whether the requested action is one that should be allowed to proceed or not.

The strength of any security system, therefore, is highly dependent upon its configuration, which is dependent upon the site's policy. Deadbolts in strong doors do a great job of keeping the bad guys out, but only if they're engaged.

Denial of service

Perhaps the nastiest of all attacks—because it's both the easiest to perpetrate and one of the most difficult to mitigate—is the denial of service attack. Essentially, these are attacks that take advantage of what is an arms race: whoever has the most bandwidth can effectively blow the other off of the network.

In the most general case, denial of service attacks simply cause the target to stop functioning. In a more typical case, a network-based denial of service attack will come in the form of a flood of packets directed at the target, where the goal is to send the target more requests than it can handle. If the target system, a web server for example, is able to process 1,000 requests per second, a successful denial of service attack would need to send the server many more requests than it can handle, perhaps 10,000 requests per second. Although the server is operating normally, it is just trying to do too much. It will be able to process a normal request from time to time, but if the flood of bogus requests is ten times the server's capacity, the bogus packets will dwarf the legitimate packets in number. The vast majority of the legitimate traffic will therefore be refused, unable to be processed, because the machine is busy trying to service the bogus requests.

As already noted, this is an arms race situation. These attacks are best directed at sites that have comparatively little in the way of capacity to handle such loads as would be created by an attack. The problem with launching a denial of service attack is that no one but the target will notice unless you manage to take down a very high-profile site. High-profile sites tend to have the resources to handle tremendous load.

In an attempt to solve this "problem," attackers have taken a more sophisticated view of denial of service attacks. Beginning in early 2000, we started to see a new breed of these tools, *distributed* denial of service (DDoS) tools [53]. Rather than requiring an attack to be launched from a single site against its target, DDoS tools make it possible for a large number of "drones"—compromised machines somewhere on the Internet—to be coordinated from a central, secret server. When the orders come from the central server to the drones, each of the drones—there could be hundreds or even thousands involved—start a stream of bad packets at a particular target. Because the drones are able to be coordinated, all can be launched against a single target, thus causing the flood to come in from literally thousands of directions. Even if some of the flooding drones are identified and removed, there are still enough others elsewhere on the Internet, in other states, other time zones, and other countries, that stopping the flood is almost impossible.

If the target *does* have the resources to handle a steady stream of bogus packets from thousands of drones, the attackers need only to add more drones to their network. This is significantly easier than adding more resources to the target. Not only is this an arms race, but it's one where the target is the only one paying, and the advantage is on the side of the attacker.

Equipment hijacking

For almost two decades, the networks that became today's Internet were friendly places, where everyone helped each other, and we could trust each other to some degree. Those days, sadly, are long gone.

It also used to be true that anyone taking over functionality of a system without authorization was either an otherwise friendly fellow administrator being mischievous or a student of one type or another being mischievous. Sadly, this also is not a safe assumption anymore. Particularly of interest is the insecure deployment of IEEE 802.11b wireless networks: it's now possible for attackers to get connectivity on others' networks without needing to do any more than getting close enough to the network.

Thanks to its adoption by the mainstream, the Internet is no longer the domain of scientists, engineers, and hobbyists. We now have an Internet full of the very same people whose idea of a job is trying to sucker people less bright than themselves into working in pyramid schemes or stapling signs like "Make $1,500 part-time or $5,000 full-time per month!", "Lose 30 Pounds in 30 Days!", and "Herbal Viagra!" on telephone poles near the stoplights of high-volume intersections.

Greed and laziness combined into a single personality is a dangerous thing.

It is this very sort of mentality that leads to the huge volume of unsolicited bulk email and articles spammed all over Usenet. The perpetrators of this nonsense are largely unconcerned with anything but the piles of money that they've been promised to receive by the people higher up on the pyramid than they are. Issues like who pays for the bandwidth, whose machines have to handle the processing load, and who deals with all of the bounces, replies, and complaints are irrelevant to these people, as along as they themselves aren't paying. Diverting others' equipment for one's own use has come to be known as *equipment hijacking*.

This disregard for anything but self-interest, combined with visions of big wads of cash being piled up on their dining room tables, leads to an entire industry of parasites whose idea of a job is sending as many copies of "advertisements" as possible while simultaneously forcing others to do the work.

Until sometime in 1997, it was standard policy for a mail server receiving email to forward it on to the appropriate place, even if it had no connection to the sender or the recipient. The idea was basically "someone sent some mail, it wound up here by accident, so I'll forward it along to the right place." Blood-sucking spammers took advantage of this cooperative spirit and began to clog email servers around the Internet with the drivel that they were pushing out to every email address they could find or guess. Naturally, this led to a reversal in policy to a more defensive stance, where mail servers would refuse to process mail that didn't originate from one of their users or that wasn't able to be delivered directly.

Man in the middle

Internet email has often been likened to a postcard. Anyone who happens to be in the middle of the sender and the recipient who cares to look at the postcard can read the message written on it. This analogy is quite accurate.

Man in the middle generally refers to a classification of attacks that are possible because the attacker is logically between the sender and recipient. Historically, someone in such a position on a network would have the ability not only to read, but to interject and to alter the data on its way.

Although it is not possible to protect messages on a computer network in quite the same way that we protect postal messages (with an envelope through which the attacker cannot see), we do have some good options available.

Digital signatures can help us to trust that the message we received is the same message that was sent to us, in much the same way that a seal pressed into hot wax on a message was used to indicate the genuineness of a message in past centuries.

Encryption of the messages makes it possible for the sender and receiver to communicate in front of others such that no one else can understand what's being exchanged, in much the same way that two people who speak a language that no one else knows could communicate without fear of others understanding what's being said. Both digital signatures and encryption are applications of a larger field generally known as *cryptography,* the art of message encoding. *Cryptology* is the science behind cryptography.

Steganography is the art of communicating secretly, so not only the contents of the message are secret, but the fact that a message has been passed also remains secret. Steganography is especially useful when used in conjunction with various cryptographic techniques, thus making it possible for two parties to communicate without anyone knowing, but also being able to ensure that the message as received is the same message that was sent and that should someone have stumbled across the communication's presence, he would not have been able to read it.

Social engineering

People are the weakest link in the security chain for almost every system. Blackmail, bribes, and threats of other harm are extremely effective means of coercing people to do things that they normally wouldn't. Furthermore, if they can find ways around the security systems in place, they'll often exploit them, simply because it's more convenient.

Perhaps more difficult to understand is *social engineering,* a means of fooling people into doing things that they shouldn't. For example, an attacker could call a user on the telephone, claiming to be a system administrator in the throes of a difficult computer problem that's hurting the company. If the attacker is convincing enough, he might be able to trick the user into revealing information that he couldn't obtain otherwise, such as a username, a password, a number to call, the name of a person in charge, or something else that could be used to penetrate the system more deeply.

Trust is dangerous to assume. In daily life, we place so much trust in so many things without even thinking about it. We trust that the taxi driver is going to get us to our destination. We trust that he's not going to go by way of the moon. We trust that if he does, we should be able to get matters settled with the cab company. We trust that if that doesn't work, the legal system will give us some recourse. We trust that if the matter goes to court, we'll get a fair hearing and have our grievances satisfactorily addressed.

Many people do not lock their workstations because they trust the people they work with—if they're able to get into the building, they must be legitimate. Instead of making each person entering a limited-access area swipe an identity card, the first person will unlock the door and hold it open for the rest. We could probably spend the rest of eternity enumerating examples.

The basic issue is that because of their trust, people in the system are undermining the security precautions that are in place. In so doing, they are defeating the protection that would otherwise be provided by the systems in place. An attacker who looks and acts like he belongs is probably going to be assumed to belong.

Social engineering attacks tend to be increasingly easier to perpetrate as the number of users increases. In targets with very small user populations, people tend to know one another, and pretending to be a new guy is pretty difficult. On the other hand, impersonating a telephone company employee probably isn't too difficult.

The point of social engineering is that it's an attack against basic human tendencies: that we trust and want to help people who appear to be "on our side."

Prevention

We're going to discuss prevention in much more detail later in the book—Part II is devoted to the topic—but we'll take a look at it here. There's an old saying about the relative values of prevention and cure that seems apropos in this context.[3]

We've taken the time to understand such things as what threats we're facing, who might be behind them, what we're working with, and building privacy. Having this understanding, we're ready to consider what we're going to do to frustrate our attackers' plans.

Management

A very large part of what we're going to do is really a *management* issue. In everything that an organization or an individual does, a level of risk is present: risk of failure, risk of succeeding and finding oneself in a position that can't be managed, risk of loss, risk of life. What constitutes a risk? What sets of risks do we worry about and what do we say are "too expensive" to manage or "too unlikely" to spend our limited resources addressing? How do we balance our risks against the rewards? Every individual, household, company, and government deals with these issues, whether realizing it or not.

These questions are answered by management in the form of *policy.* In the policy, risks have been identified, which issues we address has been decided, and a set of guidelines has been established that will allow us to go about our business without needlessly exposing us to risk. Everything from document retention policies to vacation policies are all about balancing all of the pressures that are put on the organization that try to pull it in so many different directions.

As noted earlier, in essence, a policy is a statement of what will and won't be done. Policy that no one follows is at least as useless as having no policy at all. In practice, it's probably worse, for the same reason that a bogus cryptography program is worse than none at all: it is likely to give people a false sense of security, preventing people from staying on their guard. Any organization whose management believes it's protected by virtue of a good policy, but whose employees' actions ignore the policy, will have a serious problem.

Among people who concern themselves with policy enforcement, there are essentially two schools of thought:[4] One says that additional policy is the answer and another that says policy must be enforced through other means.

---

[3]   Note, too, how skillfully I made the point without resorting to an explicit restatement of the cliché in question.

[4]   One school, which breaks everything into two groups, and another that doesn't.

Enforcing policy with policy

Although the idea of enforcing policy with more policy might initially sound ludicrous, it's really the most common type of enforcement. We have varying levels of policy, articulated in such means as government constitutions, federal laws, state laws, and municipal laws. Another set of policy deals with such things as the company's mission statement, its high-level objectives, and its day-to-day procedures manuals.

The Enforce Policy With More Policy school of thought basically says: "Do this. If you don't, we're going to subject you to our disciplinary policy." Bad boys get reprimanded verbally and in writing, put on probation, and might even be (gasp!) *fired*. Interestingly, the worst case scenario for people doesn't seem like much of a deterrent, given that everyone is working "at will" these days and is theoretically able to terminate the working agreement—or to have his working agreement terminated—without notice or recourse. With the way that a huge number of companies are set up, you can work hard or goof off the whole time and it won't make one bit of difference. Either way, you can get tossed out the door when, after blowing a bazillion dollars to monopolize Internet access to Mars, the company learns that there just isn't any market for providing connectivity to uninhabited planets.

Bureaucrats seem to love this approach, though, and its results can be found everywhere. Corporate policies are often little more than long lists of things that employees shouldn't do, what will happen to them if they violate the policy, and how the company is basically allowed to do anything that it wants. There are more than a few people who seem to think that people are basically lazy and won't do anything unless threatened.

The second big Enforce Policy With More Policy crowd is the U.S. legal system. Rather than actually preventing anyone from being able to listen in on telephone calls, we'll just make it *illegal* to do so. When someone actually makes a move to make it *impossible* to tap the phones, well, we'll have none of that! It's already illegal! Besides, how will police catch child pornographers and terrorists? In the hours following the tragic September 2001 terrorist attacks on Manhattan and Washington DC, we heard a great deal about how vulnerable a free society is to attackers, with some going so far as to say that it was time to surrender our freedoms in the name of safety. Benjamin Franklin offered some advice that seems especially apropos here: "They that can give up essential liberty to obtain a little temporary safety deserve neither liberty nor safety."

The argument that making something illegal or against some policy will prevent it from happening is complete nonsense. One needs only to consider such laws against alcohol, drugs, and weapons. Since these laws have so effectively eliminated substance abuse and violence from our society, it hardly seems fair even to consider using something other than policy to enforce policy.

If you outlaw _____, only outlaws will have _____. (Try it for "guns," "cryptography," "civil liberties," "privacy," or anything else.) The argument works. People who believe otherwise are delusional. I acknowledge that this might well have some distasteful consequences, but the basic fact of the matter is that policy alone isn't enough to enforce policy. It's just not enough. The good news is that we have another alternative, one that's especially attractive online: using technology to enforce the policy.

Enforcing policy with technology

The other school of thought believes that a better approach to policy enforcement is to make policy, and what is generally possible, more closely in line. Returning to the example of a wiretap, if Alice and Bob want to talk without Mallory being able to tap the line to hear what's happening, instead of making it illegal, actually build the system so that Mallory cannot tap the line, or communicate in such a way that even if Mallory does tap the line, she can't do anything with what she hears. Cryptography has a perfect application here.

This approach does require more up-front thought and it does often require a bit more up-front cost. The long-term costs of this approach, however, are significantly less.

Consider another example. Instead of merely having a policy not to let Internet-based users reach your employee salary data, why even make it possible for Internet-based users to reach your employee salary data in the first place? If you don't want your customer database to be read by someone who breaks into your web server, why do you provide full access to your customer database from the web server?

Enforcing policy with technology recognizes two fundamental truths:

- Computer systems fail.

- People make mistakes.

As long as computer systems fail, they're going to behave in ways that we don't expect. We can't rest all of our security on a single point, because that point will—at a time we can't predict—fail. People also make mistakes. With or without realizing it, they break policies, they misunderstand things, and they sometimes do exactly the opposite of what they should. There is nothing revolutionary here, either. But, if we fail to recognize this basic fact and to build our systems recognizing it, our systems are going to be vulnerable to being used by people to do the Wrong Thing more often and more quickly.

We can limit the damage of failure in several important ways, which we discuss in significant detail in Part II, "The Problem."

Once the fundamental issues have been determined, like what theories will be used to manage risk and to prevent breaches of policy, we can consider how to enforce that policy. Beyond the issue of management, other means for prevention include system configuration and architecture.

Configuration

As mentioned earlier, configuration is the means by which we communicate policy to the devices we're using. Firewalls need to know what our access policies are if they're to enforce them. We tell the firewalls what those policies are by way of configuration. The same is true for other devices: routers, switches, host operating systems, and everything else out there on the network.

Despite being so terribly important, it's something that is very often overlooked. People often set their configurations poorly, without giving any consideration to side effects. Whenever a user wants to do something and some security software or system prevents it, the user complains, and very often, a configuration change is made on the spot to allow the user to do what he wants. Never mind that what the user wants has actually enabled a huge avenue of attack to outsiders.

Configuration just isn't about keeping people contained in their little cells: it's an implementation of the policy. A change in configuration—unless it's made to bring the system in closer alignment with the policy—is a step away from policy compliance. An organization whose practices don't match its stated policy is in danger of believing it has a level of security that it does not have.

Configuration is a big deal.

Architecture

Even systems with the best configurations are going to be bound by some limitations. It's the nature of technology; if an attacker manages to break into a given host, the attacker likely has access to the hosts that are available to that system. Recognizing this is important in the context of architecture—what components to put where.

If you don't want someone to be able to read every corporate secret that you have by breaking into a single machine, then *don't store all of your corporate secrets on one machine*. If a web server needs to be able to write records into a database, then *give it write access to the database*. If it doesn't need to have the ability to write overtop of existing records or to read records, then *don't let it read records*.

These are basic precautions against abuse that are straightforward to take, if designers and implementors will spend that little bit of extra time to set things up properly in the first place—so that they enforce stated policy. Unfortunately, in practice, very few bother to take these straightforward steps, thus leaving themselves and their organizations wide open to all manner of attack.

We have covered a lot of ground here. We've gone through the concepts of security, what agents are and how they apply to our development of computer systems, policies, threat models, and have taken a quick look at prevention. Earlier, we discussed privacy, and its relevance for building secure systems. Now we're going to take another look at privacy, from the perspective of users out there on systems designed for use by the public.

CHAPTER 4

Online Privacy Concepts

WIDESPREAD ADOPTION AND SUBSEQUENT DEPENDENCE upon technology, where privacy is essentially a non-consideration, predictably caused significant abuses of privacy, which then led to a great degree of fear about online privacy.

Interestingly, personal privacy in electronic records is something that has been given significant consideration well before mainstream acceptance of Internet technology. International organizations, namely the United Nations [183, 184], the European Union [59], and the Council of Europe [37] have given significant attention to the issue. Much of what they have to say is highly relevant to online privacy in the way that we think of it today. Rather than building on that work, however, much of today's online privacy debate is centered around efforts to build consumer trust in the Internet's technology. The point of these efforts is always to address public fears that might stifle proliferation of online—particularly web-based—commerce.

This approach, preferred by organizations reacting to public fears, strikes me as well-meaning but potentially dangerous. Why do we spend so much time and effort building trust in technology instead of spending that time and effort in building *trustworthy* technology?

Either way, we're going to need to put forth significant time and energy. Using the first approach, we're essentially engaged in an extensive public relations campaign that is designed to make people feel confident about Internet safety and security. Where possible, breaches that occur will need to be addressed with assurance that little damage was done. Where it's clear that damage is significant, we'll need to assure the public that precautions have been taken to avoid future problems. Whatever we do, it'll be for the purpose of making people believe that the risk of exploit is remote and that whatever might happen won't happen to them. In other words, public trust is itself an end.

Using the second approach, we're spending time and energy on building systems that are designed to withstand the attacks that will be launched against them. These are systems that acknowledge that failure will occur and are designed to deal with such failure safely.

Perhaps the most significant difference about being focused on building systems that are *worthy* of trust is that it is the security of the system itself—that is, the specification and compliance to policy—that is the goal. System safety is the end. What's interesting is that a safe system will tend to earn the trust of its users. We can win public trust this way, as well, but it's a side effect of doing the job the right way in the first place.

Both approaches get us to the same place: public trust. The question is whether it makes more sense for us to get there by working to maintain the facade of security or actual security. I obviously advocate the latter position.

No doubt privacy advocates will come and go, as will self-proclaimed standards bodies, and everyone else trying to define what privacy means in practice. Numerous standards for online privacy have been proposed from various sources, each with its own strengths and deficiencies.

Specific privacy standards, if they're to be effective, need to enforce the central theme of privacy: informational self-determination. Many groups have proposed sets of principles that should be able to enhance privacy. When evaluating any set of principles, it's worth asking the following short list of questions.

- Are there any significant concepts missing?

- What exactly is the problem that is trying to be solved?

- How workable are models based on these concepts?

- Do these issues go far enough to address the problem fully?

Rather than measure some of today's proposals against these questions, however, we will discuss high-level privacy principles that seem to emerge whenever privacy is being addressed, whether online or offline. These principles fall into several groups: data collection and handling practices, data correctness, and policy compliance.

Collection and Handling

Data collection—in a very general sense, any time that a datum comes under our control—is obviously central to the issue of privacy. We can't give away secrets we don't have, but we can give away things in our possession, either intentionally or by accident. *Handling*—what we do with the data in our control—will also help us enforce the policy that we think we're using.

Privacy principles that help us in our data collection and handling practices are notice, choice, minimization, use, security, and classification.

Notice

If we're to build a system that's privacy-aware, its users must understand that data collection is taking place. In many real-world systems, *notice* is pretty obvious. For example, when you're trying to get telephone service established at a new location, the phone company representative will ask you some questions. You know to whom you're speaking, and you know what information you will reveal before you do it. You have the opportunity to object before giving any information. Notice is built in to the transaction.

As will be discussed in greater depth in Chapter 7, the nature of the Web makes it possible for data collection to happen in more places than users realize.

For example, let's take a typical case of a web-based search engine. When a user points a browser to a search engine, he knows that he's having a conversation of sorts with that search engine's servers. As would the client, the server will have some memory of that conversation, in the form of log data.

What a user might not know, however, is that some of the images on that search engine are not coming from the same server as the rest of the content on that site. The user could very well be unaware that he's having a conversation with a *marketer's* server and that now the operators of the marketer's server—in addition to the search engine's—have the ability to see how the search engine is being used.

Another thing that users might not realize is that in many cases, when they make a connection to a marketer, the marketer is tagging them uniquely with an HTTP cookie. Once a unique tag has been given, anonymity is lost; the user becomes pseudonymous. The user can be known by that unique tag in place of his name and can build up reputation.

Sidebar: HTTP Cookies

Cookies tend to be a central theme in many of the debates regarding online privacy. In the context of the Web, cookies are simply an arbitrary string of text attached to objects downloaded from servers and requests made by clients.

Web developers can use cookies for many things. Individual user preferences can be stored in the cookies, for example, or other data to preserve a transaction's state. The critical privacy issue with cookies tends not to be the cookies themselves, but how they're used. In many cases, instead of using cookies to store preference or transaction data, developers will use cookies to give users unique ID numbers.

Some have naïvely called for the elimination of cookies out of concern for privacy. Eliminating cookies will do nothing to solve the privacy problem, because the issue isn't really cookies, but how they're used: giving unsuspecting users unique numbers and correlating their activity online. If cookies were not used for this purpose, other technologies could be.

It's not the technology that's the problem; it's the technology's application. We'll discuss cookies, including history and privacy safeguards, in Chapter 7.

Marketers will often defend these practices by suggesting that they're providing adequate notice in the form of education campaigns and disclosures on their web sites.

The essential question here is whether this is meaningful "notice." Is it all right to tell someone out of band that something is happening? How would someone know to go to the marketers' web sites in the first place? How many "education campaigns" have you seen?

I built a dossier on you. Click here if you don't like it.

Another serious problem with marketers' use of notice is their explanations of how things work, they manage to destroy important distinctions between anonymity and pseudonymity. They describe the transactions as anonymous, failing to recognize that the kinds of attacks against a user's online identity relevant to pseudonymity are applicable in the case of marketers who uniquely tag the people who see their ads. Are marketers lying? Do they fail to understand the nature of data? Are they fooling themselves?

In any case, these aren't the people that I'd expect to be in a position to make such wide-reaching decisions about so many people.

Marketers are by no means unique in anything for which we've criticized them here. Nevertheless, comparison of getting telephone service to web-based advertising serves as a good example of how technology has taken notice of data collection from obvious to nearly invisible.

Choice

Once people have been served with notice, they need to choose for themselves whether they prefer the benefits of the system over its risks. Returning to the example of establishing phone service, you might be asked for a datum like your Social Security number, but you have the ability to choose whether to reveal it.

In web-based applications today, *choice* is generally implemented not in the form of proper nonparticipation, but in the form of taking on a pseudonym that is shared by all of the people who do not want to be tagged uniquely. The usual pseudonym in that case is "OPTOUT" or some variation.

Here, we would do well to consider another question, whether the choice is *meaningful*. That is, is this the choice that people want? Do we have an appropriate set of options for them to use in making the decision?

Reconsidering the question of whether to provide your Social Security number to the phone company can help us understand the issue of meaningful choice. Thanks to notice, you know that they're going to collect your Social Security number and are going to put that into their records on you. If you don't like the practice, you can object.

You now have a choice: do you give your Social Security number to the phone company? If choosing yes means that they'll do something you don't want, that's not a viable option. If choosing no means that you won't be able to get service, that basically means that you are presented with the choice of whether to have your privacy invaded or to go without phone service.

That kind of choice is not meaningful because neither option is viable.

If you are a Web user and you don't want to have third parties keeping records of your activity, you are presented with the option of opting out of the system. This, however, isn't a meaningful choice, because it doesn't stop what you find objectionable: keeping records of your activity. Thus, questions regarding the use of opt-out systems persist. We're going to discuss the use of opt-out systems and their privacy implications in Chapter 10.

Minimization

All of us have heard the advice not to carry large amounts of cash. Few question this wisdom; the reason behind it is obvious: cash is easy to steal and to use directly. Recognition that a thief cannot steal what you don't have will move you not to carry more money than you need. This is the principle of minimization.

In the context of privacy, *minimization* basically means not collecting more data than you need. Further, minimization means not keeping data you do collect longer than you must.

These practices are perhaps most commonly implemented through corporate documentation retention policies. Such policies generally define a lifespan for documentation. Essentially, anything not actively needed is destroyed, unless it is deemed appropriate for archival. Archived documents are cataloged so they can be easily found. This process contributes to efficiency in the organization, because folks know right where to look if they need something, and if it isn't there, they don't need to bother trying to find it. This process also reduces the company's exposure to certain legal risks that could come as a result of litigation that includes document discovery. Opposing legal counsel cannot discover damaging documentation that has been destroyed after its lifespan has expired.

When we're designing systems, we must think carefully about our requirements and what we have at our disposal. We do well to follow these principles, because they go a long way to making our systems safe. Not only do we show respect for our users this way, but we avoid turning our systems into targets by attackers who would try to take such data illicitly.

Use

The reason that so many people would object to the phone company collecting Social Security numbers (or at least being annoyed by it) is because the phone company doesn't need it. Social Security numbers are identifiers used for people to pay into and to draw from Social Security.

When we start looking at data in our possession and think we can use such data however we see fit, we run significant risk of violating the privacy of the data owners. If we're talking about a database full of clients, we're talking about violating our clients' privacy.

Decisions about what data people will allow us to have are made on, among other things, what we're going to do with the data. You and I might exchange some schedule information in the course of negotiating schedules so we can be in the same place at the same time. It's rather doubtful that you'd give me your schedule so that I'll know when the best time to rob you would be.

Because the matter of use is so critical to the decision of whether to give us a datum, we need to pay close attention to this matter. Privacy policies are an effective way to address the matter of use, defining what can and cannot be done with data collected under that version of the policy. In practical terms, posted privacy policies greatly simplify the job of managing data usage. Rather than needing to specify exactly what we're going to do with any datum that we might collect at the time that we collect it and then needing to keep track of which data were collected under which statements, we can define a version of the policy that covers all of what we're doing. When we're collecting any data, then, we can simply refer to our policy—hopefully, we'll specify what part is most immediately applicable—and users will be able to get the information they need in order to make an intelligent, informed decision. We, then, have a simplified mechanism for tagging the data in our possession—a version of the privacy policy that applies.

We're still left with the basic problem, however, of being able to identify exactly what part of the policy—the context under which we collected the data—is applicable. The most straightforward way is classification.

Classification

Classification of data is a powerful tool in the protection of privacy. Classification of data allows us to identify different types of data and type-specific handling practices. This principle is widely acknowledged, particularly in the handling of data that relates to financial transactions, religious or political beliefs, health, and sexual life.

Sidebar: Who classifies what?

Our consideration of privacy and security in the context of designing and implementing systems offers us a potentially tempting trap: top-down design. Classification is one area where the folly of top-down privacy design can be seen.

Let's specifically consider a case I just raised: one's religious or political beliefs. Although such beliefs are largely recognized as private—even sensitive—data, we cannot simply assume that such data are sensitive and always build safeguards for that type of data. This is particularly true if we're confronted with conflicting requirements that make us specify whether one classification of data should be given greater attention than another type.

The reason we cannot make a rule and apply it across the board is because there are many among us who have chosen to become political or religious activists, spending a great deal of time and energy speaking their minds on such matters. Spending time and effort to build systems that protect the privacy of Bill Clinton's political beliefs would be pointless.

The most private datum in one person's life might be the most public datum in another's. Our goal of informational self-determination requires that we don't decide for our users what is private and what is public.

Developing categories that make sense for one application might not make sense for another. Although there are some obvious categories that might suggest themselves across a wide variety of applications, we shouldn't be too quick to draft a list of categories and assume that we've covered everything necessary. Neither should we develop a list of "special cases," a few categories that we can identify and then assume that everything else belongs in some other "more general" category.

Our present discussion reminds us of the previous chapter's remarks about access control, specifically the design and implementation of discretionary access controls. Indeed, that's precisely what we're talking about.

The larger the number of categories we develop, the better we're going to be able to classify data. It's also noteworthy that any particular datum can be applicable for more than one category.

An obvious example of how categories used to classify data need not be mutually exclusive would be in looking at life on earth. If we have categories like human, primate, mammal, fish, male, and female, we can see how we might have something that belongs to the categories female, human, primate, and mammal.

Classification can be an effective tool to help us to identify data in our control and to manage such data according to policy.

Security

Many privacy guidelines—though failing to go into elaborate detail—specify that information collected should be reasonably well-protected against attack. Clearly, the general idea is that data collected shouldn't be easily stolen.

This is an interesting point, because of the nature of information. That is, once a datum is stolen, it can *never* be recovered. If someone steals your car, and the car is found, it can be returned to you, and the thief no longer has the car. If someone steals your Social Security number, he can return to you the media on which the information is stored, but if he's made copies and given them to others, any of whom might have made additional copies, the information has effectively been made public. You cannot "reclaim" your Social Security number.

As discussed previously, when determining how to protect something, one of the key issues in building in that protection is its *value*. No one with any sense is going to spend more money protecting an asset than its value, or more specifically, what the cost of losing it would be.

Here are some questions to consider: what is the value of information about you to data handlers? Do they value information about you as highly as you do yourself? Will they take the same precautions as you to protect information about you? There is, of course, significant incentive for them to protect information about people. Exposure of information about people would certainly cause some public relations problems and there's potential loss of some competitive advantage with the publication of information they might consider proprietary.

There are many data handlers, of course, but let's zoom in on a specific category, online marketers. Certainly *in aggregate,* there's a great deal of value in information about users, but what about on a transaction-level basis? How careful would the marketer be inclined to be on the level of a single transaction? How about a single user?

Let's consider a example. If Alice and Bob are involved in litigation, Alice might claim that evidence material to the matter at hand is contained in Bob's browser history. A court might then issue a subpoena for Bob's browser history. Bob could disagree and move to have the subpoena quashed.

Now imagine that in the same litigation, Bob's online activity is contained in databases maintained by a marketer. Instead of sending the subpoena to Bob for his browser history, the court can deliver the subpoena to the marketer to get basically the same data. When would a marketer fight a court's subpoena to access certain information? How much might a marketer spend to fight such a subpoena?

If marketers holding data would not go to the same lengths as the individuals whose activity created the data, we have a vulnerability. A chain is only as strong as its weakest link. Information is only as safe as its weakest repository.

Data Correctness

Data are most useful when correct. We can tolerate some error, but in general, the more erroneous the data, the less value they'll have. Two specific practices arise to address the matter of data correctness: access and rectification. Neither is rocket science: it's a simple matter of providing some mechanism for audit.

Access

When we're collecting data about people, we need to be able to provide those people access to the data that we're collecting. Many systems that collect and report information about people are not very resistant when it comes to the insertion of malicious data.

Credit records are a source of frustration for many a privacy advocate. These records are not warranted to be correct, but they're often taken as fact. If you have some falling out with a vendor who turns out to be incompetent or malicious, you might find that invoices that used to be sent to you are now being sent through a collection agency and are showing as blemishes on your credit record.

To provide a means to relieve many of these problems, credit reporting agencies offer consumers access to their own records. This provides a means for consumers to review their records and, in effect, lets people see what others are "saying" about them, or their credit worthiness. Additionally, such review provides greater opportunity to detect fraud, which is, of course, in everyone's best interest.

Similar ideas have been bantered about in the context of records collected and maintained by third parties about consumer activity on the Internet, namely web marketers' logs and user profiles.

As it turns out, this is an area where Internet marketers have a real problem. In theory, access means that people whose activity created records in the marketers' systems should have the ability to access the information.

The reason that there's a real problem is that many of the data in these databases are pseudonymous. How does one prove that he's the "legitimate" user of a particular pseudonym? The key into the databases will be the value that the tag uses to identify the user to the system. But how can we tell the difference between someone who has a "legitimate" key and someone who simply guesses at a tag ID or steals it from somewhere else?

Where records are verinymous, one needs only to prove his verinym, which is easily done through standard identification mechanisms (like presentation of government-issued identification).

As a result, unless you're willing to make records about yourself verinymous, you don't get access. It's not unlike wanting to keep your Social Security number private but being told that you must reveal it to receive phone service at all. The options are so absurd that the choice is meaningless.

Rectification

Closely related to the issue of access is the ability to annotate and to challenge data included in the profile. This is true in the case of credit records; not only do you have the ability to get ahold of your own credit record, but if you find blemishes there that should not be there, you have the ability to contact the maintainer of the report and to contest the accuracy of the report.

This system is hardly perfect, but a potential creditor reviewing a credit report with blemishes is much less likely to be concerned about the individual's credit worthiness if the blemish is contested. Of course, if there's a new blemish every quarter of the year, each of which is contested, that might tip off a creditor that the consumer is likely to point an accusatory finger at someone else when a bill remains unpaid.

This matter of allowing people to comment on the records kept about them is quite important. It's also one that will come up again when we consider the workability of a model for protection of privacy that relies on privacy-sensitive consumers to opt out of the offensive tracking machinery.

Policy Compliance

Finally, the last area of privacy concepts is the matter of *policy compliance*. A policy that someone isn't following doesn't do anyone any good. In fact, it might be worse than nothing at all, giving a false sense of security and being the basis for what turn out to be very bad decisions by the end users. The two issues that we're going to see here are verifiability and remedy.

Verifiable Compliance

Of course, when someone gives a statement about policy and what will and won't happen with particular types of data, a service has been done to the users of the system. Particularly when we're dealing with leaky channels like the Web—to be discussed in the next chapter and in more detail in Chapter 7—we need to consider the issue of *verifiability*.

Verifiability is so important in the context of leaky environments because there is so much room for error and abuse. Returning once more to the phone company's collection of a Social Security number, they say that they're not going to give it to anyone or do anything with it but key their database, but how do we know? Unless we're granted access to the system itself and we have the expertise to be able to audit the technology and the day-to-day business practices, we're just not going to be able to verify their compliance to their policy.

It is this desire for compliance guarantee that has spawned what appears to be a whole industry of privacy auditors and privacy seal programs. Though well-meaning, these kinds of efforts very often miss the point: no matter how complete, an audit cannot verify anything except that no violations of the policy were found at the specific time that the audit was taking place. Particularly where human error or computer malfunction have the ability to cause a policy violation, the potential for policy violation exists. For certain types of data—whether one has an embarrassing medical condition, for example—even a small likelihood of policy violation might be too much.

Verifiable policy compliance is most useful when used in combination with other privacy concepts like minimization. If a site doesn't take more data than it needs to process my request, I can verify that. If a site takes more data than it needs but relies on elaborate policy and technology on the back-end to prevent further exposure, I have very little means to verify that. Verifiability, like choice, must be meaningful.

Sanctions and Remedies

One particular means to make privacy policy meaningful is to provide additional impetus for policy compliance. Although when dealing with privacy, it's not possible to recover fully (if at all) from privacy breaches, some remedy can be offered. The most obvious type of remedy would be some sort of compensation to data owners when privacy is violated.

I think that the term "remedy" is actually somewhat misleading, because it suggests a returning to the pre-violation state, which cannot really be done. It's worth mentioning here because it's something that does arise throughout nearly every discussion of privacy and what it means, whether the participants are governments, human rights groups, or online privacy advocates.

In my view, such remedies are useful for establishing monetary figures that help us to understand just how much we should put forth in the protection of certain types of data and how to determine when the risk of holding such data is greater than the value that we'd hope to get from having them in our possession.

But "remedy" after the fact is no substitute for avoiding the problem in the first place.

We have taken a fairly high-level look at privacy, considering principles and practices that emerge when looking at requirements for protecting the privacy of individuals.

These principles are not strictly related to consumer privacy, however. Always remember that privacy is important not only for individual consumers, but for systems that want to remain resistant to attack. When we're designing and building systems, we therefore want to look at these principles when we're evaluating how our systems will talk to each other and to others.

To round out our understanding of these principles and why they're necessary, we're going to look at specific threats to privacy. When reading about the threats, consider how principles discussed in this chapter would resist these threats.

CHAPTER 5
Threats to Privacy

INFORMATIONAL SELF-DETERMINATION—THE ABILITY FOR A datum's owner to decide who may and may not have it—is the concept that we want to keep in mind when considering privacy. In this chapter, we're going to consider privacy from a different perspective: how to attack it, how we can overcome the natural barriers that prevent us from taking control of information away from someone else.

Looking at privacy from both the standpoint of how to enforce it and how to erode it will be helpful in completing our understanding of the problem. Identifying threats to privacy isn't just a simple matter of negating our list of privacy principles. We're going to look at several issues in connection with data gathering and handling that affect privacy adversely: centralization, linkability, data excess, leaky channels, and secondary uses.

Centralization

One of the biggest problems that we have in making use of data—turning them into information—is putting everything together into some kind of a form that will allow us to examine what we have and to be able to retrieve it later.

Businesses often complain about how their data are scattered throughout the organization and how difficult it is to put things together so that one can examine what's happening all the way across the company. IT departments spend time and effort trying to deal with effective data backup strategies, which are seriously complicated by the inability for the backup systems to reach the data. When people leave the company, trying to learn exactly what has happened and where things stand can be difficult.

Having lots and lots of data all over the place isn't especially helpful if it's all in the form of pieces of paper inside of "in" and "out" boxes on everyone's desk. Sure, you can find out what's happening, but only by going to each desk and examining the contents for the Right Stuff. The problem is that it's a view at the wrong level—it doesn't scale to the enterprise level.

Enter databases. Now, instead of having to keep lots of forms on paper and to catalog everything that's there manually, we can build systems that will store everything in a single place. Because the database is electronic, we can store much more data in much less space; what used to take room after room of boxes full of documents now can be stored on a single hard drive. We can build systems where data can easily be extracted. We can run queries that will examine huge amounts of data and return the appropriate responses to us based on what the database retains about things. We can have all of the data go into a central place, and people can work against that central data repository from wherever they happen to be, so there's never any concern about what data live where and how they can be accessed.

We can leap tall buildings in a single bound.

Databases are marvelous inventions. Packrats can now collect absolutely everything all in a single place where they can extract data and do enough analysis to make their eyes bug out of their heads, rather than just filing it all someplace in their offices. And how often do people go nuts with databases? The more stuff that's in them, the more useful they are, so they start putting *everything* into a single database.

Having a large central database is like giving the entire company a massive, nearly perfect collective memory of all of its transactions, in every context and with every level of informational sensitivity.

Let's think about what this means in terms of privacy.

Consider what this would mean for your bank's ability to do business with you. Now, instead of dealing with the same person at the bank, the person who gets to know what you're about and what kinds of things you're likely to be interested in, the organization can effectively assimilate that person's knowledge of your preferences and interests by tracking all of your activity at a sufficiently detailed level. Every time you engage in a transaction at the bank, that transaction finds its way into some data repository someplace, which can then be used later to determine your reputation. How much did you deposit? How much did you spend? These are pretty mundane questions, but over time, these data can turn into significantly more interesting information. For example, from such data, one can tell how often you change jobs. When you change jobs, how much of a change in salary does it take? What kinds of companies do you work for? Large? Small? How often do you take vacations? Where do you spend your money? How important is a fine home to you in comparison to the kind of car that you drive, the kind of clothes that you wear, or the kinds of places you eat? How much of your income do you spend on each of these things? How does that compare to other people?

Reputation, in the context of a database, can take on a completely different kind of meaning thanks to the ability for the database to remember so much about you. These are the kinds of things that individuals with whom you deal might be able to determine if they stopped long enough to think about it, but even in that case, they'd probably tend to forget. With a database, there's now a virtually limitless place where these kinds of facts can be stored. And the access to these facts isn't limited to such things as an individual's imperfect memory, the number of transactions that such a person has actually engaged with you directly, and the degree that these kinds of things pass through the hands of an individual.

Using a database, facts about the account's activity can now be compiled not only for actions in which a teller is involved, but all spending habits (thanks to credit, and now debit, cards), all deposits (things like the number of accounts that are making payments to this one and the frequency and amount of those deposits), and even investments of various types that are handled by the same bank.

Credit cards are especially interesting to consider in this context. Credit card companies have a great deal of data to work with, going much further than the basics needed for the transfer of money from one account to another. Neural networks are employed to analyze the likely future performance of individual accounts [92] as well as to determine interests and other information that could be useful for marketing purposes.

Not to be confused with cerebral computers.

Compilation of detailed records on client activity can be found in other types of businesses as well. People who purchase things at various stores leave little trails of data behind them in many cases.[1] It's rare that people carry around enough cash to make purchases even for things like clothes. With the proliferation of easy access to the credit and debit card networks, even the grocery store is a

---

[1] Although done unintentionally, the trail might turn out to be not unlike the trail that Hansel and Gretel left behind them. Sure, it'll help you find your way back, but what else might it make possible?

common place for people to use "plastic" instead of cash. People want discounts, and many stores are happy to provide cheaper goods—as long as customers are willing to let the company look over their shoulders. Shopping "clubs" of various types—where you need to have a membership card to get in and to make your purchases—are popping up all over the place. Even grocery stores are getting into this act now. The whole point of all of these systems is to watch people at an individual level to determine what kinds of things people buy each time they come to the store, what kinds of purchases people will make over time, and to learn other things about the makeup of the household. For instance, people who buy baby formula are going to have certain demographic characteristics that could be used to predict what kinds of purchases they're likely to need at various points in the future.

By keeping data long enough, marketers will be able to predict the need for things like baby food, toys, and even school supplies. Knowing this kind of information is extremely helpful to marketers who want to be able to customize their messages as much as possible to each individual in order to make the average advertising cost per consumer drop by reducing or eliminating advertisements to people who are unlikely to react to them. A household buying denture supplies is unlikely to act on coupons for baby formula.

The point here is that no matter what kind of business, no matter what kind of customer, there are a great many things that are being done in order to help each organization have a better understanding of what it is doing and with whom it is interacting, by centralizing all of their data, putting everything into a single database. Some value is indeed derived from this—including lower costs and greater convenience—but at what cost?

It's the collection of all of the data in a single location that helps us to make the most of the data available to us, even being able to make sense of complicated and sometimes even contradictory data. When we're talking about data collected about people and their activity, we're not just talking about having "better data" or being able to offer more convenience to our customers.

Having all of our data in one place will allow us to read between the lines, even learning things that are true but that users of the system have not explicitly told us. The users of our systems own the information about their lives. We are therefore presented with a question: Do we invade our users' privacy if we are able to infer things they haven't told us, thanks to our database's ability to create for us an effectively perfect memory?

An important aspect of centralization is the ability to access the proper record—the key needed to reach the correct datum. Each system will have a key for an individual's records. If those keys are assigned and maintained by the operators of each system, they'll almost certainly be different for each system. Having many different systems use the same key to maintain records has an important privacy penalty: linkability.

Linkability

Very closely related to the issue of centralization of data is the issue of *linkability*. Having all of the data in the world in the same place doesn't do any good unless there's a way to find the needle in your proverbial haystack.

In typical database systems, the needed data are referenced by some sort of symbolic name—the aforementioned key—just as we access elements of a hash table in programming languages by symbolic name. The issue is that the *key* used is generally local in scope, which is to say that if the database is relational, the key will be unique to that table.

We're dealing with a scalability issue here: because the key needed to access the data is local in scope, different scopes could have different keys to access the same information. For example, my health insurance provider might tag all of my records as belonging to "insuree 12345," my employer might tag all of my records as "employee 0," and my dentist might tag all of my records as belonging to "patient 54321."

I have some level of protection against unnecessary comparison of my records from various sources and compilation of the information into larger "meta-dossiers" of my activity in these three realms by the simple fact that it's computationally expensive to link these things *en masse* and the results are probabilistic—matches might be bogus.

If, however, the identifier used for my records becomes standardized, we have increased the scope of that key. The same key can be used to access records in numerous databases. That is, now when my dentist tries to talk to my health insurer, they can use a single key to access records that will allow them to engage in a simple transaction showing that the dentist needs to be paid so much for a procedure done to this particular insured patient. If my employer uses the same identifier, things get even easier, particularly when solving problems such as trying to figure out why the insurer is claiming that the employee isn't covered.

In the United States, we have such an identifier: the Social Security number (SSN). Originally deployed for the sole purpose of identifying Social Security beneficiaries to the U.S. Government, the SSN is now a universally-recognized identifier that, by default, is smacked on top of everything from income tax records to credit reports and from employee records to patient records. The ubiquity of the SSN makes it possible for vendors—and now even the marketers to whom vendors sell this kind of information—to identify people uniquely.

This great convenience comes at a very serious cost, one that the persons about whom this information is being gathered, stored, and traded, have not knowingly agreed to bear. That is the ability for others, with relatively little effort, to be able to find detailed information about individual lifestyles.

In the United States, as in many places around the world, there are laws that theoretically protect people from "stalking," a crime whereby someone watches another, compiling information, generally for the purpose of harassment or to harm the target.

If someone sits in front of another person's house to learn his schedule and follows him around to see where he goes and when, what he buys, how much he spends, and what things he's likely to find of interest, at some point, he's quite likely to run afoul of the law. If he doesn't, but the practice gets to be common enough, people are going to start clamoring for recourse against this kind of activity, resulting in stronger laws forbidding it. Nobody wants to be watched like that. Hardly anyone would disagree that compiling this kind of information about someone is *dangerous* to the person about whom the information is being collected.

So what's the difference between following someone around and noting everything that he does and surfing the electronic record of his existence? *Scalability.* People don't generally worry too much about this kind of thing, at least on a very large scale, because it's just too expensive and time-consuming to do it. The data are not valuable enough per person to justify the kind of expenditure needed to compile them. People *can* and *do* compile this kind of information, though. Rather than doing it "by hand" (or physically) they do it electronically. Marketers and their organizations like the Direct Marketing Association (DMA) do indeed purchase a huge amount of information from all kinds of sources.

These data are centralized in databases maintained by state bureaus of motor vehicles, credit reporting agencies, and many others. As noted earlier, they don't become terribly useful until we have a key to link everything together. Social Security numbers are one such key. Other keys can be made up of various types of data, including things like addresses, telephone numbers, or combinations of things like sex, month and day of birth, and phone number. The vast majority of Americans can be uniquely identified by combining sex, month and day of birth, and five-digit ZIP code. The notion of linkability is very interesting because the more data that one collects, the more likely it is that he'll be able to find *something* that can be used as a key to correlate which transactions belong to the same persons.

Think back now to our discussion of nymity in Chapter 2. If you engage in a transaction without using any name at all, you have anonymity. If you engage in a transaction with a name that cannot be tied back to yourself, you have pseudonymity. If you engage in a transaction with your true name, you have verinymity.

Linkability is essentially the issue of nymity, the ability to maintain reputation. The more widely used a particular key is, the wider the scope of the reputation, and the more complete the theoretical dossier for that key.

A recent real-world example of linkability can be found in the case of Ted Kaczynski, who admitted to being the Unabomber, a pseudonymous mail bomber dedicated to stopping the development of technology. Unabomb was the name given to the case by the FBI; notes sent by Kaczynski were sent in the name of "the terrorist group FC." After the pseudonymous publication of his manifesto, a great deal of analysis was made of the writing, indicating an intelligent, educated author. In the end, a relative recognized the unique style, which led to the linking of the Unabomber's identity to that of Ted Kaczynski.

On the Web, HTTP cookies are the most common state management mechanism. In practice, these are also the means by which users' activity online is tracked and users' reputations built. As touched on in the previous chapter, many sites online use cookies to store unique identifiers—pseudonyms. Just as a pseudonym made it possible to connect all of the Unabomber's crimes together, a pseudonym can be used to connect all of an unsuspecting user's activity on a particular site. Just as a large enough set of data to analyze made it possible to link the Unabomber pseudonym to the verinym Ted Kaczynski, we just might be building systems that are eroding the privacy of our users much more seriously than we imagined. We'll discuss this in considerably more detail in Chapter 7.

Too Much Information

As the number of data in one's possession increases, so does the number of things he can do with the data. Collecting more information than is necessary for the purpose of the transaction makes it possible for the transaction to be used as a means to another end. This is the basic principle behind the science of *data mining*. Data mining is essentially searching through huge sets of data, looking for things that might not be immediately obvious. Although we've already discussed a privacy issue of credit cards (centralization), it's worth giving them another look here. The collection of information other than that which is necessary to complete the transaction allows profiling of cardholders. Interestingly, one of the consequences of having credit card companies collect enough information about transactions that they can profile users is the ability to sort through those data, to find anomalous transactions, and to use the technique to keep a lid on fraud [181].

Another strange side effect of collecting too much information is that it can make the collector a target of attack. In such cases, the data collector isn't itself an especially interesting target, but it has some datum needed for the bad guy to do his dirty deed. Thus, an attacker might target the data collector. We'll consider one such example in detail: a system that needs to use passwords to authenticate users.

User authentication is accomplished by giving each user an independent password and each user keeping that password secret. Thus, when a user gives his password, we can determine whether it is the same password that is associated with that user account.

Use of a password will give us some level of certainty that the person typing the password is the person we think it is, because the chances of someone guessing the right password are pretty slim. How slim? Well, if a password made up of ASCII characters—all of the unaccented Latin letters, numbers, control characters, and punctuation—we're dealing with seven-bit bytes, giving us a total of 128 possibilities (2^7) for each letter.[2] If the password is up to eight characters in length, we're dealing with 128 possibilities for each of the eight characters, yielding a total of over 72 quadrillion (128^8) possibilities.

The most straightforward solution to this problem would be to have the user set his password and to have the system store it someplace. When the user authenticates, we'll just pull up his password from our secret file and make sure that it matches what the user typed.

Think carefully about the requirement here: it isn't that we read the password or understand it. The requirement is that we compare the token that the user gave to the token in the user's profile. Couldn't we accomplish the same thing by looking at certain *properties* of the token and comparing those properties? Indeed, this is exactly what we do in order to compare the correctness of a file—we use some sort of *checksum*.

Depending on the properties that we're examining, we could have something that's very weak and easy to defeat, or we could have something that's very strong and difficult to defeat. A simple case of comparing properties would be to look at the number of letters in the password. However, this would be weak and easy to defeat. Rather than having to give the correct password, an attacker would merely need to give a password with the same number of characters. The number of attempts that would be required to break the system by brute force—by trying every possible combination—would be too small. Rather than having only one out of over 72 quadrillion possible tokens work, a successful brute-force attack of the system would take only eight attempts.

The relative difference in the strength of comparing an eight-character ASCII password and using our trivial character-count checksum is too great to make our checksum mechanism workable. There are more sophisticated checksum schemes available, such as the *cyclical redundancy check* (CRC). CRC, though more sophisticated than our byte-count scheme, is still much easier to defeat than brute force against the space of possibilities.

Still more sophisticated than checksum mechanisms like CRC are *cryptographically secure hash functions*. These functions, such as MD5 [167] and SHA1 [173], work the same way that other checksums work: they take some kind

---

[2]   These numbers are theoretical; we're ignoring certain practical matters like the probability of certain characters coming up being greater than others and other things that would actually make an attack against the system work better than plain ol' brute force against the entire set of combinations. Basically, in practice, you'd be able to identify certain combinations as being more likely than others and work your way through the entire set of possibilities, starting with the most likely, working toward the least likely.

of input and produce a simple output. There are two important properties of a hash function's output:

1. The original cannot be determined from the output, and

2. Comparing the output of the hash should be just as strong as comparing the original.

If we use a hash function that produces a 56-bit output, a brute-force attack against the hash—trying every possible hash output—will be the same strength as a brute-force attack against the password itself ($2^{56} = 128^8$).

If we can use a hash function this way, we can use this as a reliable means of determining whether the password given was correct, *without actually knowing the password itself.* Here's what we do: when the password is set, we run it through the hash function and we store the hash. When the user presents us with a password as a means of authentication, we run that password through the same hash function and we compare the result of the hash with the stored hash result. If the hash output of both functions match, the user has given us the same password as the one stored in his profile.[3]

Because we've taken a step back from our requirement and not implemented the first solution that popped into our heads—storing the password someplace to compare it with what the user typed—we actually found a way to implement a system that had just as much strength, but kept us from having to collect a datum that we didn't really need.

Consider the datum in question—a user-selected password. Who owns the password? If the user created it, wouldn't the user own the password? If we're storing a datum, we're presenting a certain risk to it: exposure through error or malice. If we're putting a datum that's not ours at risk, aren't we denying the datum's owner the ability to determine who knows it? Haven't we violated the owner's privacy?

Aside from the issue of risking exposure, why go to all of this trouble instead of just using policy to assert ownership of the datum and keeping the password itself on file? For one thing, we have a practical problem: despite what we tell users, they continue to use the same password on various systems. Thus, if someone can collect a password from a user account, the same password could be applied to other systems where the same user has accounts, which would result in a significantly greater likelihood of breaking into the account, simply by virtue of reusing the password. If we don't need to know the datum to achieve our objective, we're better off knowing the datum. If we know too much, *we* can

---

[3] There is actually a probability of *collision*, where two different inputs will result in the same output. There are means of dealing with these cases but we don't need to get into that level of detail in hash function operation. The point here is to demonstrate that we needn't know a datum to determine whether the user knows that datum.

become the target of attack, since the knowledge that we possess would be very valuable to an attacker.

Leaky Channels

In many ways, the "leaky channels" problem is basically a twist on the "too much information" problem just described. The big difference is that instead of having more information than necessary to complete the transaction, too much information is being sent or stored not only to the participants in the transaction, but those kind of data are also running a significant risk of being sent to others inadvertently or deliberately.

A good example of a leaky channel is the Web's protocol for shuffling data from host to host, HyperText Transfer Protocol (HTTP) [65] and its good friend HyperText Markup Language (HTML) [162]. As we discuss in Chapter 7, the Web has essentially no concept of privacy in its addressing schemes. Web addresses are logged in many places: on clients, servers, and proxies in the middle. Web addresses are passed from one transaction to another in a completely different context with no warning. Despite the complete lack of care in the privacy of these addresses, they can provide a great deal of detail about a transaction, even including reusable authentication credentials.

In the case of the Internet today—particularly the World Wide Web—leaky channels is one of the biggest problems we have. When systems are not designed with privacy in mind, we can wind up doing a lot of things that might seem to make sense in the context of other requirements (perhaps like reliability, in the form of redundancy). A protocol might be very "chatty," for example, giving a great deal of state information that should—theoretically—already be known by the other side. Such information could be used by the other side to make sure that the session is still sane and that everything is moving along as it should. However, such information could also have some other consequences if it were to be observed by nonparticipants in the conversation.

Secondary Uses

Perhaps one of the biggest and most significant threats to privacy is the idea of using information that has been obtained for a particular purpose in another way. Returning briefly to the discussion of Social Security numbers—a favorite example of all manner of things-gone-wrong for privacy advocates—we can readily see the kinds of risks that come about from finding additional uses for data.

Social Security numbers were, of course, originally assigned by the U.S. Government for the purpose of collecting and then paying Social Security.

Of course, once people began to get Social Security numbers, which were assigned by a centralized authority—the U.S. Social Security Administration—and theoretically unique to each person, other uses for the number soon began to present themselves. As a means of identification, we saw SSNs make their way into other areas of government [74], including the collection of income taxes. For the Internal Revenue Service (IRS), an individual's tax ID number—which he must give to anyone who pays him for his services—is his Social Security number. Employers began to use the number as the key for their employee databases, since they needed the number for tax purposes anyway, and the number was supposed to be unique to each person.

Most state bureaus of motor vehicles require one to divulge his SSN to receive a license to drive in the state. Financial institutions began to use the number as a means to identify people uniquely for reporting and examining credit histories. Universities began to use them as student identifiers and employee IDs. Marketers began to buy the information from various sources, using the number to key their databases.

Soon, the SSN became the *de facto* means of identifying people in the United States. Unfortunately, at the same time that the SSN began to increase in usage for purposes other than Social Security, few of the organizations that were building extensive databases of personal information keyed by SSN were giving any thought to the consequences of their actions. Few were putting any real security measures in their systems, building their systems and policies with the assumption that if someone knows an SSN, he must be the SSN holder or an authorized agent.

Originally intended for a single purpose, the SSN became a nearly ubiquitous identification number. From that point, it began to change yet again into a single token that would serve the purpose of identification as well as the purpose of authentication.

Now the situation that we have on our hands is that we have built an entire information infrastructure that is susceptible to all manner of fraud, a very common manifestation of which is now *identity theft*. The idea is basically this: an attacker gets enough information about his target to be able to impersonate his target to some select organizations. Those organizations are likely to be involving credit in one form or another, thus allowing the criminal to engage in commerce under the identity—and with the credit history of—the target. Identity theft is becoming increasingly common.

One of the biggest facilitators in the identity theft crime is the sloppy data handling procedures that have been in place for decades now by organizations whose livelihoods heavily depend upon this kind of customer information. Without giving appropriate consideration to the nature of what they were dealing with, they let "feature creep" take over and the SSN turned into a single key needed to gain full access to the proverbial kingdom.

Recognizing this situation, there has been a lot written about identity theft in the past few years. Even the U.S. Federal Reserve has recently issued guidelines to financial institutions to get such organizations to take more active roles in protecting the privacy of their customers.

This is an interesting position: to hear marketers and others tell their story, they have an interest in protecting the privacy of people whose information is stored in their machines. It's in their best interest to make sure that nothing bad can happen to people by virtue of being in their databases. In no event would any organization want to be the means by which an individual is brought to some kind of harm, or put at needless risk. This is their side of the story, but the great irony is that it's this very thing that is allowing crimes like identity theft to be perpetrated. Despite all of the lip-service to individual privacy, to many of these organizations, it's a lot easier to write off fraudulent activity against their accounts than it is to build systems that prevent these problems in the first place by their design.

What we don't hear about is all of the damage that's left in the wake of this kind of crime. Hard-earned credit histories are severely damaged, reputations can be hurt, and the process of going about engaging in daily pedestrian commerce can be significantly harmed or even brought to a complete stop because someone was the victim of a crime like identity theft. The data handler thinks that the problem is solved, by writing off the amount that was stolen and not forcing the victim to pay the bills that someone else created in his name. However, for the victim, there are still many unsolved issues, and will be many unsolved issues for years after the problem has been "addressed" from the perspective of the organization.

Finding other uses for SSNs started us down a slippery slope, and the mess in which we now find ourselves—including a financial system unnecessarily vulnerable to fraud—is a direct result of refusing to succumb to the threat of creeping featurism. These threats play off of each other well. Our consideration of the Social Security number is an excellent way to see how such issues as linkability and secondary uses contribute to loss of privacy.

Feeping creaturism is a different animal altogether.

More generally, recall what we've discussed. Note centralization: we have huge amounts of data kept in relatively few places. See linkability: the use of the same identifier for various systems makes it possible for us to merge dossiers to form even more complete records. Find data excess: collecting and storing more data than that needed to complete the transaction results in not only the risk of lost privacy, but also threatens to make the data collector a target for attack. Observe leaky channels: protocols that have little or no concept of privacy volunteer tremendous amounts of information about system users, contexts for links, and can even pass sensitive data like authentication credentials to unrelated third parties. Finally, consider secondary uses: people who agree to surrender information for one purpose can find that their information is being used for quite another purpose.

Looking back over what we've covered so far, we've considered why privacy is important and some theory behind privacy, including properties of data and access control. From there, we considered policy enforcement, online privacy principles, and then threats to privacy. We're ready to look at the problem of building online systems that are privacy and security aware. We do just that in Part II, "The Problem." Our first discussion in that context will be secure system design principles—guidelines that should be followed in the development of any system that claims to enforce any kind of policy.

Part II

The Problem

CHAPTER 6
Design Principles

THE STUDY OF COMPUTER SECURITY is by no means new. Principles of secure design are not unknown. Yet as discussed earlier, as technology moves forward in so many other areas, it seems that we are making no progress at all, or are actually falling behind when it comes to systems that are safe and trustworthy.

Interestingly, many people think that "security" is a synonym for "invincibility." This concept of security is deeply rooted. Consider the Russian word for security: *bezopasnost*. It literally means "without danger." When we talk about building trustworthy systems, we're not talking about systems in which there is no danger, but we're talking about systems that you can reasonably believe will not come back to get you after you've decided to place your trust in them.

In essence, the difference between computer system *bezopasnost* and "trustworthiness" is really one of perception. Correct or not, to many people, security is about the elimination of risk to whatever degree possible. Trustworthiness is more broad, but generally it's about the elimination of *surprises,* particularly unpleasant surprises. Unquestionably, security is a significant part of trustworthiness, but trustworthiness also includes things like reliability and manageability with requirements that go beyond security's "don't let attackers alter your state."

The Need for Secure Design Principles

Anyone who has ever developed anything knows that designing and implementing systems that operate correctly is difficult. When we're confronted with a specification, we look for ways to solve the problem, but will often do so in such a way that we enable some other functionality. For example, we might decide that if we're going to be able to do business, we need the ability to send and to receive Internet email. Few businesses with such a requirement would actually get connectivity that would enable *only* email—they'll get something that *includes* it, along with access to the Web, and any other service that runs atop Internet Protocol. Although this connectivity addresses the requirement, it does so by enabling a huge level of connectivity, not only for your machines to the outside world, but for the outside world to your machines.

Although in many cases, our bosses and our customers will see such systems and think that we're doing a good job, perhaps by solving multiple problems at once, the fact is that if we're providing functionality that has not been specified and analyzed, we're actually introducing a *risk* into the system. It's some other connection, some other element that can fail, or some way to use the system beyond what we've considered when thinking about how to keep from giving away the store.

We therefore need to concern ourselves not only with *minimal functionality* (solving the specified problem) but also with *maximal functionality*. Concern about maximal functionality means that we're not going to stop after we've asked the question, "Does this system do *X*?" but that we're also going to ask the question, "What else does it do?" Some of these design principles might seem redundant, but in reality, they're different perspectives on the same theme: deal with the system one feature at a time. Doing several things at once and otherwise being too clever are great ways to get ourselves into horrible trouble.

To illustrate, we'll return to an example raised in Chapter 2. We touched on an argument against absolute privacy made by Scott McNealy in a *Washington Post* article [125]. He suggested that sacrificing privacy can sometimes have significant appeal, for example, building cars that provide driver medical information and vehicle location data to authorities if an airbag is deployed.

Following the publication of McNealy's article, discussion ensued on the *Cryptography* mailing list. Security expert Win Treese raised the need to consider whether tradeoffs in privacy for the ability to get help are being made explicitly or implicitly. He further proposed three systems.

1. A system that tracks Scott at all times and calls for help if there's an accident. Scott pays for this service in the form of lost privacy. The service provider can also benefit from the system by making use of the information collected.

2. A system that is designed to help in the case of an accident, implemented in such a way that it tracks Scott all the time. Someone might later figure out that the system contains additional data that can be somehow used.

3. A system that is designed to help in the case of an accident, whose design explicitly collects only the information needed to perform its task.

In this example, we see three different approaches to exactly the same problem. In the first case, we're looking at a system explicitly designed to collect data in order to provide some benefit, perhaps to multiple parties. The second case is implemented such that such data are collected as a side effect. The final case is one explicitly designed not to collect more than it needs.

Looking at the systems all around us, we find many examples of the first and second cases. Systems do a lot of data collection and storage these days. Were we to perform an extensive study of systems in the wild, I believe we would find that most systems collect way more data than they need, and it is after such data are collected and stored that someone figures out how to use those data. The case studies that we consider in more detail in Chapter 8 tend to show that this is a very common way of viewing system design. Clearly, collecting additional data as a side effect is a quagmire of nasty problems.

The obvious question that we must raise at this point, then, is why we don't just build systems that collect everything, figure out what to do with everything collected, and move forward from there. As already discussed, privacy has long been viewed as a basic human right. Privacy by definition—informational self-determination—is a matter that must be decided on an individual basis, for oneself. We as an industry cannot seriously claim that we're reasonable and professional if we're building systems that are designed to deny users an internationally recognized basic human right.

We're thus left with only one viable option: building systems not to collect more data than they need to do their jobs. This means that we must change our perceptions about system functionality; we must concern ourselves not only with minimal functionality, but we must be sure we understand the system's maximal functionality. Instead of merely meeting our requirements, we must ensure that we meet them exactly.

Without further ado, we'll move on to the secure design principles themselves.

Saltzer and Schroeder Secure Design Principles

The 1975 Saltzer and Schroeder paper [168] outlined design principles of secure systems. The principles they presented have shown themselves to be timeless principles that apply just as much in today's world of many devices talking to each other over networks as they were in the days of many users per machine. We're going to consider these principles here, in detail. As we go through each, we're going to consider what the principle means, some examples, and why we care. Our examples will draw heavily from our experiences in everyday life and from network-enabled computing systems. Our discussion will focus less on security, in favor of trustworthiness.

An advantage to using these principles is not only that they give thorough consideration to secure system design, but that they are widely cited, giving us a common vocabulary with which we can discuss secure systems meaningfully. Our discussion here is for the purpose of understanding how to build systems that are privacy-aware. Our examples and discussion of these ten principles, therefore, will be focused on privacy and enforcing it.

Economy of Mechanism

The first of the Saltzer and Schroeder secure design principles is *economy of mechanism*. This principle actually goes back much further than 1975.

In the fourteenth century, William Ockham[1] proposed the principle that has come to be called *Ockham's Razor:* "Pluralitas non est ponenda sine neccesitate." Literally, the phrase means "entities should not be multiplied unnecessarily," but the principle is most often taken to mean "keep it simple." In physics, this Razor is used to establish priority: given two theories for the same thing, study the simplest one first.

For our purposes, it is worth noting that there is a practical limit to how simple things should get. Albert Einstein warned, "Everything should be made as simple as possible, but not simpler." Simplicity and elegance go together well, but it does not necessarily follow that the more simple something is the more elegant it is. Taken together, simplicity and elegance form a balance that is admired everywhere, and for good reason.

Simplicity has many beneficial side effects. Simple solutions will tend to be:

- Easier to understand in their entirety;

- Easier to review from beginning to end;

---

[1]   In Ockham's Latin, his name would be written *Occam*.

- Easier to analyze in their interactions with other things in the deployment environment; and

- Implementable in fewer lines of code, with fewer lines of configuration, and with fewer dependencies.

The result is that it's easier for us to ensure correctness and exact conformance to specification.

Here is an example. Suppose that we have a need to transfer a file from one system to another. The only interface that we have is serial, the kind of interface we'd use for a modem. We could implement a system that would work like this:

- Source calls the target on its modem.

- Target answers the incoming call.

- Source gives the target some identification and authentication credentials.

- Source then transfers the file to the target using some trivial protocol.

- Source tells the target that the transfer is complete.

- Source and target both hang up their modems.

This is something that could be written with relatively little code and that code would be straightforward for others to review. Even if we had a very high security requirement that made it necessary for us to analyze not only our scripts that would make this process work, but also the underlying code that supports it, there's relatively little code for us to analyze.

Contrast this with the amount of code that would be active to accomplish essentially the same objective over a typical Internet connection. In addition to the serial interface and the file transfer code, you would have to examine code that would handle:

- ISO layer 2 services (e.g., Ethernet drivers)

- Device drivers for the Ethernet cards

- The means of tying layer 2 services to layer 3 services (e.g., Ethernet to IP, using something like ARP)

- The IP stack in the operating system

- The TCP support in the operating system

- IP routing

That's an awful lot of code that comes into play in order solve a relatively simple problem. This, of course, conveniently neglects to point out that certain things that could be transferred over a typical Internet connection simply wouldn't be feasible to do for other reasons, including cost, in our simple manner.

Interactive media like the Web depend upon a constant connection for usability. Although you *could* send HTTP messages over our simple system, instead of taking seconds, it could take anywhere from minutes to days to get a single web page.

The point is that there are multiple, often conflicting, requirements that need to be considered. In our simple example of a need to transfer a file from one system to another, our solution *is* feasible, and therefore worth considering. But this is the reason that we specify our requirements; we might quickly decide that a trivial or "old" way of doing something isn't appropriate because it's not as flexible or "can't do as much" as some newfangled general-purpose solution. Keep in mind, though, that unless we've considered all of that additional functionality, we're only introducing unassessed risk into the equation.

Note that the first principle we're considering isn't strictly simplicity, it's economy. Economy means that we need to make efficient use of our resources. Our trivial file transfer mechanism solves the problem that was originally stated. Adding new functionality could become difficult and costly. Economy of mechanism will therefore mean that we strike a balance between simplicity and functionality.

Fail-Safe Defaults

Imagine this design for a nuclear weapon launch mechanism: an electrical circuit is responsible for keeping the weapon from launching. A break in the circuit or a loss of power will launch the weapon. Would this be a good design?

It might be said that a nuclear weapon station would have plenty of backup power and that an interruption in service would mean that the site had been attacked successfully.

The problem with this, obviously, is that there could be numerous other reasons for an interruption in power. Even if we do assume that the station was attacked, it doesn't stand to reason that the pre-programmed destination of the weapon is that of the attacker. Imagine that a developing country takes issue with the United States. If this country were to attack another nuclear power such as Russia, particularly the sites that are most likely aiming their weapons at the U.S, it would be an effective means to get Russia to do their dirty work. Simply take out the power on the Russian stations and wait for them to assume that they're under attack, and off the Russian missiles go.

Consider a bank vault. If its door is open and the building loses power, should the vault use its remaining backup power to close the door in a locked position or would it be alright for there to be no additional power, leaving no means to lock the door?

The question of *default behavior* is an important one, because the default behavior is typically what we'll see a system do whenever it fails.

And systems do fail [146].

The question is, will they fail into a position that's safe or into a position that's unsafe? Although we can easily see how this is applicable in the case of nuclear weapons or bank vaults, do we consider the same kinds of principles when we're designing systems that hold information?

If we're running a search engine, unless we look at every submission to the search engine by hand and peruse the sites included in our indices regularly, we can't really be sure to what we're linking. If we have been given a directive from management that we need to make our search engine "safe for kids"—i.e., no links to anything highly controversial or illegal to give to minors—a simple way to do that would be to have one of the options of our search be whether to limit our results to "safe for kids" links.

In this context, we're looking at the second of our design principles, *fail-safe mechanisms*. So what do we do by default? Do we make our searches include everything by default or do we limit our results to "safe for kids" links unless the user specifies otherwise?

Perhaps we want to make the user's choice persistent, so that he doesn't need to choose a non-default option every time that he conducts a search. The obvious solution to this problem in a Web context is to use a persistent cookie that will tell our search engine what the user's preference is every time that a search is submitted. The question arises again: which behavior is default, and which behavior do we use if the cookie is not present?

The choice for a fail-safe system is to fall into the position of absolutely greatest possible safety if the correct safety level cannot be determined. In this case, it means that our searches are going to need to be "safe for kids" unless the user affirmatively specifies otherwise. A user whose choice is not to restrict search results has, therefore, made an explicit choice, not had the choice made for him. If the user's cookie that stores the preference is lost—perhaps because he's using a new browser or new computer account—the user will have to assert the choice to be less safe again.

A great debate is raging at present with regard to the default behavior associated with such things as cookies and data collection practices on the public Web, particularly in connection with online advertising. The debate is opt-in versus opt-out. We discuss this in significantly more detail in Chapter 10, but this is something worth considering in this context. If we're going to be able to protect consumer privacy online, given the principle of fail-safe defaults, should we collect and profile the information by default, forcing consumers to assert that they do not want to have their data included in this kind of thing? Or does it make more sense not to collect the data by default and to require that users explicitly state that they want to participate in the data collection and analysis?

Complete Mediation

Complete mediation means that every time we request access to any object in the system—whether some piece of memory, a file on the disk, or a device—permission to access the device must be checked. By requiring that we include access control as part of the process of accessing any object, we're forcing the system to have the notion of access control included in the system's core, rather than as an add-on. This is extremely advantageous, since add-ons are often straightforward enough to circumvent.

One place to which we can look as an example of complete mediation is the Unix filesystem. Each device on the system, file on the disks, and even (in some systems) each process on the process table has an entry somewhere on the filesystem. Each entry includes several important properties, namely:

- Ownership by both user and group, with more granular specification available in many, particularly commercial, implementations

- Permissions, specifiable in such things as access to read, to write, and to execute at the very least

Thus, whenever a process in the system attempts to access a file or even a device, the ownership and permissions of that object's entry on the filesystem will perform the mediation and determine whether the requested action should be taken. If permission is granted by configuration, the action proceeds. If permission is not granted, the system will return an error (EX_NOPERM).

Having the ability to perform complete mediation on the filesystem is extremely useful and, particularly in the case of implementations that allow for highly granular permission specification, effective.

However, having all of the security features in the world won't do a system much good if the system administrators don't take advantage of those features. When we're writing applications, we do well to understand what features the operating system can provide us and to take advantage of all of those features that will help us.

When we're building applications that run locally, for local users, it's generally a lot easier to take advantage of the features of the operating system. When we're running services that are for use by network users, we seem to forget that we're dealing with a completely different environment, one over which no one has control. When we get a connection from a machine, for example, we can't really be sure that the machine is what it claims to be, since IP provides service for identification, but not authentication. When we get a packet that looks like it came from our application running on another machine, we really can't be sure that it wasn't really generated by a hostile application. When data are being directed to a dæmon on our server, we can't be sure that an attacker hasn't initiated the connection in an attempt to exploit some bug in our software or the operating system underneath.

We could enumerate examples all day. The point that we need to remember is that building applications that work on local, controlled environments is fundamentally different from building applications in the large, for potentially any user anywhere on the network. We must recognize the difference between what we can believe about our environment when running on a local machine and when offering our service to the world.

A concrete example we can use for driving this point home would be a web site that needs connectivity to a back-end database. Many system designers will look at ways to integrate web functionality with the database system itself. Others will look at ways to provide the web application access to the database through some standardized mechanism like SQL.[2] Each of these might seem reasonable upon first thought, but when looking at the secure design principle of complete mediation, we see that both approaches fail to consider security.

Perhaps the easiest way to see the folly of integration would be to consider the system in a mode of failure. A bug in the dæmon that services the request could influence the behavior of the database itself. If, on the other hand, we have a mechanism in the middle the mediates the connection, we can focus on ensuring that mediator's correctness and provide sanity checking, thus preventing hostile code from being able to reach the dæmon where a vulnerability could be exploited to undermine the system.

Standard access mechanisms, like SQL, have an additional risk. Rather than running only the risk of providing potentially hostile forces direct access to the dæmon, it's also possible that a data-borne attack could cause the exposure of data. Introducing the mediating program would allow us another point for enforcing policy. Here, we can ensure that the only kinds of SQL statements allowed to make it to the database for evaluation are valid by our policy. The advantage we have in a case like this is that if an attacker manages to break into the web server that talks to the database, requiring such access to go through a mediator would prevent the attacker from formulating queries that would reveal information that the web server would not need. Thus, even though an attacker has broken through a layer or two of protection (such as a firewall and the host security), there is still no advantage. It isn't until the mediator itself is broken that the attacker could send the database a `SELECT * FROM *`.

---

[2]   By the way, that's "S-Q-L," not to be confused with SEQUEL, which is another, different, database access language.

Open Design

When we discuss *open design,* what we're talking about is a design that is not secret. A system with open design is one where the design is published and widely available for review and comment, just as open source code is published and widely available for review and comment. Let's take a look at how well this principle is understood in very general terms.

Some computer software vendors, Microsoft most notably among them, loudly and proudly proclaim that their offerings are "more secure" because their implementations are trade secrets, protected by the law of intellectual property and lawyers willing to chase after anyone violating the owner's intellectual property rights. Some computer security system vendors have even taken up this side of the argument. Many people buy this line (along with the proverbial hook and sinker) and look with disdain at offerings like Linux and BSD Unix. The question remains: does secrecy of implementation result in higher or lower security? Microsoft isn't the only organization in the world that seems to think that secrecy of source code means greater security.

Law in the U.S.—namely the Digital Millennium Copyright Act (DMCA)—codifies this mindset, making it illegal even to attempt to circumvent a security feature. People foolishly imagine themselves protected by this sort of thing. Whether you're talking about the secrecy of source code or outlawing reverse engineering, you're after the same thing: security through obscurity.

In most security circles, you'll hear, quite rightly, that security through obscurity is no security at all.

Of all of the areas of computer security where the goodness of open design is proclaimed, cryptography is especially noteworthy. It's easy to develop a cipher that one cannot break oneself. It's hard to develop a cipher that others cannot break. Therefore, instead of pursuing a comparatively simple business model of inventing a cipher, building it into a product, and taking it to market, responsible cryptosystem developers follow a much longer, harder path to market.

A cipher is first developed to address some sort of specification: that it should be good for *these* applications, that it should have *this* level of flexibility, that it should be *this* fast, that it should be easy to implement in software, and so on. Developers of the cipher will then apply known cryptanalytic techniques to look at their own work from the perspective of an attacker. Ciphers are going to have certain properties: that they process their data in blocks of *so many* bits, that they use keys of *this* length, that they run through *this many* rounds before spitting out the results.

After a cryptologist has implemented a cryptosystem and has analyzed its performance against well-known attacks, he might decide that it seems to show some promise. At this point, he'll publish the algorithm in its entirety so his peers in the scientific community can study the algorithm. Algorithms that seem to be the best candidates for actual use or that are novel in some way are most likely to get the attention of other cryptologists. Others might find new avenues of attack. Some might try new variations of already well-known attacks. Some might find successful results on weaker versions of the algorithm, perhaps one with a reduced number of rounds.

An algorithm that has gotten this kind of attention and has generally fared well in the face of serious analysis will begin to get a reputation as a worthy challenge. The longer that an algorithm stands in the face of analysis, the greater its reputation will be and the greater the level of trust that will be placed in it.

The reason for all of this work is straightforward: no matter how big your organization, no matter how smart your staff, there are more smart people working outside of your group than there are in it. In general, the more analysis that something receives, the greater the likelihood that its problems will be discovered and fixed. This is true in cryptography, and it is true in all areas of security.

Anyone still inclined to believe that hiding the details of implementation and its source code results in greater security would do well to consider the example of Microsoft. Despite being the largest software company in the world, with pockets deeper than virtually any other organization known and having so much riding on its software, the company that made Internet email-based worms possible doesn't seem able to stem the tide of security advisories about its products.

Reasons for this situation are many, but we're picking on Microsoft here merely to demonstrate a point: keeping source code a secret hasn't kept Microsoft out of CERT advisories.

Separation of Privilege

In Real Life (whatever that is), when we give someone a piece of paper, we're granting him essentially complete control over the paper. The ability to read it, to modify it, to copy it, even to destroy it. When dealing with computers, we have a nice feature that we don't have when using paper: the ability to separate privilege. Rather than giving someone "ownership" or "stewardship" of an object, we can grant the necessary access on a very granular basis. The well-known Unix permissions of "read," "write," and "execute" provide a useful means of sharing information to certain sets of users. Newer Unix implementations that include the concept of filesystem Access Control Lists (ACLs) give even greater separation of privilege.

What this means in practice is that if we are developing a system that will grant access to certain data, we need to specify what kinds of access the system will support. The more granular we are, the better. With no separation of privilege, we would need to grant each user with need to use an object for any reason complete stewardship of the object. As far as our security is concerned, we're back to using paper.

With a high separation of privilege, we'd have the ability to specify which users may and may not

- Read: learn a datum and its meaning;

- Copy: duplicate a datum;

- Modify: change a datum;

- Add: create a datum;

- Delete: mark a datum to be removed; or

- Expunge: destroy a datum that has been marked for removal.

There are probably many more that would make sense. The point is that when a user needs the ability to add records to the system, it isn't necessary also to grant him the ability to read the records in bulk after the fact or to remove them from the system. Someone (or something) responsible for making backups might have the need to copy everything in the system, but not necessarily to read anything or to to delete anything.

This leads us into our next issue . . .

Least Privilege

Least privilege is an extremely important principle. In practice, this means don't give any more privilege to someone than he needs to accomplish the specific task at hand.

As an example, let's consider the use of credit cards. Our requirement is to provide a simple, convenient mechanism for one party to transfer funds to another party without needing to handle cash. In general, this kind of thing can be done by check, though this can be something of a hassle, and the relative ease with which one can produce bogus checks is fairly high. It'd be nice to be able to do this in a way that one could actually verify the funds' availability and transfer the money. Credit cards are nice because it's possible for the merchant to put the transaction through immediately. If the funds are unavailable or there is reason to believe that an unauthorized person is attempting to make the payment, the transaction can be rejected on the spot.

If we then ask the question, "Does the system satisfy its requirements?" we're quite likely to answer, "Yes." If, however, we step back and ask the question, "What else does it do?" we're going to find some very interesting answers.

Use of a relatively constant and fairly easy-to-learn token—the credit card number itself—introduces some interesting possibilities, namely reuse of that token. For "security reasons," completion of the transaction will generally be dependent upon another token, one that changes every two to three years—the card's expiration date. Additionally, cards where a transaction is attempted with the wrong expiration date attached are shut down after a few unsuccessful tries—we'll say three tries for the sake of this discussion.

One might think that we've been able to address our requirement without introducing too much risk into the system. Since there are twelve months in the year, and cards are good for three years from their date of issue, we're looking at a maximum of 36 possible expiration dates. With only three attempts to guess the expiration date before the card will be shut down, we might feel pretty safe about the way that our cards are being used. Even if someone is able to get ahold of the number, the attacker has a one in 13 (that's three in 36) chance of guessing the valid expiration date, which would be required to use the card.

The problem is that the attacker doesn't have to try 13 different attacks on a single card to reach his goal since chances are that one attack against each of 13 different cards will get the same result—without triggering an alarm that something fishy is happening. People who would illegally use a credit card don't generally care *whose* card it is—as long as it isn't one that can be tied back to them.

Return to what we're talking about: not giving someone more information than he needs to do his job. If what we're trying to do is provide a means to pay for something, if we're following the principle of least privilege, we're going to give only information that will work for the present transaction. Trying to use the same token again would not work. One possible means of doing this would be to transfer money into a specific account for a specific purpose and to give the merchant the token to that account, which holds only enough money for that transaction, and which will be closed as soon as the transaction has been completed.

In many situations with computers, however, this principle isn't as cumbersome to implement.

Let's consider a second example, a computing example. For the sake of "ease," a system administrator might decide to login to his own workstation with a privileged account, like root on Unix machines or Administrator on Windows machines. A sysadmin would have a much easier time of going about his work this way. Configuration changes, software installation, and other routine administrative tasks could be done directly, without the need to go through hoops to get additional privilege.

Windows NT is best written "Windowsn't."

In practice, though, few people do this, because everyone—generally, even the people who still insist on doing it—knows that working that way puts the system at risk. In multiuser systems, users generally are protected from each other, and users who get themselves into trouble tend only to be able to hose their own data. To destroy someone else's data or to make the system unstable will often require additional levels of privilege. Thus, if a user is running a stupid piece of software, it will be limited in what damage it can unleash on the system. If, however, the program is being run with the privileges of a superuser, there will be essentially no limit to the amount of damage that something poorly written (or an ill-considered command) can do to other users and even to the system itself.

A third example might be in the issue of system configuration. Suppose that you have a web site that you're running. You need for your HTTP server to be able to read the content off of the filesystem in order to serve it to the clients. In many cases, people will make the ownership of the files on the filesystem match the user of the HTTP server process. This, however, violates the principle of least privilege. The HTTP server does not need the ability to write, to delete, or to remove any of those files. It needs merely to have the ability to read those files. A web server with a bug that can be exploited by a hostile client can only have its HTML files overwritten if the HTTP server that's being tricked into executing a command will have the authority to write over top of that file.

Following this principle will force us to ask the fundamental question: what, exactly, does this piece of the system need to be able to do? Knowing the answer to that question will then allow us to provide exactly that level of functionality—and not a single bit more. This one obstacle is extremely effective and terribly under-used.

Least Common Mechanism

Another principle that will help us to avoid building systems that can be used against us is *least common mechanism*. This means that we shouldn't create components that run exactly the same for everyone and provide everyone with exactly the same thing. This is the security-conscious way of saying what other software experts will tell you to do for other reasons: build modular code.

An operating systems example of this principle in practice would be in the development of a general-purpose utility. In a Unix system, one might implement a feature in the kernel, in a library against which "userland" programs may link, or in a function that is local to the application itself.

Addition of the functionality in the kernel might be desirable for performance reasons, perhaps for convenience, or just because the user wants to be able to say that he's written "kernel code." This is problematic, however, because code that runs in the kernel cannot be readily seen by a running system. A function that goes out to lunch when invoked will cause the kernel to fail. A function with a memory leak will cause the system to run out of RAM.

Kernel failure would be bad.

These kinds of problems are limited to some degree if they're implemented as library functions because a program that uses the function in user space can be killed by the system, thus reclaiming resources or at the very least, stopping the waste of resources. If this is true, one might argue that the obvious thing to do to limit the damage further would be to make the function local to one's own program, rather than providing the functionality to the rest of the system. This would be carrying the idea to the extreme, however, because although it's true that it would make the reach of bugs in the function even more localized, the amount of damage that would be caused by such a bug is roughly the same: a process would be goofed up. Its means for recovery would be the same: kill the hosed process.

Thus, we have no real "win" in the case of implementing the function locally in the program itself. We do have several losses, however, by comparison to the provision of the function as a generic feature that's available as a library. By increasing the potential for dependency on the code, we're increasing its importance, providing greater economic justification—whether we're talking about real money, funny money, or just plain ol' time doesn't matter here—for taking the time to build it correctly and to review it for defects.

One more example that we can use would be the case of connecting to a database. As we're building web-based applications, we see the need to build them such that they'll be used by many different persons, each of whom would have his own identity in the system. In such a system, if we rely on a single interface to a database, one where all connections to all parts of the database are handled through a single interface with the same privilege for every request, we have provided a common mechanism for functions like "add harmless record to database," "download every record in the database," and "scramble everything." Least common mechanism would dictate that we provide interfaces to the system such that if one were subverted, the attacker would not be able to do any more than that interface would allow. The compromised mechanism can't be used as a mechanism to do other things to the target.

Of course, we're advocating principles that complement each other well; such a design would allow us to enforce other principles like separation of privilege and complete mediation. We're building in layer after layer of functionality, rather than providing all of our functionality in a single component that can be compromised. Not all of our secure design principles, however, come down to the question of technology.

Psychological Acceptability

In general, the biggest problem that we have in building and deploying secure systems is our user base. Many just don't want to know anything more about any technology than they need to avoid getting fired from their jobs. Others would take more of an active interest in how all of this stuff works if there were some way to educate them reasonably. In either case, we end up with a user base that is clueless.

Even beyond dealing with the "clueless user" problems, we have to ensure that we build systems that people will not view as obstacles to getting things done. If our users don't accept the systems we build, no amount of "security" that we build in will prevent compromise, because they'll just work around whatever safeguards we put in place. Security can be viewed as a spectrum, just as we saw with nymity in Figure 2-1. On one end of the spectrum, we have complete security and on the other, we have complete access.

It has been said so often that it's almost a cliché now—but not often enough outside of security circles, so I can get away with it here—that a completely secure system is one where all of the data on its disks are encrypted before it's unplugged from the network, turned off, unplugged from its power supply, locked in a safe, and thrown to the bottom of the ocean. Even then, given enough time and money (that's "dedication" when we're talking about the resources of an attacker), that system might not *really* be secure. The problem with this kind of system is that it's not very usable. What's the point of having a computer if it isn't usable to *anyone?* We need to make the system do something useful for its intended user base.

On the other extreme of the spectrum is complete access. The computer will happily do anything that anyone tells it to do. Give me a listing of all of the users on the system. "Here you go." Dump the contents of the company's customer database and give it to me in a nice pretty format. "No problem." Tell me the salary and employment history for each of the employees. "Here you are." Reformat your drives and reboot. "Sure thing." The problem, of course, with complete access is that it does nothing to prevent the system from being abused by people who should not have the authority to get at the information it contains or even to protect itself against the most trivial of attacks. Neither does it prevent any accidental damage, such as that which might come from a poorly implemented program.

This might sound pretty silly, but in fact, complete access has been granted in a wide variety of production systems. Take, for example, single-user computer operating systems; no concept of access control. If you're on the machine, you must have authorization to do absolutely anything you want. This isn't something that was limited to the early days of "home computing." Even "business" microcomputers had this problem—look at DOS and Windows as examples. All you needed was the ability to type and you could make the computer do anything that it was capable of doing. Of course, with the advent of voice-recognition technology, it wasn't even necessary to have access to the keyboard. Simply shouting loud enough at the right time would be enough to make the computer do something stupid.

This isn't merely a theoretical problem. A great example appeared in a 1999 issue of *Computing* [6]. A representative of a company with a voice recognition product prepared to demonstrate their product and asked the crowd gathered to see the demonstration to be quiet. Someone in the back of the room shouted,

"Format C Colon Return!" Someone else shouted, "Yes, Return!" The software worked perfectly, reformatting the primary disk on the demonstration unit, requiring that the machine finish its format and have all of its software and data reinstalled. Another great example of complete access was the IBM PS/1, with the infrared keyboard. Aim your keyboard at your office mate's machine, hit Control, Alt, Delete, and watch his machine reboot.

Work Factor

The cost of circumventing a security system is sometimes called its *work factor.* This is most commonly seen in cryptosystems. The fact is that all ciphers are ultimately susceptible to the problem of someone guessing the right key. The way that we prevent that attack from being a reasonable one is by making the number of possible keys so big that it's not practical for someone to try every single combination.

A simpler example of the same principle is a bicycle combination lock. Imagine such a lock having one tumbler with ten positions. Would the lock be secure? The amount of time that it would take to try each position to see if it will open the lock is not significant. Thus, its work factor is very low—you only need to try ten possible options. At the rate of one per second, that's probably a ten second job.

Consider the same combination lock, having two tumblers with ten positions each. Instead of having $10^1 = 10$ possible combinations, there are now $10^2 = 100$ possible combinations. By adding another tumbler, we've increased the work factor by an order of magnitude.[3] Now instead of taking ten seconds, the job will take 100 seconds. Add another tumbler and we get $10^3 = 1000$ possible combinations, etc.

This principle is exactly what we deal with when we're working with cryptosystems and we're trying to define how secure a cipher is. By the time we're working with a cipher in a production system, it should have undergone significant peer review and commentary to be sure that the brute force attack is the most effective attack. This is also why it's unwise to deploy a cryptosystem that depends on an algorithm that hasn't been studied widely and hasn't been able to stand the test of time.

Open Design!

Algorithms like the Data Encryption Standard (DES) [140] have proved to be quite strong. After decades of inspection, the best avenues of attack are brute force. There are now variations of DES that increase its key length from the original 56 bits. Once such variant is 3DES, which will increase the effective key

---

[3] Since there are ten positions on each tumbler, each subsequent order of magnitude is *ten times* the previous. Combinatorics is the friend of people who want to address such attacks.

I'm not spelling out 2^{168}. That's much too silly.

length to 112 bits[4] or 168 bits, depending on how it's implemented. However, it is notable that at 56 bits, the key length of DES is short enough that computers today can break DES keys by trying every single possible combination. The first public crack of a DES key by brute force was by Rocke Verser's DESCHALL team in 1997 [46]. Since that time, other, faster DES-key–cracking machines have been built [121].

It's important to remember that brute-force attacks aren't necessarily the best attacks against a system. In practice, it's extremely difficult to build a system where a brute-force attack is the best. Just as we can use bolt cutters to defeat a bicycle combination lock of any number of tumblers in under a second, we can often apply other methods to defeat cryptosystems with huge key lengths. Key length is important, but only if the cryptosystem can last through all of the other attacks that we'll apply to it. Most cryptosystems can't, even in theory. Essentially, none can in practice, thanks to such modern wonders as virtual memory (read: "swap space might have an image of some pages of memory with the clues we need to break the encrypted file"), temporary files, and other goodies that are enabled by the operating systems on which we're trying to run these things.

So, in practice, calculating work factor can be difficult, because we need to identify each of the avenues of attack and then figure out how much it would cost (in terms of time, money, and effort) to circumvent that attack. If we can make it necessary for an attacker to spend more resources than the target is worth, our job is finished. Work factor is what helps us to determine that.

Compromise Recording

In some cases, it might not be as important to prevent an attacker from obtaining something as it would be to make it readily apparent that an attacker has done his deed, or to record the act of compromising the system. The reason this is useful is because cost is something that must be considered not only by attackers, but also by defenders.

If we have some physical documents that we want to store safely, we might do so by keeping them in a building that has some basic security systems in place: locks on the outside doors, other locks on inside doors, and perhaps a lock on the file cabinet where we keep the documents.

---

4   Since bits are binary units, our "tumblers" have two possible positions; a 112 bit cipher has $2^{112} = 5{,}192{,}296{,}858{,}534{,}827{,}628{,}530{,}496{,}329{,}220{,}096$ possible keys. For the curious, that's "five decillion, one hundred ninety-two nonillion, two hundred ninety-six octillion, eight hundred fifty-eight septillion, five hundred thirty-four sextillion, eight hundred twenty-seven quintillion, six hundred twenty-eight quadrillion, five hundred thirty trillion, four hundred ninety-six billion, three hundred twenty-nine million, two hundred twenty thousand, ninety-six."

In such a case, we might decide that we're going to defend against someone trying to get into the building, against someone in the building trying to gain access to the floor where our office is, and against someone on our floor gaining entry to our office. But if such a person can gain entry into our office, we might figure at that point, it's all over: there's no stopping the attacker now. This is a time when we might want to have one final mechanism that will not stop the attacker as much as it will leave an audit trail.

One choice available to us might include a closed-circuit video camera pointed at the door. The attacker can destroy the camera, but not until after he goes through the door and gets his picture taken and has the image saved somewhere else. An excellent example of this principle can be found as a result of the 1982 Tylenol tragedy. Drugs on store shelves were vulnerable to being taken, tampered with, and returned to the shelf. Making the containers tamper-proof was too expensive, but the same benefit could be derived by a simple foil seal. If the drugs had been reached, the seal would be broken, giving us evidence of compromise.

No system is immune to all avenues of attack—even theoretically "perfect" systems—so the idea of recording a compromise in some way is very helpful for us to reconstruct what's happened, perhaps to make the recovery easier, and at least so that we don't continue to believe that a compromised system is safe. Sometimes, we can even use this as a means of exercising some legal recourse.

A commonplace technological example is one of the newest and most popular tools in data security: the intrusion detection system. By recording what's happened, we can have some evidence to suggest how the attacker broke through—thus giving us a feedback channel to improve the system—and giving us the heads-up we need to react appropriately.

One thing to remember is that the mechanisms that we use for compromise recording are themselves imperfect. An attacker can write raw traffic to a network to make it look like something that isn't happening is happening. The systems to record the compromise can crash or otherwise fail. Sophisticated attackers might even be able to render the data recorded by the system useless, making it impossible to tell which—if any—data can be believed.

Putting the Design Principles to Use

Use of secure design principles can help us make tremendous steps forward in building systems that resist failure. We do well to keep these in mind any time that we're involved in design or implementation—irrespective of whether management realizes that security must be built in. Once again, our ten principles are the following:

Memorize this list. That's an order.

- Economy of mechanism

- Fail-safe defaults

- Complete mediation

- Open design

- Separation of privilege

- Least privilege

- Least common mechanism

- Psychological acceptability

- Work factor

- Compromise recording

Consideration of secure design principles is unfortunately not common in undergraduate curricula. We therefore have a large number of folks working on building systems without ever having given serious consideration to the construction of systems that would not be vulnerable to attack. Hopefully, our tour of the Saltzer and Schroeder principles has proved eye-opening. We have gone a long time building systems without giving serious attention to the issue of security. Exceptions to our ability to avoid security has largely been confined to specific industries like banking. Secure design principles have long been necessary where security is a requirement. What we're discussing now isn't new; but the requirement for security is now present in more systems, affecting more systems developers.

As the Internet has become ubiquitous, the nature of the applications that we have built has changed dramatically. Most of the software that we've been building over the years has been confined to individual machines and used by users in whom we have some level of trust. Our deployment environments are no longer the desktop; we're deploying into the Internet, where users of our systems aren't always people we can trust.

We're now going to consider the Internet as a deployment environment.

Deployment Environments

BECAUSE OF THE UBIQUITY OF the Internet and the Web, we're going to focus specifically on this environment for deployment. One of the most interesting things about the rise of the Web is that it has significantly broadened the concept of what a software "developer" is. Someone who designs and implements web sites might not be someone with a computer science background—in fact, it's quite likely that the background is one of art or graphic design—but it is someone who will have tremendous influence on how information, and even sensitive information, will be handled in practice. This is why it's important for us to try to bridge this gap that we have between information science's state of the art and what we have in practice.

With this chapter, I hope to help bridge the gap. Our discussion of this material should be useful and relevant to a wide audience. Technical readers shouldn't think that they can skip this material; what's covered here is very important to building secure online systems. Less technical readers shouldn't be put off by what follows; where we delve deep into technicalities, summaries, footnotes, and marginal notes accompany the text so that no one should miss the point.

To understand the Internet as a deployment environment for web applications, we're going to need to discuss relevant details of the Internet's architecture. We'll cover what makes the Internet run, the domain name system, and the World Wide Web. We'll pull apart relevant parts of the Web: its addressing scheme (Uniform Resource Indicators), the markup language that defines almost all web documents (HyperText Markup Language), the protocol that delivers web content (HyperText Transfer Protocol), and mechanisms for preserving state (including HTTP cookies).

Internet Architecture

Many computer networks are networks of computers, or hosts, as illustrated in Figure 7-1. An *internet* (common noun) is any network that is based on the *TCP/IP protocol suite*, which we will discuss momentarily. The *Internet* (proper noun) is a specific global network not of hosts, but of *networks*, like that shown in Figure 7-2. So the internet in Figure 7-1 can well be part of the Internet shown in Figure 7-2. Each network, when connected to an Internet-connected network then becomes a part of the Internet.

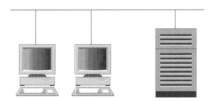

Figure 7-1. A Network of Hosts

Each host on the network must have a unique address—an *IP address*—so that traffic can be directed to it, just as each house on a street must have a unique address so that mail can be directed unambiguously to it. IP addresses are indicative of where the host is on the network, networkologically, rather than geographically.

Routers are special-purpose computers that connect networks together, looking at such things as source and destination IP addresses to determine where to send packets to direct them to their final destination.

Figure 7-2. The Network of Hosts—Part of a Network of Networks

The Protocol Stack

In the previous section, we mentioned networks that are built using the TCP/IP protocol suite. What exactly does this mean? First, let's cover some definitions. *IP* is Internet Protocol, which ties together everything that makes up the worldwide network of networks we call the Internet. *TCP* is Transport Control Protocol and typically runs over IP. Together, these make up the building blocks for most forms of Internet communication.

To understand exactly what we're talking about, we're going to take a look at a fundamental concept of networking: the protocol stack. The most typical model used to discuss protocol stacks is the International Standards Organization Operating Systems Interconnect (ISO OSI) seven-layer model. Table 7-1 depicts the protocol stack, giving some examples from the TCP/IP protocol suite to demonstrate where they fit in the protocol stack. These layers are numbered from the bottom to the top, so physical is layer one and application is layer seven. More complete descriptions of each layer will follow.

Table 7-1. ISO OSI Seven-Layer Protocol Stack with Examples for Each Layer

OSI Layer	Examples
Application	Sendmail, Eudora, Outlook
Presentation	Message (RFC 2822)
Session	SMTP (RFC 2821)
Transport	TCP
Network	IP
Data link	Ethernet IEEE 802.3 Link
Physical	10base-T, 100base-T, Gigabit Ethernet

We're simplifying somewhat here, since by strict interpretation some protocols in the TCP/IP suite provide some services from one layer and some from another. Since most TCP/IP networks at some point connect to the Internet and email is the most common use for the Internet, we've chosen to specify some email-centric examples.

Microsoft LookOut.

Application layer manages the interface from the application on down. In typical systems deployed today, this functionality is provided by some combination of operating system and application. Common examples would include programs that are used for processing mail, both on the client and server side, like Sendmail, Eudora, Gnus, and Microsoft Outlook. Examples from the Web would include Mozilla, Internet Explorer, and the Apache web server.

Presentation layer provides the semantic transformations so that both ends of the session (or "conversation") can understand what's taking place. For email, this includes the format of messages: such things as the necessity for a From and Message-ID header. In the context of the Web, this would include HTML, the actual structure of the document. Such things as encryption and compression are also addressed at the presentation layer.

Session layer is responsible for control of the session. Establishing new sessions, keeping them active, and tearing them down when finished are all features of the session layer. Examples of the session layer would include SMTP for mail, NNTP for news, and HTTP for the Web. Many, many other examples exist.

Transport layer provides transparent data transfer services. Error recovery and flow control are provided here. It's worth noting that in OSI, reliability of the communication is provided here. However, in the Internet context, not all transport layer protocols are reliable. UDP (User Datagram Protocol) [157], for example, provides no such guarantee. Reliability comes with a price, typically in the form of overhead, and for such things as streaming audio, missing a frame or two won't matter.

Network layer is where the data flow is managed across the network topology. Issues like how to get traffic from one place to another are handled at the network layer. The most common example of a network-layer protocol is IP, the Internet Protocol.

Data link layer is where the control over the data flow and format over physical networks are defined. Ethernet's data link services are present here. Ethernet (MAC) addresses are defined here, as is the means by which network interface cards in machines on the local area network communicate.

Physical layer is where data transfer physically occurs. This can be optical, electronic, mechanical, or anything else. Wires, interface cards, and all the stuff you can touch go here.

The stack is always the same, but the protocols in use differ from job to job. It's noteworthy that TCP and IP—employed for almost every Internet communication—are toward the middle of the stack. As a general rule of thumb, the further from the middle you go, the more protocols are available at each level. Toward the application layer, this is due to the varying nature of the jobs that we're trying to accomplish with the network. Toward the physical layer, this is due to the varying types of networks and physical topologies that exist in a global network of networks.

On the Internet, at OSI layer three, we have IP. The services provided by IP to higher-level protocols are straightforward, including source and destination addresses, packet length, and a lifespan for the packet (represented as time to live, or TTL). Whenever you're pushing data from one part of the Internet to the other, you need those services, so IP is going to do the job you need. If we move up a few layers, however, we can see that not everyone uses the same software to read email. Some people prefer Outlook, others prefer Netscape, and still others prefer Eudora.[1] The beauty of the protocol stack is that it lets us identify on which layer our communication is really taking place, so we can standardize *there* instead of at the application layer all the time, always requiring that everyone use the same software, the same computers, and the same networks. We work with specifics on both ends of the protocol stack, working through layer after layer until we get down to a very generic layer, one that ties everything together. On the Internet, that layer is the network layer.

Let's consider an example in detail. If we follow an email message from Alice, who uses Eudora, to Bob, who uses Netscape, we'll be able to see the value of the protocol stack illustrated a bit more clearly. Alice will compose her message and click the "send" button. Eudora will format the message to meet a set of requirements for Internet email messages, most notably RFC 2822 [91]. This standard articulates a presentation-layer protocol, defining the semantics for a message.

Eudora will then take that RFC 2822-formatted message and send it to Alice's mail server over a protocol known as *Simple Mail Transfer Protocol* (SMTP), defined in a standards document known as RFC 2821 [176]. SMTP is a session-layer protocol, so it includes things like how to initiate the conversation, how to identify the sender and the recipient, and what to do with errors like unknown user bounces.

Of course, Alice's machine and the mail server don't communicate telepathically. The operating system of Alice's machine—Windows, say—will break the

---

[1] Hackers, of course, run the likes of Gnus and VM under their favorite Emacs implementation.

SMTP session into a stream of TCP packets. The TCP packets will include data like which service port to use to initiate the connection, an identifying number, and which packet comes next in the stream.

We now have a message split into a series of TCP packets, but TCP packets don't know how to get from one machine to another on a network, since TCP is a transport-layer protocol. Windows on Alice's computer will then tack each TCP packet and put it inside of an IP packet. IP packets know things like source IP address and destination IP address.

Alice's computer is connected to a network connection in her office: an Ethernet connection. Alice's Windows will take each of the IP packets and place them inside of an *Ethernet frame* so that the packet can go from Alice's computer to the router that will forward the packet to its destination across the local Ethernet. Alice's computer will communicate with the router using the Ethernet data link layer protocol, identifying things like the Ethernet address of Alice's machine and of the router. Obviously, the Ethernet frame will be sent from Alice's machine to her router over the 100base-T wiring that physically connects all of the computers and routers in the building together.

Alice's mail server will follow the same process to deliver the message to Bob's mail server with the SMTP protocol. Once Bob's mail server has the message, Bob can fetch the message with a transport-layer protocol like IMAP4 [40]. Bob's Netscape mail client will then be able to understand the RFC 2822-formatted message and display it to him in a familiar form.

Note that by standardizing at the right level for the job, Alice and Bob are able to communicate over completely different types of networks, with completely different computer types, and with completely different software. The only requirement is that their machines can physically communicate with something that can eventually get them to IP and that their software can agree on the format of the data to be exchanged and get it put into a packet that can transfer over the IP network.

This is the most important concept of the protocol stack: the ability to address problems at the appropriate layer of abstraction.

It isn't necessary for us to understand each of these layers in great detail, but it is important that we're familiar with the concept. We can reference it when we're looking at a protocol to understand what service it needs to provide and what services it relies upon.

Note that different network types and protocol suites can have different ideas about how many layers there are and in other comparatively minor details. Several models, including a four-layer model and a five-layer model, exist specifically for TCP/IP. We're discussing OSI in part because it is recognized universally and because it provides good granularity.

There are many protocol suites, each of which can generally be explained in the context of ISO OSI, although different protocol suites usually have protocol

ed *is the standard editor.*

—ed *manual*

stack models that fit their particular stack's implementation more closely. Some other protocol suites that are worth mentioning include CCITT, SNA, XNS, DECNET, Appletalk, and NetBIOS.

Even if we don't work with these protocols directly—and even if we can be thankful for avoiding working with them—it's useful to know that they exist, as understanding how other systems approach the same domain of problems is important in coming to a full understanding of the problem at hand and seeing what the tradeoffs of various design decisions are.

Armed with an understanding of the protocol stack, let's consider why Alice doesn't need to know what IP addresses are in order to get her message safely to Bob.

The Domain Name System

Computers like numbers. People prefer names. Imagine if, instead of typing a logical name like `dmoz.org` into your browser, you had to type an address like `192.168.210.28`.[2] Not only are such addresses generally more difficult to remember, but as the physical architecture of the network changes, and as people move their sites from one place to another around the network, their underlying IP addresses change.

> **NOTE** *This isn't just a nice theoretical feature. During the writing of this book, systems at my company changed IP addresses thrice, thanks to the arrival of Digital Subscriber Lines (DSL) to our area, changes by our DSL provider, and then a move to a T1 circuit prompted by the implosion of our DSL provider's business. Through all of this, nobody noticed any changes, since email addresses and web sites—as defined by their logical names—continued operation.*

To allow people to deal with logical names, rather than physical network addresses, Internet hosts must be named. Each logical name on the network must also be unique. Originally, site names were some simple abbreviation like MIT-AI, SAIL, and OSU-CIS. When there are very few hosts on the network—all places with big research facilities—the possibility of collision isn't too high.

Originally, the mapping of logical names to physical addresses was maintained by a file called `HOSTS.TXT` that was shared by every site on the

---

[2]   With the adoption of IPv6, it'll be significantly worse, since instead of having to deal with four 8-bit quantities, we'll have four 16-bit quantities to make up each host's address.

network [115]. As nodes on the network grew, maintenance of the file of hosts became too difficult. The solution that stuck was a hierarchical system that would allow *zones* to be delegated to the administrators of the sites, who could in turn delegate sub-zones to local network administrators, ad infinitum.

The *domain name system* (DNS) [136] can be pictured as a tree, where the base of the system—its "root"—is written as a single dot, as shown in Figure 7-3. Zones just under root are known as Top-Level Domains (TLDs). Examples of TLDs are NET, EDU, COM, ORG, MIL, GOV, and INT. Other TLD examples include the two-letter country-code domains, one for each of the countries of the world, such as US, IE, RU, FR, DE, and AU.

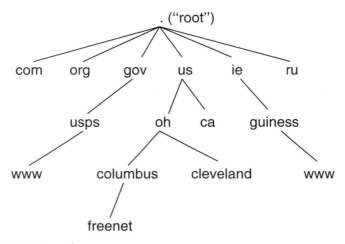

Figure 7-3. DNS Hierarchy

Each of those domains has a registrar—or a group of registrars—responsible for handling requests for zones in their respective domains. One example of such a domain would be OH.US, OH being a subdomain of US. OH.US could in turn delegate domains like COLUMBUS.OH.US and CLEVELAND.OH.US. COLUMBUS.OH.US could then delegate domains further, to organizations inside of that locality, such as FREENET.COLUMBUS.OH.US.

Hierarchical DNS is extremely flexible and provides us several important capabilities. Thanks to its hierarchical nature, DNS allows us:

- To delegate zones to the appropriate level of administration; there's no need for a single, central authority that handles all changes for all networks on the Internet.

- To name hosts whatever we like within our own namespace. Thus, names that are logical indicators of the host's functionality, for example, mail, news, or www, need to be unique only within their own zones. The result is that we can have both `web.mit.edu` and `web.interhack.com` without requiring that MIT and Interhack fight over the name `web`.

There are plenty of other benefits—like balancing the load of directory queries across a large set of servers—as well, but a full discussion of those benefits would be well beyond the scope of this book.

DNS is covered in much greater detail in Paul Albitz's and Cricket Liu's book *DNS and BIND* [1].

World Wide Web Architecture

The World Wide Web [10] (also known as "WWW," "Web," and "W3") is a collection of transport-layer through presentation-layer protocols that define a means of pushing bits around the Internet and formatting them for presentation to the user. In general, when we talk about "the Web," we're talking about the global public Web that sits atop the global public Internet. We needn't restrict our consideration to this view however; these issues are relevant to any network that uses this collection of protocols. Particularly if there is any kind of connection between one's private web and the global public Web, these matters are for serious concern.

> **CAUTION** *Readers who do not develop applications for the public Web might be inclined to think that this advice doesn't apply to them, since their network is private. Some might even reason that they're behind a corporate firewall and are therefore safe.*
>
> *Developing applications that exist solely on internal networks doesn't eliminate your need to give consideration to secure application design and implementation. Most attacks against a network occur from within. Additionally, the presence of a firewall is no guarantee that outsiders won't have access to some part of your system or something that your system assumes is safe. Intranet developers need to give these matters just as much careful consideration as the people developing things to run "out there in the wild." No one is safe from attack. The question is this: how will your systems fare when—not "if"—they're the target?*

It's important to remember that as with the rest of the protocols on the protocol stack, each of these protocols depends on the services provided by lower-level protocols.

Although web applications are typically implemented using such protocols as HTTP and markup such as HTML, that isn't necessarily always the case. Besides these relatively newfangled mechanisms, we also have some comparatively oldfangled protocols—like FTP [161] and plain text—implemented in most browsers. Furthermore, the Web's addressing scheme includes definitions for protocols like FTP and Gopher [4]. This can complicate matters for us considerably, since it increases the number of protocols that we need to understand in order to be able to render a good assessment of the relative security and privacy merits of a web-based application, at least in theory. In practice, though, almost everything is done with the newfangled stuff. We'll discuss the oldfangled only briefly.

To understand the Web, we're going to walk through the entire process, from the perspective of the user.

Addressing Objects on the Web

Objects—it doesn't matter whether they are files or server-side programs—anywhere on the Web are identified uniquely by a standardized addressing mechanism. Before we jump directly into how it works, we're going to review a few concepts to make sure that we understand exactly what we're talking about.

Pathnames: Finding Local Files

Finding a way to identify each file on a global network can be a challenge. The concept of *pathnames*—an "absolute" file location—is by no means new. Any operating system supporting the concept of a hierarchical filesystem (i.e., the ability to have directories or folders on a disk) understands the notion of a pathname. Absolute pathnames indicate how to reach a given file no matter where you are on the filesystem. Relative pathnames indicate how to reach the file from where you are at present.

Different operating systems that support this concept visually represent pathnames in different ways, as shown in Table 7-2. Although the notation is different, the functionality is identical.

Table 7-2. Various Operating Systems' Directory Separators

Operating System	Directory Separator
Unix	/
DOS, Windows	\
MacOS 9	:
MacOS X	/

The result is that we have the ability to use the filesystem to categorize things and to place things that logically belong together in the same "place." Thus, we can have two different files on the filesystem called .plan if we place each in a different directory. For example, consider Figure 7-4. We can reach one copy of .plan as /home/cmcurtin/.plan and the other as /home/gfe/.plan. The two might be two copies of the same file, or they could be completely different files.

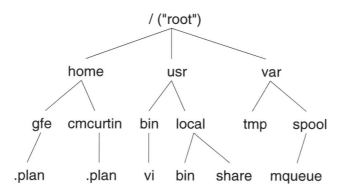

Figure 7-4. A Filesystem Hierarchy

Working Just Like DNS

Our hierarchical filesystem gives us a flexible way to reach any file on the filesystem. There are significant similarities between the domain name system and filesystem hierarchy. Just as we can have two different administrators running a web server called web, we can have two different users maintaining files called .plan inside of their own namespaces. In DNS, level separators are the dot character, exactly as slash is the level separator on Unix filesystems. Thus, www.w3.org has elements on three levels, just as does /home/cmcurtin/.plan. In DNS, each level to the right gets you closer to the root; on the filesystem, each level to the left gets you closer to the root. Aside from these minor differences, they work identically.

Making Object Names Globally Unique

Once we see that hierarchical filesystems allow us to identify any file on a computer system uniquely and that the hierarchical DNS allows us to identify any computer system on the Internet uniquely, we can see the next logical extension: unique identification of any file on the Internet.

This is accomplished by qualifying the pathname further, to include the host. A detailed specification for how this is done exists [12], but we'll cover the highlights here.

There are three important terms when talking about web addressing schemes.

URL Uniform Resource Locator, the typical scheme for addressing documents on the Web [12].

URN Uniform Resource Name, a more logical, as opposed to physical, means of identifying a document [130]. URNs are required to be persistent.

URI Uniform Resource Indicator, the most general way to talk about web addresses. Some addresses are URLs, some are URNs, but all addresses, whether URLs or URNs, are URIs [11].

Here is a sample URI with all of its parts populated:

```
http://user:password@foo.example.com:80/bar?baz=quux&lang=en#blarg
```

These parts are:

http is a scheme that identifies the protocol by which we're going to speak to the server, which we'll name a few tokens later. Some common schemes include http, mailto, ftp, https, news, and file. Many others are possible [75, 86, 122, 147].

user is the name of the user the client will present to the server for authentication purposes.

password is the password the client will present to the server for authentication purposes.

> **WARNING** *Just in case you're wondering, no, sticking an authentication token in a URI is not a good idea. There's an important lesson here: the possibility or the standardization of a particular practice is no guarantee of its prudence. Later revisions of the standard explicitly point out that inclusion of authentication tokens in a URI is a Bad Thing.*

foo.example.com is the name of the host to which we're initiating the conversation.

:80 shows the port number on which the server is running its HTTP server. If you don't know what ports are, you can imagine a server as a post office and a port number as a specific post office box. Once the mail gets into the building (the correct server), it still needs to be directed to the correct box (port) for the intended person (program, service, or dæmon) to get the message.

/bar is the pathname of the object—usually a document, but it can also be a program that will be run on the server and will dynamically return a document, as is probably true in this example.

?baz=quux&lang=en is the "query string"—input to the program. These are name/value pairs. Thus, when the program bar is run on the server, it will have the variables named baz and lang populated with the values quux and en, respectively.

#blarg is a specific point in the document. This is generally used to link to points of a long document.

Not all parts of the URI are mandatory. Other legitimate URIs include

- http://www.@stake.com/[3]

- http://www.google.com/search?q=cmcurtin&btnG=Google+Search

- file:///home/cmcurtin/.plan

- ftp://ftp:cmcurtin%40interhack.net@ftp.sourceforge.net/

Notice that in the FILE URI, the name of the hostname is empty. This is possible since the FILE access method will just open the file on the local filesystem; there's no need to specify a host.

Particularly for web developers, URIs are well worth understanding in detail. For our present purposes, though, we've covered enough to show what the components of URIs are and why they're important: a relatively simple string of text can be used to identify something on the Web completely uniquely. This is a critical piece of the solution to providing easy access to information online.

The obvious question that arises at this point is, "What do we do with URIs?" Of course, we could publish them in books and card catalogs, but that would fail to take full advantage of what options are before us. The most common use of URIs is in the links made from one document to another, the property that makes the Web, well, the Web. Those links are most commonly found in documents presented in HTML [9, 162].

---

[3] I like the http://www.@stake.com/ URI because it's a demonstration of a cool little trick to make it look like something it's not. The name of the company is "@Stake." They use the domain stake.com. When constructing a URI, they can use the user name www. so they can build a URI like http://www.@stake.com/. The client will connect to the server stake.com and send the user name www. when it makes the connection.

HTML, Architecturally

The HyperText Markup Language (HTML) has been key to the successful adoption of Web technology. HTML is a language for defining electronic documents *logically* rather than *visually*. Another fundamental property of HTML is the ability to cite other documents. One type of citation is the hyperlink—the ability to present an element of the document as "active," such that if it's selected, the user will be taken to another document. An example of HTML can be found in Listing 7-1.

Listing 7-1. The Source for Our Sample HTML

```
<!DOCTYPE HTML PUBLIC "-//W3C//DTD HTML 4.0 Transitional//EN">
<html>
  <head>
    <title>Some sample HTML</title>
  </head>
  <body>
    <h1>Some sample HTML</h1>
    <p>
      Here's some text in a paragraph. We can make a
      <a href="http://web.interhack.com/">link</a> to another
      item on the Web. We can also specify a dependency,
      perhaps an image, like this one.<br>
      <img src="/img/main/interhack_logo.gif"
       alt="INTERHACK">
    <p>
      The end.
    <hr>
    <address>
      <a href="mailto:cmcurtin@interhack.net">Matt Curtin</a>
    </address>
Last modified: Wed Jun 20 22:18:29 EDT 2001
  </body>
</html>
```

Elements like <P> (paragraph) and <H1> (level one header) define logical page components. Elements like <A> (anchor) define an active page area. One of the options available in an anchor tag is HREF, a hypertext reference, the address—as a URI—of the reference we're citing.

Another type of citation falls into a category that might best be generally described as a *dependency*. A dependency would be another object on the Web—perhaps some HTML, a stylesheet, or an image—that the web browser needs to fetch in order to render the page as described.

While the HTML source itself seems relatively straightforward, when interpreted by a client and presented for the user, the document can then come to life.

In Listing 7-1, we have some text that is described by the markup in the document itself. We have a document head and body. In the head, we have a title. In the body, we have a level one header, a few paragraphs, a horizontal rule, an address, and some anchor tags that provide links to other objects on the Web. One is a link to the site at web.interhack.com and another is a link that will allow someone to compose email to the document maintainer.

To render the page into something intended for the user, like the sample HTML shown in Figure 7-5, the client will need not only to see these elements and to understand them, but it will also need to make another download. The IMG tag tells the client that an image is needed and where the image can be found. Before rendering the page, the client will download the image from the specified URI.

Figure 7-5. Sample HTML, Displayed in a Browser

To view this single "page," then, the client had to make two separate downloads: one for the document source and another for its dependency.

We'll soon consider why the specification of dependencies is so important when we're thinking about privacy.

> **NOTE** *Because URIs allow objects to be specified anywhere on the global Web, it's possible to build a page in HTML that will have dependencies on other sites, even sites that are under different administrative control. There is no way to prevent someone from linking to your documents. This is a feature of the Web. There is also no way to prevent someone from putting dependencies on your images from their site. This is also a feature, but one with some important side effects.*
>
> *Despite being a feature of the environment, some—notably the operators of commercial web sites that want to maintain absolute control over the user's experience from beginning to end across the site—have attempted to stop the practice of linking. Some have gone so far as to file lawsuits [114].*

HTTP: Pulling Stuff from the Net

HyperText Transfer Protocol (HTTP) [66] is by far the most common protocol for moving objects around the Web. Despite its name, the protocol is responsible for getting not only hypertext, but also images, sounds, and video from one machine to another. In general, if an object is moving across the Web, it's doing so over HTTP.

HTTP Anatomy 101

HTTP messages—like messages sent over protocols for email and for news—have two components: a header and a body. We will look at some HTTP traffic and dissect it. If you have ever wondered how these things *really* work, you're about to find out.

> **NOTE** *Do not confuse the HTTP header with the* HEAD *element of an HTML document. HTML specifies a document's structure and content. HTTP is a protocol for getting an object from one machine to another.*

Let's consider a trivial HTTP session. We're going to work at the layer of the protocol, not the user interface layer.

> **TIP** *You can use the Telnet program to impersonate essentially any TCP-based client. Most of the time, people use Telnet to establish a terminal session with a remote machine. However, this is basically creating a TCP connection to port 23 of the server. Note that instead of logging into a machine with a command like* `telnet servername` *it's possible to specify that optional second argument to get the same behavior, i.e.,* `telnet servername 23`.
>
> *You can talk to any TCP-based service this way.* `telnet servername 13` *will connect your client to the "daytime" service that might be running. The server will report what time it thinks it is over the socket.* `telnet servername 17` *will connect the client to the quote-of-the-day service on servername. If the service is running, it will return a random quote to the requesting client.*
>
> *HTTP generally runs on port 80. Thus,* `telnet servername 80` *will connect to port 80 of servername in exactly the same way that a web client would. You can then type exactly what a web client would send to the server to get the server to process the request.*

First, we establish a connection to the web server:

```
$ telnet servername 80
Connected to servername.
Escape character is '^]'.
```

Many protocols begin with some sort of banner or greeting from the server telling the client what to expect. HTTP is not such a protocol. Once we have been connected, the server will stare at us until we tell it what we want. One option is to grab the header on the site's root document.

Whenever we send something to the server, we'll need to send a valid HTTP message. That means we'll have a header, separated from the body by two carriage return–linefeed (that's \r\n in C-ish languages) sequences. The body of our requests will be empty in most cases. For example, consider the request:

```
HEAD / HTTP/1.0
```

After we type the above and hit return twice, the server is likely to respond with something like

```
HTTP/1.0 200 OK
Server: CL-HTTP/70.23 (Macintosh Common Lisp; 3.7.0)
Content-type: text/html
```

Note that its response is also an HTTP message: a header followed by two carriage return–linefeed sequences and then the body. Each message, whether from the client to the server or the reverse, is a valid HTTP message.

It is important to recognize that HTTP is a stateless protocol: it has no notion of a multistep process or need to remember where in such a process it is. A client asks a question and gets an answer. The conversation is finished. If the client wants to know more, it'll ask another question. The server will just answer questions, not having any idea what questions that client asked previously.

In our trivial example, we sent just the minimum necessary to get an answer back from the server. We sent the request method, the object name, a query string, and a protocol version number. A more typical HTTP client request will include significantly more header information, including such things as the URI of the page that is linking to the requested object, a cookie [113] if one is present, and authentication tokens [67] if they're present.

Sidebar: The Referrer

HTTP 1.1 improved the standard, but not its spelling.

The HTTP Referer [sic] header has a curious history. In addition to having incorrect spelling specified in HTTP standards and consequently in every web application, the header itself has been the source of a significant amount of headache.

Its original purpose was to help people understand how the Web was being built—who was linking to whom. The header was also helpful in finding broken links. In the days that preceded the mainstream adoption of the Internet, this seemed like a fairly reasonable thing to do. Just about everyone on the Web was actively involved in building it, and everyone knew just about everyone else.

As more and more applications became available on the Web, facilities for such things as database queries became more commonplace. As the Web became more useful, more people began to use it, and soon, the Web was full of applications for many purposes, with many people building and using these applications—not all of whom necessarily knew or had much reason to trust each other.

Version 1.0 of HTTP—not the first version of the protocol, which had no concept of a version—mandated that clients specify their referrer. In the general case, this wasn't much of a problem. It did present many problems, however, as sites began to specify dependencies in their documents on third-party resources. Because of such privacy concerns—not to mention outright security concerns because URIs can contain authentication tokens—version 1.1 of HTTP reversed its position, allowing clients to specify referrers, but not mandating that they do, and even strongly discouraging their use where encoded data might be sensitive.

For example, if we followed a link from www.example.com to web.interhack.com, Netscape's Navigator version 4 might make a request that looks like the following:

```
GET / HTTP/1.0
Connection: Keep-Alive
User-Agent: Mozilla/4.76 [en] (X11; I; SunOS 5.6 sun4u)
Host: web.interhack.com
Referer: http://www.example.com/
Accept: image/gif, image/x-xbitmap, image/jpeg, image/pjpeg,
  image/png, */*
Accept-Encoding: gzip
Accept-Language: en
Accept-Charset: iso-8859-1,*,utf-8
```

The question now becomes how the server answers that mess.

HTTP Message Body

When the client is sending data to the server, there are several methods available. The most common, which we have just seen, is GET. The client simply tells the server to send a particular resource. The server replies, answering with a header, as we've seen, and with the actual results of the request being contained in the HTTP message body. For example, in response to a straightforward query for our sample HTML file, the server would send it back to the client something like the following:

```
HTTP/1.0 200 OK
Server: CL-HTTP/70.23 (Macintosh Common Lisp; 3.7.0)
Content-type: text/html

<!DOCTYPE HTML PUBLIC "-//W3C//DTD HTML 4.0 Transitional//EN">
<html>
  <head>
    <title>Some sample HTML</title>
  </head>
  <body>
    <h1>Some sample HTML</h1>
    <p>
```

```
            Here's some text in a paragraph. We can make a
            <a href="http://web.interhack.com/">link</a> to another
            item on the Web. We can also specify a dependency,
            perhaps an image, like this one.<br>
            <img src="/img/main/interhack_logo.gif"
             alt="INTERHACK">
          <p>
            The end.
          <hr>
          <address>
            <a href="mailto:cmcurtin@interhack.net">Matt Curtin</a>
          </address>
Last modified: Wed Jun 20 22:18:29 EDT 2001
        </body>
</html>
```

The HTTP body can also be used to submit data from the client up to the server. The most typical case for this usage is in the submission of data from an HTML fill-out form. Examples of HTML forms can be found everywhere. Essentially, every time you can enter some text, select a button, or pick an item out of a drop-down menu, it's handled by an HTML form. Viewing the page source for any web search engine should show you an example of at least one form in use.

Form data can be submitted by either the GET or POST method. If no method is specified explicitly, GET will be used. Form data submitted by GET are included in the target URI. In the case of the form in Listing 7-2, if we submit foo@example.com to the form, the client will make a GET query for the URI http://example.com/sub?email=foo@example.com.

Listing 7-2. HTML Form Source

```
<!DOCTYPE HTML PUBLIC "-//W3C//DTD HTML 4.0 Transitional//EN">
<html>
  <head>
    <title>A page with a form</title>
  </head>

  <body>
    <h1>A page with a form</h1>
    <p>
      This page has a form.

    <form action="http://example.com/sub" method="get">
      <p>
```

```
      Give us your email address!
      <input type="text" name="email">
    </form>
  </body>
</html>
```

If instead of `method="get"` we specified `method="post"`, the client would make a `POST` query for the URI `http://example.com/sub`. Rather than including the submitted data in the URI itself, the client will send the data in the body of the HTTP message.

HTTP Cookies

Although HTTP is itself a stateless protocol, there are times when applications we build on top of HTTP require state. Perhaps the most common example in the context of the public Web is the electronic shopping cart.

HTTP's notion of a session is trivial: a client tells the server the name of the object it wants and the server returns the object along with a status code. There simply is nothing else. No greeting, no setup, no teardown, just enough for one message in each direction. To get the idea of what this would be like, imagine calling a vendor on the phone. Each time you want to learn something about a product, you call the vendor and ask for the details on a given product. The vendor tells you the answer and hangs up the phone. So you call back to say you want to purchase it and the vendor tells you how much it is and then hangs up the phone. You call back and say what you want, how you intend to pay, how much you're expecting to pay, where to ship it, and everything else needed to reduce the vendor's response to "OK, it's on its way"—before hanging up the phone.

This is exactly what the Web was like initially; there was no easy way for the server to remember where it left off with the client.[4] Rather than extend HTTP to support the idea of carrying on a conversation, where the client and server could open a channel and communicate, developers at Netscape chose a simpler solution: add a header to HTTP that the server can use to tell the client, "Remember this token and give it back to me the next time we talk."

They called this token a *cookie*. Cookies—and the name cookie—have long been in use in the hacker culture [163]. At least since the 1980s, cookies were in use as a simple token that would be passed from one process or machine to another. A Real World example of a cookie is the claim check you get with your dry cleaning. You give them your clothes and they give you a cookie—a piece of paper with a number printed on it, a number useless outside of the system that issued

---

[4]   A rather crufty workaround has always been possible, inserting a session identifier—essentially a cookie—into the URI itself.

it. You can return to the dry cleaner later and give them the cookie that they gave you. Seeing that cookie, they'll be able to pick up your transaction right where it left off.

There are a few important properties for HTTP cookies that we'll want to note.

- **Origin** indicates the domain or the server which set the cookie.

- **Domain** is a boolean field indicating whether the cookie should be active for all servers within the domain.

- **Path** is a string used for URI matching, as described later.

- **Secure** is a boolean field indicating whether the cookie is "secure," and thus restricted to travel only over encrypted channels.

- **Expiration** is the cookie's expiration date.

- **Name** is the cookie's name, to disambiguate in case one server or domain has several cookies set on each client.

- **Value** has the contents of the cookie.

If we're trying to implement a shopping cart, we have a few different options for how we're going to use cookies. First, we could just take whatever data the client needs to be able to present us and put it in the cookie.

> **NOTE** *In fact, when the feature was first introduced into Netscape browsers, I had a web page that would allow readers to customize the view. They could choose their own colors for foreground, background, and other elements of the page. When they'd set their preference, I'd write the preferences into a cookie and hand it to the client. When the client asked to see the site again, it'd pass the cookie to my server. My server would read the cookie and then dynamically generate HTML to make the colors match the preferences.*

In other words, we could put a bunch of name/value pairs in the cookie, some "remember this" token, or anything else that we like, given some limits on the storage space available in the client's implementation.

Initially, because of limitations in the cookie's ability to store nontrivial amounts of information, people began to store a "user id" in the cookie. Then when the user would return to the site, the server would read the cookie, and could learn all of the active state data by making a query to a database. This prevented running into the kinds of problems that would come about by trying to store too much information in a single cookie (making it truncate), and also made it possible for people to store a great deal of preference information (such as a customized news or search engine page) without needing to store everything in the cookie itself.

Undoubtedly, this was a much better idea than trying to store everything on the client.

What happened, apparently without anyone noticing, is that the client lost its anonymity. Instead of just being some client out there on the Internet, the client had a name, a pseudonym. As the user would continue to use the client and would continue to pump more and more information into the system along with that pseudonym, the user's privacy eroded, and thus began the slippery slope of subtle web privacy invasion by web server operators.

How is giving someone a name an invasion of privacy? Remember that stuff we covered in Chapter 2? Privacy is informational self-determination. If the client didn't explicitly grant the server permission to correlate all of the data from all of that user's visits, he could very well argue that his privacy has been invaded. Not because anything learned by the server was by itself sensitive or even "personally identifiable," but because the user was denied the opportunity to decide for himself what information about his visit is being saved.

We can see how easily we moved from anonymity to pseudonymity. And we did it without anyone noticing.

> **NOTE** *IP address would be a constant token, but there's no guarantee that the address would be used by a single user or that it would remain constant. As such, there was a token, but how good it would be for user identification isn't clear. Apparently it wasn't good enough to avoid the need for the HTTP cookie. This isn't complete anonymity, because at least for a short period of time, the IP address would be a name, unique either to a user or to a very small set of users. This would be "weak anonymity," or short-term pseudonymity.*

An interesting design decision went into the creation of HTTP cookies. Three criteria were established for having the client determine whether to send the cookie along with any request; if any one is not true, the cookie will not be sent with the request. These criteria are:

- Originating site must match

- Path must match

- If the client from client to server is not encrypted, the "secure" flag on the cookie must not be set.

To determine whether the site matches, there are two tests:

- The site part of the cookie matches the host part of the URI. So, if you're visiting a site at foo.example.com, this test will pass if the cookie's site part matches `foo.example.com` exactly.

- The site part of the cookie matches the domain part of the URI and the cookie is set as a "domain cookie." To be a valid domain for the cookie, it must have two dots in it if the top level domain has three characters (for example, the most abstract domain cookie allowed for `foo.example.com` would be `.example.com`) or three dots if the top level domain has two characters (e.g., `freenet.columbus.oh.us` can set a cookie for `.columbus.oh.us`). Note that because country-code domains have varying levels of depth, in the case of the geographic part of the US domain hierarchy, it's possible for one site in a locality to set cookies that can be read by other sites in the same locality. Sadly, few other than hobbyists use US domains, opting to waste tremendous resources by grabbing domains that require load on the root nameserver, so in practice, this isn't much of a problem.

Sidebar: My Solution to the Domain Conflict Problem

In an attempt to deal with the demand for domain names exceeding the available workable domain names, more TLDs are being added. In addition to the venerable COM, NET, and friends, we now have such TLDs as INFO and BIZ.

This is precisely the wrong thing to do.

I say say that we should get rid of all three-letter domains except INT—the "international" domain, reserved for things like UN or NATO that do not have a logical home inside of a country code—and push everything into country-code domains. The US domain is well structured to put every business, government entity, non-profit organization, and individual that wants to have a domain online in a sensible way. Apparently too sensible for there to be any hope of widespread adoption.

In addition to there being a match for the site, there must be a match for the Path element. Basically, this is just a substring that must match some part of the request in the URI. The idea is that multiple applications can be present on a single site and you can keep the cookies from getting mixed up by restricting the cookie to a specific set of URIs on the site.

If the search engine runs from `www.example.com/search/` and the news section runs from `www.example.com/news/`, there could be two different cookies active, both for the host `www.example.com` and one with a Path element of `/search/` and another with the element of `/news/`.

The idea is that this will prevent the client from giving every server it talks to every cookie. As we've seen, there are limitations to how well these protections will work, so some care is necessary in their use, even with their safety mechanisms.

It's worth noting that a new specification for HTTP session management [113] has added some additional features to cookies, including the ability to document their intended use, to specify handling of data returned with cookies by proxies, and ports to which the cookie should be limited. As of this writing, the specification is an IETF standard, but the newer features are not universally implemented. Additional safeguards are recommended in Best Current Practice documentation from IETF [138], but again, are not widely implemented.

Cookies sound harmless enough. Even noting that we've slipped from anonymity to pseudonymity with most sites' use of cookies, we still need to consider what the big deal is, and why this is a problem worth our attention.

Invading Your Privacy

Privacy invasion is generally a question of how much data can be compiled about an individual. Nobody cares about a random datum being disclosed—unless the datum itself is sensitive, like a Social Security number or a credit card number—but the ability to profile, to correlate all of these data together to form a more complete picture of the person behind the nym, is both powerful and extremely distasteful to the profiled. (Technically, Social Security numbers and credit card numbers shouldn't be especially sensitive, but because they are often misused as both identification and authentication tokens—when was the last time someone scrutinized the signature on the back of your credit card?—they have become sensitive.)

We're going to talk about data leaks here. A data leak is exactly what it is in the context of a company secret: someone legitimately privy to the datum tells it to someone else. These kinds of leaks in business can move stock markets. These kinds of leaks in governments can have tremendous influence over handling public relations and diplomatic ties. These kinds of leaks online can compromise privacy.

Online privacy—the complicated issue that it is—boils down to two theoretically simple issues:

- Centralization of the little leaks that happen all over

- Circumvention of what protection there is

Alice is going to do some web surfing today, and we're going to watch what happens very closely. As we walk through these examples, we're going to see that everything third parties learn things about users on a web site can be put into one of three categories:

By design. Systems can be built specifically for the purpose of collecting some type of datum. For example, if search terms that Alice feeds into a search engine appear in the resulting page's URIs for banner ads, that's a leak by design.

By consequence. Some things are leaked as a result of the deployment environment—trying to do what we're doing in the environment where we're doing it has some consequence. Establishing a direct connection to a host, for example, has the consequence of revealing our IP address to the target host.

By inference. Here we start to get into some very tricky issues. When we deal with inference, we're moving beyond the level of raw data and moving into the realm of information. Data tell us that Alice reads *Cosmopolitan*, *Women.com*, and *Better Homes & Gardens*. We can use inference to arrive at information—whether true or not—that the reader is female. Data might tell us that she's a regular reader of *Yahoo! Personals* and *FriendFinder*. Inference can help us to arrive at the information that she's single.

Online advertising has been the most visible point of the online privacy debate, probably the most recognizable area where this is a problem. Perhaps a more concerning application of the techniques we're about to discuss can be found in the case of surreptitious tracking of user movements. Just as we can use advertisements from third-party servers to track users, we can use invisible images—known as *web bugs* [179]—to cause clients to make the requests that leak data about the user. Additionally, such requests are sometimes generated from JavaScript code that can be written to obtain additional data about the user and to report it upstream.

Because so many are already generally familiar with online advertising (but might not know exactly what the problem is or how the privacy invasion works), we're going to use this context to study the problem. Just remember that these same mechanisms can be employed by much less scrupulous persons to do much greater damage to the privacy of unsuspecting users online.

How Online Advertising Erodes Privacy

The question of how online advertising can erode privacy is interesting because we have become so used to seeing and hearing advertising everywhere. What is it that's so special about being online that creates specific concerns about advertising online and its effect on privacy?

We're going to watch Alice use three different web sites. We'll look at what happens in each case and then at the end, we'll put it all together and see what fits into the "dossier" that would exist in the hands of the advertiser if they put together the data that they received as a result of Alice's web surfing.

The First Site

Alice goes to visit our old friend www.example.com. Trying to figure out how to make a few bucks from their site's operation, they decided to put banner ads on the site. They're not interested in managing all of that advertising and the whole business that goes with it themselves, so they've outsourced it to an online ad management company running from the domain ad.ve.rt.

Assuming a very simple site like our trivial example earlier in the chapter, we have a simple page of HTML with a dependency on one image. That image, instead of coming from the same site that the user is visiting, is coming from their banner advertising network provider.

Figure 7-6 shows the process of reading a web site that transparently introduces a third-party site that tags new users. Because this all happens behind the scenes, Alice has no indication that the banner ad is coming from the third party. In fact, there isn't anything special about these banner ads; the dependencies could be for anything that would need to be loaded in order to display the page, including JavaScript, some HTML (perhaps as part of a frameset or an IFRAME), or an image that's invisible. The use of these other elements is

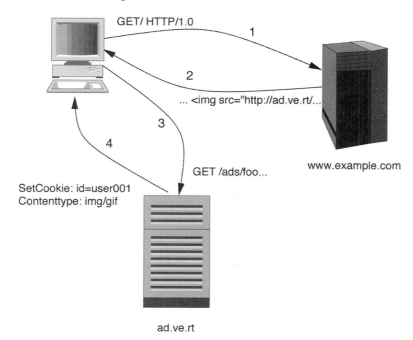

Figure 7-6. The First Site with Ads

becoming increasingly popular and is the subject of fierce debate about the privacy ramifications. The issue is that a web site that Alice is visiting has the ability to build its page such that Alice's browser also registers activity on other servers. In turn, those other servers can introduce still other servers, and any of the machines involved in the transaction can give the browser a cookie.

Here we're going to focus on the trivial case, but remember that this scales. The order of events for loading this page follows.

1. Client requests / from www.example.com.

2. www.example.com returns the contents of its "root document" (probably named something like index.html on the local filesystem). The code is shown in Listing 7-3.

3. Client parses the HTML and sees the IMG tag, so it requests the image from the site named in the SRC element of the IMG tag, which in this case is ad.ve.rt.

4. ad.ve.rt returns the image, and in the HTTP header of the response, gives the client a cookie with the Set-cookie header.

Listing 7-3. Source for http://www.example.com/

```
<!DOCTYPE HTML PUBLIC
  "-//W3C//DTD HTML 4.0 Transitional//EN">
<html>
  <head>
    <title>Example dot COM</title>
  </head>
  <body>
    <img src="http://ad.ve.rt/ads/blah.gif?site=example.com">
    <h1>Welcome to Example dot COM</h1>
    <p>
      News, goodies, and more!
    <p>
      Blah blah blah...
  </body>
</html>
```

The final step in the process is for the client to display the image in the page and to save the cookie, noting its expiration time. In practice, the lifespan of online advertisers' cookies tends to run from 10 to 30 years. If no expiration date is set, the cookie will only be active until the browser is restarted.

What happened

Code for the site `www.example.com`—a site Alice knew she was visiting—directed some element of the page to be loaded from `ad.ve.rt`. Consequently, Alice visited a site that she didn't know she was visiting. In the process of getting the content needed to render the page, she picked up a cookie for `ad.ve.rt` and became a unique user in their system. Note that the format of the request for the ad included data in the query string. This is clear evidence that the marketer designed the system to report the site that referred the ad, such that it would work even if the header that provided the referrer was disabled in the client or blocked somewhere in the middle.

Let's take a look again at the client request.

```
GET /ads/blah.gif?site=example.com HTTP/1.0
Connection: Keep-Alive
User-Agent: Mozilla/4.76 [en] (X11; I; SunOS 5.6 sun4u)
Host: ad.ve.rt
Referer: http://www.example.com/
Accept: image/gif, image/x-xbitmap, image/jpeg, image/pjpeg,
  image/png, */*
Accept-Encoding: gzip
Accept-Language: en
Accept-Charset: iso-8859-1,*,utf-8
```

Notice what is included in the header information. Any part of the request can be stored if the server is so configured. In this specific case, it includes the specific document we're reading thanks to the referrer header. Our user agent reports what it is, which version it is, and gives additional tokens to identify which edition (language edition, host operating system, encryption level, and even the architecture type of the host computer). The client reports what MIME types it will accept. If we have plugins enabled, that will usually extend the standard types of media that the client can understand, thus telling the server what plugins we have available. It'll report which languages the user can read and which character sets the client can understand.

Of course, in order to complete the TCP handshake necessary to answer the client request, the server must learn the client's IP address, or the IP address of the proxy used to make the connection. This almost always will be local to the user, at least telling us which network the user is coming from.

Many data were sent to to `ad.ve.rt` in the process of reading just a single trivial page at `www.example.com`.

Some notes on what happened

Because data are being sent from the client to the server at so many different logical levels, it's difficult for us to tell definitively which data the third party gets by design and which things the site gets by consequence of the deployment environment. Is the transmission of IP address and referrer by design or by consequence? Perhaps a good test is whether the data are being saved or used at all. The data might be sent as a consequence of the implementation environment, but if the server operators save or use the data, then they're also making the data leak part of their design. The problem with our test is that from the outside—from where Alice, whose data are being collected, sits—it's impossible to audit. At best, she can read a report from an auditor. More typically, she'll have to read some obscurely-written "privacy policy" that pretends to communicate intention, but is actually written by lawyers trying to prevent the company from getting sued. At worst, there's nothing at all to give any indication what happens to the data.

The problem here is that if Alice didn't know that the conversation with the third party took place, even the "best case" scenario is terrible—Alice has no control over what data about her are being sent or to whom they're being sent.

Of course, once the data are collected, they can just sit there—even for years—waiting to be analyzed. Such data might be used later to learn more about Alice by the process of inference.

So let's see what happens as Alice moves on to another site.

The Second Site

Moving down her daily reading list, Alice makes a visit to a completely different site: `www.example.to`. Little does she know, this site uses the same banner advertising network as does the first site. The result is that Alice reads another site, sees another ad, and makes another impression on the ad server as illustrated in Figure 7-7. Source code for the second site can be found in Listing 7-4.

On this site, the specific order of events is:

1. Browser fetches `http://www.example.to/`.

2. Site returns HTML, including image for banner ad: `http://ad.ve.rt/ads/frob.gif?site=example.to`.

3. Browser makes a new connection to `ad.ve.rt`, sending along the cookie that it got in the first connection with the ad server.

4. Ad server logs the request and returns the ad.

Listing 7-4. Source for http://www.example.to/

```
<!DOCTYPE HTML PUBLIC
  "-//W3C//DTD HTML 4.0 Transitional//EN">
<html>
  <head>
    <title>TONGA Ex</title>
  </head>
  <body>
    <img src="http://ad.ve.rt/ads/frob.gif?site=example.to">
    <h1>TONGA Ex</h1>
    <p>
      It's the Tonga sample site! Buy! Buy! Buy!
    <p>
      Hype, hype, hype...
  </body>
</html>
```

As we can see from the code and architectural diagram, the connection here is identical to what happened in the first case. We're just dealing with a different "front-end" for the banner advertiser and the specific transaction data that we're feeding are different.

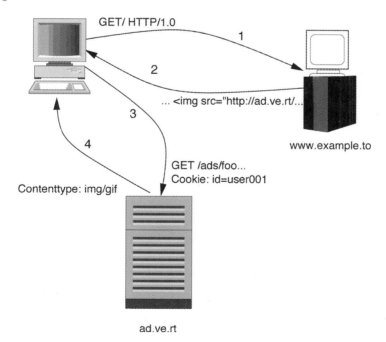

Figure 7-7. A Second Site with Ads

What happened

Since Alice is already in the system, what happened here is exactly what happened in the previous case, except instead of getting a new cookie, her browser just reported her existing one. This allowed the ad server to correlate the impression made by reading www.example.com with the one made by reading www.example.to. From Alice's perspective, www.example.to was a completely unrelated site. One site might well have been *Cosmo* and the other *Better Homes & Gardens.* Instead of giving the server some random datum, she was given a datum that can be compared with the other, and her reputation in the system is now being built.

What does the ad server know now?

Now that Alice has a two-visit-long reputation, what does that reputation include?

- Which pages she's read "at best" or which sites she's visited "at worst"

- When she visits them (the ad servers know the time!)

- Any other information she volunteers, like languages or character sets (which can hint at other languages)

- The degree of customization she's done on her browser (they know the defaults for her browser type, so if her browser is different, she's configured it, and she reports which plugins she's installed)

- Her IP address, which will tell the ad server which ISP(s) she uses, and if her company is big enough to have a network assigned to it, where she works

If we take a step back and start to think about what the ad server knows with some inference, we can start to identify things like what kind of schedule Alice has. The IP address will probably give us some idea of the time zone, so looking at that activity in connection with the likely time zone tells us if we're dealing with someone who uses the Web mostly during the day or night. We can see what kind of network we're dealing with, which helps us to understand whether we're talking about a home or office user (consider examples like AOL versus some big company's network). We can probably even infer things like how much time Alice spends at work. We can learn things like what time of day someone will or won't be at home.

None of these things by itself—in a single transaction—is problematic, but the greater the amount of historical data we have, the better we're going to be able to use it to predict the future. (Does Alice always vacation from December 21 to December 31? After a few years' worth of data, we can know.)

About this time, we usually start to hear the "don't worry" crowd point out that even by our own definition we have a pseudonymous profile. That's true. So let's hit fast-forward and catch up with Alice a little later in the day.

Visiting the Third Site

Alice just got a box of stuff she ordered. She rips open her box and therein is a product registration card that says she must fill out the card so the warranty can be enacted. Better yet, suggests the card, "Fill out the form online!" So off goes Alice to the specified URI. She submits a form with her name, address, phone number, and some magazines she reads. She hits the submit button and Figure 7-8 shows what happens.

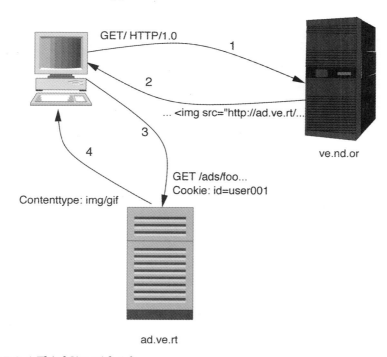

Figure 7-8. A Third Site with Ads

The order of events here is:

1. Alice's browser submits the form data from the product registration page to the site ve.nd.or with the GET method.

2. The ve.nd.or server returns a thank-you page containing an IMG tag to pull in an ad from the ad.ve.rt server.

3. Alice's browser requests the ad from ve.nd.or and puts the URI of the thank-you page into the HTTP referrer.

4. ve.nd.or returns the ad to Alice's browser, which can then render the page.

Yes indeed, the vendor has advertising on its site and there on the thank-you page is a banner ad from the friends we never knew existed at ad.ve.rt. The source for the thank-you page is in Listing 7-5.

Listing 7-5. Source for Vendor's Registration Thank-You

```
<!DOCTYPE HTML PUBLIC "-//W3C//DTD HTML 4.0 Transitional//EN">
<html>
  <head>
    <title>VendorName</title>
  </head>

  <body>
    <img src="http://ad.ve.rt/ads/4906.gif?site=ve.nd.or&area=reg">
    <h1>Thank you for registering with VendorName!</h1>
    <p>
      Now that you've registered your product with us,
      we can bury you in junk mail!

  </body>
</html>
```

So what was added to the ad server's profile this time? As it turns out, quite a lot, really. This form used the GET method for form submission, which means that the entire contents of the form were sent to the advertiser by way of the HTTP referrer. Some will object that this is poor design, that this sort of thing is really more theoretical than practical. Although poor design, this sort of thing does happen quite a lot in the context of the Web. GET is the default form submission method and many examples in books and other technical documentation show the use of GET.

This thank-you page will look something like http://ve.nd.or/reg?name=Alice %20Foo&address=123%20Neil%20Ave&Phone=818-555-1212.[5] Now everything between "here and there"—the browser's history, proxy logs, and server logs— including Alice's name, address, and phone number are there in all their glory.

---

[5] Pretend that's one long line. Ah, the joys of trying to represent data on paper . . .

For the ad server, which gets the URI in the HTTP referrer, Alice's cookie will tie this transaction to all previous transactions she has performed. Now, without her knowledge, Alice's reputation has gone from pseudonymous to verinymous. It only takes one record like this in the entire history of an online profile to make the entire profile verinymous. As a result, all of the other "non-personally-identifiable information" that exists in the ad server's database can be tied back to Alice just as easily as can this transaction with her name.

Although this kind of leak has happened in practice—and is no doubt continues to happen every day—this is a pretty extreme case. A more likely case of moving to verinymity will be in the form of leaking all of the needed information to make the verinym, one datum at a time. As of this writing, ZIP codes are often pushed into query strings—clearly leaks by design. Sites are pushed into query strings—clear leaks by design. Birthdates are pushed into query strings—again, leaks by design. (Stop and think for a moment why all of those horoscope sites online ask for your birthday instead of your sign.)

Now, imagine taking three data—ZIP code, sex (as inferred by which sites one reads), and birthday—and searching through the kinds of databases that are kept by marketers. It's trivial to put these three data together into a single "key" that can be the basis of a search in a marketer's database which would also contain name, address, phone number, and even Social Security number.

Non-personally-identifiable indeed.

The Ad Server's Database

So let's drive this point home. The ad server collects transactional data from users who browse web sites that use the ad serving network. Some of these data are leaked by design. Other data are leaked by consequence of the implementation. Any data might be useful to infer some higher-level information about the user behind the browser.

The ad server gives a unique name to each of the users, the value that's stored in the cookie. That name is associated with each of the requests that the user makes of the ad server.

Because the user has an identity in the system, the user will build up reputation and anything that is learned during any single transaction (like a real name or phone number) can be linked back to the profile for that user. As more data are collected in the profile, more information about the user can be inferred and the closer the user moves to verinymity.

All of this happens without the user's knowledge or consent.

The Internet as a Deployment Environment

Thinking "in the large" is critical. Developers have been able to get away with myopia in various settings like application-level software that runs on machines for individual users. That kind of worldview is orders of magnitude more dangerous online.

As we can see from the example of the online advertising network, it's possible to build systems that collect a great deal of information, even much more than is intended. As people continue to increase their reliance on Internet-based systems and continue to put information about themselves in these systems, we need to give very serious consideration to how we handle the trust placed in us—the people who develop and operate these systems. We would do well to consider that ill-considered moves now could make for very serious problems in the reliability or trustworthiness of our systems, even in the safety of our systems' users.

CHAPTER 8

Case Studies

OUR DISCUSSION OF SECURITY AND privacy problems can easily become too abstract to make direct application. Even when we know the issues at hand, how do we understand when we're creating a problem? How do we find remedies? Learning how to apply this information is often best done by looking at real, concrete examples. This chapter does just that: we consider systems that were actually deployed and try to understand what undesirable side effects came as a result of these systems' deployment. We continue our consideration from the perspective of system implementors and offer suggestions for improving system security.

My firm, Interhack Corporation, sponsors a research project, called the Internet Privacy Project [47], that studies Internet-based systems, attempting to understand how their design and implementation have affected the privacy of users online. When we encounter a new type of problem, we release a technical report describing the system, what problems its design present, and what steps could be taken to address the problems. This chapter will draw heavily from the Internet Privacy Project's work.

The five cases we consider include a system whose implementation involving a persistent cookie had drastic privacy consequences, two different kinds of opt-out system failures, how a web site monitoring service violated posted privacy policies, and how optimizing for convenience resulted in a tradeoff in security.

NOTE   *As we consider these case studies, it's important to understand that these systems were actually deployed to the Internet-using public. Privacy advocates are often chastised for raising hypotheticals that just aren't likely. None of these failures is hypothetical. Each of these systems had some sort of failure that resulted in some kind of privacy risk to the users of the system, often very subtle risks that nonexperts wouldn't recognize were present.*

Equally important to understand is that we make no accusation of malice. As mentioned in Chapter 3, people make mistakes. Our goal in understanding these failures is not to ridicule their designers, but to understand how they failed and what might have been done to avoid the failure. Ultimately, we should be able to learn from these failures, so that the systems we build in the future will not repeat the mistakes of the past.

Case Study #1: Centralization Unexpectedly Erodes Privacy

The Internet has often been called the world's largest library—with all of the books on the floor. Tremendous advances in cataloging and searching have been made since the dawn of the Web. Despite the progress made in navigating the Internet, it is clear that there is still a great deal of room for improvement.

Our first case study is an examination of an attempt to solve this problem in 1998.[1]

Users searching for information about a specific product, service, or organization are likely to get a great deal of irrelevant information included with

---

[1]   Dates will be important to our discussion since the scene on the Internet changes so rapidly, and some of the critical issues in these cases are non-issues now. It is necessary to understand the technical and political environment into which these systems were released.

the relevant. This has a range of consequences, from mildly annoying the user to making the Internet nearly impossible to use for research on a specific item.

Enter the notion of "smart browsing." Netscape teamed with Alexa Internet to offer users of Netscape's browser software the ability to use the Alexa service, as a built-in part of the browser beginning with version 4.06. The Alexa service was intended to help users find information that was relevant to them by asking their browser, "What's related?"

Users who clicked the *What's Related* button in any version of Netscape Communicator with the smart browsing feature would be presented with a number of sites intended to be related to the web document that was currently being displayed.

> **NOTE** *We focus specifically on Netscape's implementation of the technology, even though Alexa had a client program of its own and Microsoft's Internet Explorer now offers the functionality as a built-in. Our initial investigation focused on the Netscape implementation because it was the first to be included with standard software and was enabled by default. At the time of its initial release, Netscape offered no documentation on the smart browsing design and its implementation.*

Tell me this wasn't screaming "investigate me!"

Anatomy of "Smart Browsing"

Of course, how smart browsing was implemented is of great interest to those involved with Internet architecture, which is what roused the attention of our privacy project members in the first place and got us started in our investigation.

What appeared to be an interesting and useful feature came at a significant price: loss of control over data in connection with activity online. More directly stated, we're talking about invasion of privacy.

Communicator offered three options for "smart browsing" configuration in the browser's Preferences settings. These would load *What's Related* automatically:

- Always

- After First Use

- Never

Architecturally, the system worked just like the architecture discussed in Chapter 7 to support third-party advertising, with one key difference: instead of happening automatically, the user initiated the original connection to the third party. Figure 8-1 illustrates the interaction. Note that the user points the browser to www.example.com and then the user clicks on the *What's Related* button to initiate the connection to www-rl.

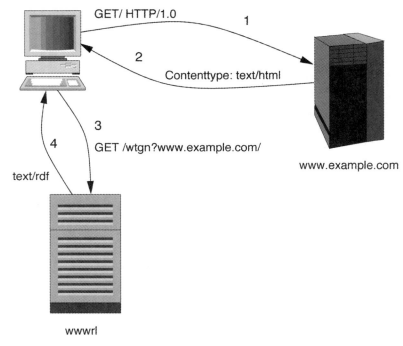

GET/ HTTP/1.0

1

2

Contenttype: text/html

3

4

GET /wtgn?www.example.com/

www.example.com

text/rdf

wwwrl

Figure 8-1. Interaction with What's Related Server

When *What's Related* loaded, we found that in addition to the normal requests, an additional HTTP session was started with the host www-rl4.netscape.com, which is one of a group of servers used to share the load. We refer to the *What's Related* servers as www-rl. This continued as the user bounced from site to site, leaving an electronic trail of his activity on the Web with a centralized server. We examined the conversation between the browser and this host for the remainder of this session.

Ring around the Internet, Packet with a bit not set, SYN ACK, SYN ACK, We all go down!

Analysis of this system was performed using a packet sniffer, a system to capture traffic on our network and to analyze it.

Current URI

In this particular case, the URI of the page that the user is currently viewing is sent in the query string of an HTTP GET request. A full request is shown in Listing 8-1.

Listing 8-1. A Netscape What's Related Request

```
GET /wtgn?www.example.com/ HTTP/1.0
Connection: Keep-Alive
User-Agent: Mozilla/4.06 [en] (X11; I; SunOS 5.6 sun4u)
Host: www-rl.netscape.com
Accept: image/gif, image/x-xbitmap, image/jpeg, image/pjpeg,
  image/png, */*
Accept-Encoding: gzip
Accept-Language: en
Accept-Charset: iso-8859-1,*,utf-8
Cookie: NETSCAPE_ID=10010014,12f8fee8
```

After performing a variety of requests, we came up with the following observations:

- URIs were reported back to `www-rl`. This included both "public" URIs and "private" URIs, i.e., those that are on an intranet, unless that URI is part of a group that has been explicitly excluded by the user by browser configuration.

- HTTP query strings were *not* included on the URI that was sent to `www-rl` in Netscape's implementation. Specifically, the URI `http://www.example.com/search.cgi?secret` would be reported as `http://www.example.com/search.cgi?`. Alexa's browser plug-in client reported the entire URI, including the query string.

Response

In response to any query, `www-rl` returns a file of the MIME type `text/rdf`. Resource Description Framework (RDF) is a mechanism for dealing with metadata on the Web, a way to aid programmatic "understanding" of pages on the Web. RDF can be used for such things as assisting cataloging agents, asserting intellectual property rights, and (ironically enough) describing privacy properties [166]. In this case, it was a definition for links that the server believed to be relevant to the URI sent in the request. Listing 8-2 shows the complete response to the request for *What's Related* to the literal string `www.example.com`. The nature of the response's content provides a commentary—interesting, amusing, or sad, depending on your point of view—on the Web.

Listing 8-2. What's Related Server Response

```
HTTP/1.0 200 OK
Content-type: text/rdf; charset=utf-8
Connection: Keep-Alive
Content-length: 00459

<RDF:RDF>
<RelatedLinks>
<aboutPage
 href="http://info.netscape.com/fwd/rl/http://www.example.com:80/"/>
<child instanceOf="Separator1"/>
<child
 href="http://info.netscape.com/fwd/rl/http://www.a.com/"
 name="The Alternative Japan Web Page! For Adults
  Over Only Please!"/>
<child instanceOf="Separator1"/>
</RelatedLinks>
</RDF:RDF>
```

There isn't anything especially peculiar about this file, except that all of its links are in the form of

```
http://info.netscape.com/fwd/rl/http://www.example.com:80/
```

This means that rather than being linked directly to the recommended site, the user would make the connection by first telling www-rl where he's going. This is the feedback mechanism which tells the server which, if any, of the recommended sites the user followed. As shown in Listing 8-3, once the client connected to info.netscape.com, it would be sent on to www.example.com by way of an HTTP redirect.

Listing 8-3. Following the Suggested Link

```
HTTP/1.0 302 NSAPI REDIRECTOR: INVALID URL
Server: Netscape-Enterprise/2.01
Date: Wed, 26 Aug 1998 04:27:47 GMT
Location: http://www.example.com:80/

<HTML><HEAD><TITLE>NSAPI REDIRECTOR: INVALID
 URL</TITLE></HEAD>
<BODY><H1>NSAPI REDIRECTOR: INVALID URL</H1>
This document has moved to a new
 <a href="URL UNKNOWN">location</a>.
Please update your documents and hotlists
 accordingly.</BODY></HTML>
```

> **NOTE** *This HTTP redirection is all happening in real time. The web browser will never need to render a redirect page, so the redirection from one server to another will be completely transparent to the user. If such redirection is done against users' expectations, users might not even realize that redirection took place.*

The cookie

Perhaps the most interesting part of the entire transaction was the presence of a cookie along with the request:

```
Cookie: NETSCAPE_ID=10010014,12f8fee8
```

Because the www-rl servers were all a part of the .netscape.com domain and there were no Path restrictions on the Netscape cookie, the very same cookie was used for browsing all Netscape sites. Among the types of content that were served by Netscape were such things as hit counters, news, developer and user documentation, and Netscape software downloads.

Frequency of the fetch

Communicator did obey the user's configuration of the option. After testing, we were able to determine that the www-rl fetches only happened after the user pushed the button. Afterward, the behavior was

- The www-rl fetch would happen for the next 1,000 requests the user made when "Always" was selected.

- The www-rl fetch would happen for the current URI and the next three pages when "After First Use" was selected.

- The www-rl fetch would happen only for the current page when "Never" was selected.

Impact

The *What's Related* feature raises some extremely serious privacy concerns, not only for individuals, but organizations that might have sensitive information leaked outside of the boundaries of their firewalls.

Here we consider some of the implications of our observations.

Leaking intellectual property beyond the firewall

Having an extremely descriptive URI, perhaps including the name of unannounced products, the people working on them, and other potentially sensitive information, is a bad idea. Something along these lines makes an excellent find before attempting a little social engineering to further compromise an organization's intellectual property.

Sidebar: Mixing Internal and External Data

Software that operates by watching user activity and reporting it back to the provider's sites poses a serious danger to the privacy of online data, possibly making firewalls essentially useless.

The 2001 SirCam worm worked by finding a file on a mounted filesystem and sending that file, infected with SirCam, to others. This malware represented a turn for the worse in the level of damage that would occur. Rather than simply infecting vulnerable recipients, this worm would also expose the contents of a file randomly selected from the user's filesystems. For weeks, people being hit by the worm were finding their résumés, business letters, spreadsheets, and other private documents effectively published. Firewalls that would allow email to flow freely through them provided no protection against SirCam.

Although SirCam was malicious, there's an important lesson from it that can be extracted and generalized: granting unrestricted access between security zones on a network—such as an internal network and the Internet—provides a mechanism for the protection between the zones to be broken. SirCam demonstrated how such software could take advantage of email.

People running software that monitors and reports their activity to Internet sites pose a serious risk to the privacy of private data on internal networks. Remember from Chapter 3 that when we are granting access, we don't grant the access to people, we grant access to their agents. In today's systems, a user with access to a file in one application can almost certainly reach the same file with another application. Even worse, finding that such an upload took place might prove sufficiently difficult, so that in many environments, no one would ever know. How would a user stop, for example, his browser from grabbing a copy of a financial spreadsheet and uploading it to an attacker's site? How would a user know that it happened?

The *What's Related* directory wasn't built by uploading complete content, as was happening with SirCam attacks and the theoretical browser-based, file-upload attack described above. However, in returning the *What's Related* directory entries for some large companies, we did see that some internal sites were included in the directories, indicating that some data flow had been taking place. Users on the internal networks of these companies would be able to use *What's Related* to identify useful internal web sites. Users on the external networks would also see the names of the internal web sites, but the firewall would prevent the outsiders from reaching the sites. Nevertheless, we might ask the question, "Just how much information about those 'related' sites lives in the *What's Related* directory?"

Finally, the same question can—nay, should—be asked about any system that uploads data from intranet users.

Looking at *What's Related* data for some large companies proved to be especially interesting, since some of the highest-ranked sites were not visible from the public Internet. For example, a user clicking on *What's Related* for BigCorp's web site[2] might find a list of related sites that are actually part of BigCorp's intranet. Users of the software with access to the internal networks would be sending "related" URLs back up to the server. Thus, some data about corporate *internal* networks made their way to an unaffiliated index, available for anyone to see.

In all fairness, this isn't the only case of URI leaking on the Web, and probably isn't the most problematic. The HTTP `Referer` header is more dangerous, as it leaks the *entire* URI, including any query string data. Poorly implemented systems that pass private data in the query string will expose their users to many sorts of privacy invasions and security risks. Some early web-based mail readers stored all state data and authentication tokens in their URIs' query strings, thus allowing attackers to read the email of users whose session URIs were leaked. The most common case for leaks of this sort is in the HTTP dæmon's logging of the document referrer.

As we discussed in Chapter 5, the danger here is that rather than having a few "juicy bits" spread randomly throughout the Internet, there is now a single place that could be theoretically used to find more information about a site's internal hosts and URIs. Mining these databases for clues about a site's internals might very well prove to be an effective method of gathering information needed to break into a given site.

The blurring line between intranet and Internet is important. Many developers falsely believe themselves and their systems to be safe because they're behind a company firewall. However, as these musings demonstrate, it is possible for data to flow outside of the firewall. Thus, instead of an attacker needing to break through your firewall to steal your secrets, he might well just be able to get your software to send the data he wants outside of the firewall to someplace he can get them.

Extremely detailed click-trails

As discussed in Chapter 7, by collecting detailed browsing data, marketers can classify an individual user and direct advertising content explicitly for that user, based on the site currently being browsed, as well as historical data collected.

Additionally, such detailed click-trails might themselves become vulnerable to various types of attack, including targets for discovery in litigation or blackmail.

---

[2]   For obvious reasons, the company sites in question shall remain anonymous.

Building a dossier

Part of the way that privacy concerns regarding cookies on the Web have been addressed is by their decentralized nature. By forcing the level of granularity on a cookie's domain, the user has the ability to give certain information to a vendor he might trust more without having to worry about the information being stored in a cookie, which could then be used by a different vendor, one that the user trusts less.

By sending a stream of URIs back to `www-rl`, each of which is accompanied by the same persistent cookie, it now becomes possible for Netscape to circumvent the privacy designs of cookies, collecting a rather complete picture of an individual user's browsing habits across the Web. The user's pseudonym for use with Netscape includes activity on other sites as well.

Adding your name to the dossier

As discussed in Chapter 2, a central theme of privacy is nymity. Users identified by a persistent and unique cookie are pseudonymous, able to have reputation. Any datum associated with the cookie will then be able to be included as part of that possible database.

Nymity is especially interesting in the case of *What's Related* because when the feature was first made available, Federal law forbade U.S. companies from distributing strong cryptography outside of the U.S. and Canada. Several Netscape products available for download were therefore limited to domestic use. To comply with Federal law, Netscape required users downloading products with strong cryptography to submit a form including name, address, and telephone number.

Similar risks have been identified in Microsoft's Passport Single Signon Protocol [110].

Given the popularity of the Netscape browser, the number of services offered by Netcenter, and thus the number of data flowing into Netscape's logs, this certainly could quickly become the most complete database of web users and their browsing habits. Again, this was all most likely taking place completely without the knowledge—much less the consent—of the users involved.

Centralization wasn't necessarily a design requirement for the system in question. Data centralization happened as a side effect of offering so many services from the same domain. The use of a persistent domain cookie made it possible to correlate all of the data to the appropriate pseudonymous users. Attempts to satisfy legal requirements resulted in pseudonymous users needing to reveal verinyms. One tiny piece at a time, the system became a huge data repository, with mechanisms needed for identifying the users behind the data. This is an important lesson: our failure to adhere to good privacy or security design principles can happen slowly, in several stages.

Remedies

The problems that we identified in this case study can be succinctly summarized as follows:

- Leaking proprietary information through overdescriptive URIs

- Providing the means for a central repository of a huge number of users' browsing habits, on an extremely granular level

- Allowing the aforementioned repository the ability to identify individual users with a relatively high degree of certainty

There are several steps that can be taken in order to neutralize the privacy-invading effects of the *What's Related* feature. In a nutshell, now that we know what the problems are, we can provide remedies for each of them. Client-side solutions for these problems are documented in our technical report on this topic [48]. What we're going to consider here is from the perspective of the implementor. If we were in the position to build the system again, how could it be done such that these problems would not exist?

At a very high level, the requirements for this system seem straightforward. Netscape built the service using Alexa's data, rather than building a system that builds the directory used for the *What's Related* service. We can therefore keep our scope narrow, focusing just on the use of the directory.

Rather than giving a full-scale consideration to the requirements of this system in Netscape's implementation, we can look at server-side remedies to the problems already highlighted.

Overly descriptive URIs

As URIs are the addresses by which web pages are identified, sending the URI to the directory location is mandatory. It would be possible, but infeasible, to build the directory into the client, thus avoiding the need to transmit the URI to another server at all. We discuss these architectural issues further in the next section.

There is no effective defense against URIs that have too much information in them. URIs should never contain data that are not considered "publishable." Intranet developers need to take special care, since the official company standards of what qualifies as proprietary probably includes things like project names, organization charts, and possibly even things like internal hostnames. Now that anyone, anywhere on the internal web, can link to external resources, it's possible for anyone to be the catalyst to leaking information that should never make it outside the firewall. In particular, internal sites might have links to competitors so that employees can keep tabs on what others in the marketplace are doing.

You might also be telling your competitors that you're keeping tabs on them, and giving them data that they can use.

> **WARNING** *This is a point that bears repeating:* URIs should never contain any datum that would be considered sensitive. *Imagine a postal address like:*
>
> ```
> Bob Smith, Serbian Language Specialist
> National Security Agency
> Central European Counterintelligence Unit
> Ft. Meade, MD
> ```
>
> *Bob might be clever, but signing up for too many magazines like that is going to get him on the fast-track to a career change.*

It's worth noting that Netscape already sanitizes the URIs that it sends up to www-rl, not including the query string or section part of the URI. Given the way that many web sites are implemented—dynamic sites, driven by a database—query strings are an integral part of the URI, making it impossible to browse much of the site without the ability to fill out forms or to query the database. This practice is popular, but isn't universally viewed as a Good Thing [79].

Centralization of user browsing habits

Centralization is one of the biggest facilitators of privacy problems. Nymity is important, since once the user is pseudonymous, he can maintain a reputation. However, pseudonymity alone isn't likely to be much of a problem. It's the collection of data and the association of those data with the pseudonym that make for the reputation.

To avoid the centralization of data indicating users' browsing habits, we have several options. Looking back at the design of *What's Related*, all of the processing was done on the server. The other extreme in design would be to put all processing on the client side.

Looking at our requirements, it becomes immediately obvious that we're going to run into several serious problems in a purely client-side solution. We consider four big problems.

Synchronicity of the data in the client with what Alexa Internet knows about the state of the Internet and its linking would be seriously impacted. Imagine someone who uses a browser that's supplied by an IS department that upgrades its browsers only once per year. Imagine people who manage their own software and have just gotten tired of downloading, installing, and configuring a new browser every two hours. Some of these folks can be running a browser that's several years old. (Ask anyone who runs a busy web site that keeps track of user agents which browsers people are using, and you might be surprised to see how many people are running with some surprisingly old software out there.) How useful would it be to have a Web directory that's two years old? Search engines have enough trouble keeping up with the Web as it is.

Plug the phrase "Not Found" or "Moved" into a search engine sometime.

Disk requirements would go through the roof. People with modems would be downloading the software and its data for a month. People on systems with disk quotas would likely exceed their quotas before finishing the download. This problem alone makes the whole idea of putting the processing on the client side completely unworkable.

Memory requirements would also be significant, since at the very least, indices would need to be memory resident for efficient searching. This could actually be managed, but would just be a ridiculous waste.

Processing requirements could also be managed, but would increase quite significantly. Now, instead of waiting for some data to shuffle back and forth across the network, the client itself would need to handle all of the processing to determine which things are and are not related. Processing speed is rarely a problem on client machines these days.

I miss my 1 MHz Apple II.

The size of the directory alone makes the client-side solution unworkable.

Another possible architecture would be somewhere between the extremes of an all-server solution and an all-client solution. In such an approach, we might be able to avoid some of the problems associated with full-blown client-side processing without getting all of the side effects of full-blown server-side implementation. This kind of architecture would avoid the problem of data centralization. However, the nature of the service we're providing—a directory—doesn't lend itself to client-side implementation for any component. What would you offload to the client and how would you keep it from requiring everything else to be on the client as well? If our plan is to move the index to the client, we're immediately forcing our disk space, memory, and processing requirements to the client to support the index.

Remember that the high-level problem we're trying to figure out how to address is how to implement Netscape's *What's Related* feature without creating a central repository of browsing history, which could become a target for subpoena or otherwise unexpectedly compromise a user's privacy. Centralization is merely one of the pieces of this puzzle. At least some degree of centralization is rather central to the feasibility of this system's utility.

So, we don't have a good option for building privacy into this system by attacking its centralized nature. Let's try another tactic, seeing how we can enforce user privacy by addressing another of the problems that the design presents: allowing identification of the directory's users.

Identification of users

Let's consider the issue of pseudonymity and its role in this system. We've already noted that centralization is critical to the privacy invasion, but as we've seen, decentralization could be prohibitively difficult. Perhaps we can find a more efficient solution to the problem at hand by attacking pseudonymity.

Because the user's nym—the Netscape cookie's value—is present for all Netcenter services, many data come into the Netscape servers for a wide variety of purposes. The secure download page was by far the most problematic piece of this puzzle. U.S. law pretty well mandated it at the time of the deployment. However, all of these features being run from one domain puts all of the data in the hands of a single entity—Netscape—to correlate the data from the secure downloads with the pseudonym, thus making the user verinymous. Because the user's name—which is often unique only within a relatively small namespace[3]—isn't all we have, not only is the profile verinymous, but it's a *strong* verinym, including name, address, and phone number. It's likely that given all three data, the user will be unique.

Looking back at our nymity spectrum from Chapter 2, we can see that this system takes many users very close to that "strong verinymity" area. Whether this is by design or by accident is irrelevant to the discussion. Our topic is building systems that have privacy as a built-in feature, not privacy by some complicated system of management and auditing.

Removal of the cookie—the nym—would be a significant step taking the user back toward the other side of the nymity scale ("strong anonymity"). Even in a transaction where sensitive data leaked back to the server, there wouldn't be a way to associate it with other data that were leaked to the system by that user. The ability to build a profile, a reputation, would be lost.

It's worth noting that we wouldn't take the user all the way back to the level of "strong anonymity." Though the user would again be anonymous, there would be enough transactional data, including such things as IP address(es) and browser type, that might be used to correlate some transactions together over relatively short periods of time. Nevertheless, given the number of clients on the net and the relatively few permutations, it would be infeasible to look at user data over a long period of time. This might be considered very short-lived pseudonymity or perhaps "linkable anonymity" [77].

---

[3] I'm not the only "Matt Curtin" who can be found on the campus of The Ohio State University, for example.

Design

In design, we need to balance all of our requirements, which are often conflicting. In this specific case, the privacy-eroding side effects result from the intersection of log data centralization and user pseudonymity. Even if one were able to spread the data into the hands of many different parties, if the users of the system are pseudonymous, any data holders could collude to build more detailed user profiles. The best remedy against the unintended privacy-eroding side effects of this system is to attack the pseudonymity. There are several options available to the implementors of the system. In any case, what we want to do is ensure that requests to the www-rl server do not include any tokens that will allow the requests to be correlated to any other activity from the client.

The most straightforward means would be to make requests a special case in the client, never including a cookie, even if the client has a cookie that matches the necessary rules for inclusion with the request. This has a significant downside, however: the term "special cases" in practice tends to be a euphemism for "kluge." Handling of special cases can get dirty in implementation and this is a frequent place for the introduction of problems. Remember Ockham's Razor; simplicity is an important goal. Handling special cases will tend to undermine simplicity.

A better solution would be to put restrictions in the cookie itself: construct the cookie with the appropriate levels of restrictions based on the host or path element such that requests to www-rl will not match any available cookies. This solution is also potentially problematic, as there are so many services offered by the Netcenter servers that it might not be feasible for Netscape to manage the operational burden placed on a bunch of product managers who all want to use the cookie for different purposes.

Probably the most straightforward solution would be to put the www-rl servers into another domain altogether. Netscape—originally known as Mosaic Communications—has other domains besides netscape.com available to it. Some other domains available would include netscape.net, and mcom.com. Arguably, this is a klugey solution, since it's a special case of a different type: all of Netscape's servers are part of the netscape.com domain, where they can easily be identified. Our solution really has both klugey and elegant parts. Putting the service in a separate domain puts a requirement on deploying the service, but it also granularizes the administrative boundaries. This is something that a well-crafted security policy can specify and an audit can verify.

Which of these solutions will make the most sense for the problem at hand will largely depend on the implementation and operational costs associated with the solution, as compared with the potential cost for not fixing the problem.

We have examined some possible solutions, including both client-side and server-side design modifications. Without being insiders to the system ourselves, it's really not possible for us to say with a high level of confidence which makes the most sense.

What we want to remember when we walk away from this problem is the process where we've taken a look at a design or an implementation and have considered what side effects are present in the system and what "accidental features" have been built-in. When we're looking at requirements and we're building and critiquing the designs we work with, we always want to keep these questions in mind.

Case Study #2: Server Bug Undermines Opt-Out

DoubleClick is a leading provider of Internet advertising. One of DoubleClick's longstanding assertions is that it respects user privacy and gives users who wish it the ability to opt out of their system. This case study considers a failure in DoubleClick's opt-out system, silently tracking users who had been told that their opt-out request had been successfully processed.

After this problem was first reported in May 2000, DoubleClick quickly moved to fix the problem. The failure is still worthy of consideration, however, because it is a good example of how systems built specifically for the purpose of adding privacy can fail. This failure raises several questions, including which default mode of behavior is most appropriate. Going a step further, this failure actually points out why the secure design principle of Fail-Safe Defaults, described in Chapter 6, is so important.

At the core of the problem was an implementation flaw in DoubleClick's handling of cookies sent from the browser. This defect could result in the user being tracked without any knowledge of this activity, contrary to the consumer's explicit action of opting out.

Tracking Protocol

In order to describe how DoubleClick set up its opt-out system, it is useful first to explain the basics of how the DoubleClick AdServer initiates tracking the consumer. Note that this works basically as described in Chapter 7, with one important difference, the "priming" cookie.

Setting the priming cookie

As illustrated in Figure 8-2, if the AdServer in the tracking domain (i.e., `.doubleclick.net`) does not receive a cookie in the request header, then a cookie similar to the following is presented to the browser:

```
Set-cookie: id=A; path=/; domain=.doubleclick.net...
```

The value of A indicates that the tracking process is being initiated. We refer to this as the priming cookie.

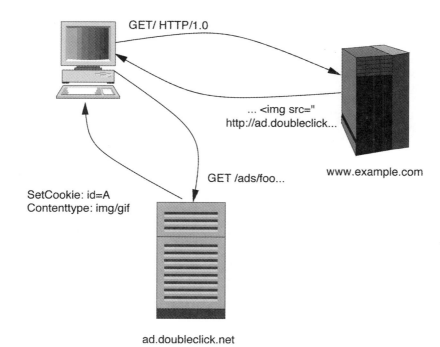

GET/ HTTP/1.0

... <img src="
http://ad.doubleclick...

www.example.com

GET /ads/foo...

SetCookie: id=A
Contenttype: img/gif

ad.doubleclick.net

Figure 8-2. Setting the Priming Cookie

Setting the tracking cookie

If the AdServer in the tracking domain receives a priming cookie (i.e., `id=A`), then this cookie is updated to a unique value. For example:

```
Set-cookie: id=8abc4321; path=/; domain=.doubleclick.net...
```

We refer to this as the tracking cookie. Setting it is shown in Figure 8-3. The next question is, "How is the cookie used?"

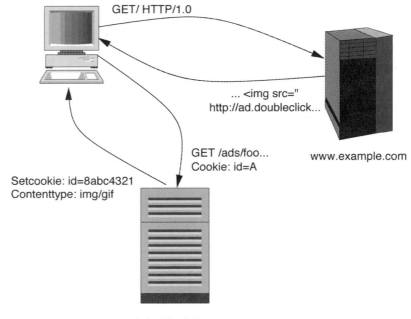

GET/ HTTP/1.0

... <img src="
http://ad.doubleclick...

GET /ads/foo...
Cookie: id=A

www.example.com

Setcookie: id=8abc4321
Contenttype: img/gif

ad.doubleclick.net

Figure 8-3. Setting the Tracking Cookie

Using the tracking cookie

If the AdServer in the tracking domain receives a tracking cookie then DoubleClick correlates the referring page and the target image into the consumer profile keyed off of the unique id as shown in Figure 8-4.

Note that there's a special exception to this rule: when the AdServer in the tracking domain receives a cookie with id=OPT_OUT, the cookie is effectively ignored, as this is an opt-out cookie.

Protocol Defect

The problem we discovered is that the DoubleClick AdServer, which initiates the tracking, violates Section 4.2 of the HTTP specification [66] concerning field name case insensitivity. Specifically, the server fails to recognize the cookie in the request header if the field name is not literally sent in the form Cookie. For example, if the field name is all uppercase (COOKIE), DoubleClick does not recognize the cookie.

Netscape 6 Preview Release 1 (PR1) sends the cookie field name in lowercase (cookie). This is ignored by the DoubleClick AdServer, and puts Netscape 6 PR1 in a constant state of priming. Therefore, the browser will never really succeed to opt out. The user is unlikely to be aware of this since during the opt-out procedure DoubleClick reports the "Opt-out completed successfully."

There are two critical issues here.

- DoubleClick's server failed to recognize a completely legitimate response from the client, a cookie header without the exact capitalization the server expected.

- The server reported that the opt out was a success, even if it wasn't.

Either of these problems by itself wouldn't be such a big deal. That they occur simultaneously exacerbates the situation, turning it into a serious failure. If the server checked before reporting success, users unable to opt out of the system would have no false expectations about being opted out of the system successfully. An inability to take the desired course of action could easily lead to an investigation of the problem, the identification of the bug, and its correction. Failure to report success even in the event of a failure is a sure sign of sloppy implementation. DoubleClick is by no means alone in this. Making assumptions that things work as expected is a common problem.

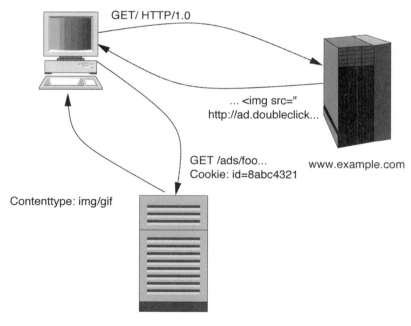

Figure 8-4. Using the Tracking Cookie

Privacy Threats

An interesting privacy breach would occur for some users after DoubleClick updated their server software to be HTTP compliant. After the fix was in place, DoubleClick recognized the lowercase cookie field name. A consumer who deliberately went through the opt-out process could, without any actions on his part, once again be tracked.

One such scenario is where a consumer went through the opt-out process using Communicator 4.7*x*. At some point, he updates to Netscape 6. The next time the consumer visits a site which uses DoubleClick for ad serving, the opt-out cookie is replaced by a priming cookie.

Another scenario is that if someone temporarily tries Netscape 6, the DoubleClick priming cookie will be put in the cookie store in place of the opt-out cookie. If the user goes back to a previous version of Netscape, the user will have been opted back into the system without knowing it.

Either way, when the user resumes normal browsing activity, he'll come in contact with DoubleClick ad servers once again, and the priming cookie will be recognized and replaced with a pseudonymous `id` tracking cookie.

Remedies

In response to the problem, DoubleClick modified its server software to understand the `cookie` header to be the same as `Cookie`. Interestingly, as of this writing in October 2001, headers with other capitalization, like `COOKIE` and `CoOkIe`, are handled incorrectly.

The solution to this problem is strict adherence to the specification.

Although our discovery was made using a preview release of Netscape 6, it's important to note that many programs are available for fetching data from the Web. We must recognize the importance of building to the specification, rather than to behavior expected on the basis of experience. In the context of the Web, this argument is most often made in the case of HTML, and building Web content in such a way that it will not require a specific client to view. The argument, however, carries down to a much deeper level. Even down at the transport and session layers, it's important that specifications be followed in order to allow the greatest possible interoperability.

Case Study #3: Client Design
Undermines Opt-Out System

This case study demonstrates how the client's handling of persistent cookies can have unexpected privacy consequences in opt-out systems. Again, a key issues to consider here are default behavior and interaction between client and server.

Recognizing the handling of HTTP cookies can have adverse privacy ramifications, many web client implementors have chosen to make cookie handling optional. However, an apparently short-sighted implementation of Netscape Communicator's cookie handling resulted in an inadvertent (and potentially unnoticed) tagging of users by these tracking sites, even after the user explicitly chose to opt out. Netscape Communicator seems to assume that if you *ever* configure "Do not accept or send cookies" that you will *never* want to re-enable any previously stored cookies in the future. In Netscape version 4, when the user disables cookies, the browser deletes the entire client-side database of cookies.

One case where someone might wish to use cookies selectively would be a privacy-conscious user who surfs the Web without cookies enabled. Such a user might want to allow the handling of cookies on particular trusted sites. For several years—between the introduction of HTTP cookies in Netscape 2 and the release of browsers such as Netscape 6 that have cookie management features—the only way to allow selective cookie use was to toggle the browser's preferences, defining globally whether to allow cookies. Thus, someone who wished to browse the Web anonymously but used one site for customized content would need to toggle the browser's cookie settings frequently.

If a user were to opt out of a tracking system such as DoubleClick's, and then to disable cookies, the opt-out cookies would be deleted. Once cookies were enabled again, the user would again be tracked, despite just having opted out before changing the browser's setting.

Systems Tested

Our discussion has been focused on the cookie handling mechanism for Netscape 4. Netscape 6 implements a different cookie management scheme entirely, which is not subject to this type of failure. Internet Explorer 5.x stores each cookie in a separate file and does not delete them when cookies are disabled. Opera 4.0 Beta 3 stores cookies in a single file but does not toss them when cookie acceptance is disabled.

Better Cookie Management

Netscape 6 provides a very nice solution to the cookie management problem. Ultimately, cookies are useful and do benefit the end user. The problem is that the user needs to be able to make informed decisions about what kinds of cookies will be accepted, from whom, and for how long.

Version 6 of Netscape has dealt with this problem by including the user-selectable option for the browser to remember the answer to the question. Thus, if `example.com` tries to set a cookie, I can tell my client, "No, do not accept the cookie, and furthermore, never accept this cookie." Never again will I be pestered about the `example.com` cookie. This allows the user to choose for himself which cookies he'll accept, returning the control of the user's nymity to where it belongs: in user's own hands.

Case Study #4: Service Model Creates Privacy Holes

Coremetrics provides a service called *eLuminate* where Web retailers can have their site usage and customer data outsourced easily. Rather than buying a product and dealing with the data in-house, or turning over web server logs, site operators can include some code in their pages that will enable Coremetrics' *eLuminate* service. The implementation of this model requires that the sites instruct the users' browsers to send an extensive number of data to Coremetrics for collection and analysis. As a user gives information to a site, typically during the process of making a purchase, that information is being sent not only to the vendor who needs it to complete the order, but to Coremetrics, whom the vendor has introduced into the transaction.

We might now say that this is typically done without the knowledge of the user, but as more sites include privacy policies that specify data handling procedures, it becomes less clear about what users can reasonably expect. In any case, whether one would fault the user for not reading the privacy policy or the company who had it written by lawyers whose intention was to prevent the company from being sued, is not especially relevant. We're focused on the technology.

It is noteworthy that these data are very detailed and include specific data like what's being purchased, the user's name, mailing address, email address, and phone number.

The system is implemented by embedding JavaScript[4] code into the vendor's web site that will cause a connection to be made to Coremetrics with a specially crafted query string that will report such details in a standardized format for easy

---

[4]   JavaScript is a language developed at Netscape. Its standardized name is ECMAScript. There is no connection between JavaScript and Sun's Java Programming Language.

entry into a database. This fetch is implemented as a request for an image, a blank, one-pixel GIF—what is commonly known as a "web bug" [179].

Sites Investigated

During our investigation between May and June 2000, we studied eight web sites' use of *eLuminate*. A list of those sites can be found in Table 8-1.

Table 8-1. Sites Sending Personal Information to Coremetrics

Site	Leaking Name, Address, Phone Number, or Email?
www.toysrus.com	√
www.ashford.com	
www.fusion.com	√
www.dxcart.com	
www.exofficio.com	
www.getplugged.com	
www.inchant.com	
www.lucy.com	√

NOTE *Of these eight, only two leaked data like a name, address, telephone number, or email address. All sent data about the activity of the user to Coremetrics, including such information as what products the user was browsing and the price of these products. Importantly, every time that such data were reported, they contained the same eLuminate cookie, which would allow all activity on all Coremetrics clients' sites to be correlated into a single user profile. Thus, even though only two sites sent Coremetrics the user's name, once the name was associated with the profile, the activity of that user on all eight sites could be linked with his name.*

It is also noteworthy that from our perspective—as an outsider who can see only what eLuminate is collecting from us—we have no way to know whether such correlation is taking place. Coremetrics claims not to do this and we have no evidence to suggest that it does. The possibility, nevertheless, is there, and we have no way to tell if such correlation has begun.

Coremetrics clients' sites commonly make use of banner advertising networks, which can leak data about the user's activity to still other third parties. Table 8-2 shows a list of other third-party sites, whether those sites can identify a user from request to request through the use of cookies, and the sites that introduce these third parties into the transactions.

Such prolific leakage seems to suggest that user privacy is a low priority, perhaps not even being given any consideration.

Table 8-2. Non-Coremetrics Third-Party Sites

Third-Party Site	Cookies?	Referred By
switch.avenuea.com	√	www.toysrus.com www.lucy.com
a1896.g.akamaitech.net		www.toysrus.com www.lucy.com www.getplugged.com
a1428.g.akamai.net		www.getplugged.com
medals.bizrate.com	√	www.fusion.com
view.accendo.com	√	www.getplugged.com
ad.doubleclick.net	√	www.petstore.com
207.178.130.149	√	www.getplugged.com (?)
partners.quokka.com		www.fusion.com
service.bfast.com	√	www.fusion.com www.lucy.com
209.24.233.190		www.fusion.com
ad.linksynergy.com		www.fusion.com
www.dxcart.com	√	www.inchant.com

On the Topic of Data Collection

Such detailed data gathering raises several questions, the central themes of which are "How much is too much?" and "Who decides?" We address these briefly. We want to emphasize that we are not accusing Coremetrics of malice to the Internet population. However, we believe the risks presented to be serious—much more serious than Coremetrics itself seems to believe—and worth the attention of everyone who uses the Web.

As for *why* this is happening at all, it's best to consider Coremetrics' business. Coremetrics provides a means for web site operators to outsource the job of collecting and analyzing web site data. Instead of providing a *product* that will serve this function, Coremetrics provides a *service*. Thus, there is a need for Coremetrics to be introduced into the conversation between the client and the server.

This is a crucial point. Note that in our earlier discussion of the ability to include elements in a web page from anywhere in the world—the very feature that makes this sort of thing possible—we concluded that this is indeed a feature, and not a bug. It does not necessarily follow that any connection to a third party is "evil." The questions that we must consider are:

- What is the purpose of the connection?

- What is the connection intended to allow?

- What else might such a connection allow?

We know that the purpose of the connection is to allow Coremetrics to collect the data needed to perform the service it's been engaged to perform. We know that the connection is intended to allow the user's activity on the site to be followed very closely, thus allowing Coremetrics to show on a per-page level, which things are apparently working and which are not. Even customer data like name and address are included in the job that Coremetrics has been engaged to perform.

This leaves us with the question, "What else might such a connection allow?" This is an important question to consider, especially by organizations inclined to outsource functionality. Failing to understand the technicalities of a service offering could have unforeseen consequences, particularly with respect to the risks that organizations place on their customers.

Despite attention to security and privacy, use of the system still has significant ramifications.

Sidebar: What Coremetrics Is Doing Right

Clearly, Coremetrics has given the matter serious consideration and is engaged in a serious effort to address consumer privacy concerns. Perhaps the most interesting of Coremetrics' approaches to privacy management is its two-level opt-out system. Rather than providing only a mechanism to opt out of all data collection and tracking, Coremetrics offers an option to opt out of the recording of "personally identifiable information."

Privacy Complications

Although Coremetrics does clearly explain what it's doing—once you know that information is being collected by a third party and you know which third party to investigate—there are several problems with the *eLuminate* system with regard to the privacy of individual Web users. We again wish to stress that we are discussing what is *technically possible* and what *can happen*. We simply cannot be sure of what actually is happening. Our discussion along these lines is important, because this helps us to understand how we might be able to build the system such that there is effectively no difference between what should happen and what can happen.

Collects everything by default

One of the biggest issues here is that information is being collected about surfers of Coremetrics' clients' sites without their knowledge and before they have the opportunity to decide whether they want to be tracked. Additionally, since users have not seen any descriptions of what's happening, they don't have the opportunity to see to what degree they're being tracked. Even those who don't mind banner advertising networks are likely to find the collection of their name, phone number, and email address to be extremely invasive. The fact that *eLuminate* returns an invisible web bug instead of a visible image, perhaps one that would take the user to a description of *eLuminate* and a list of exactly what data were collected in the transaction, is strong evidence to support the assertion that this system was designed to work without the users' knowledge. Indeed, were the system drawing too much attention to itself, it would be a nuisance and could make the system unusable. So how quiet is quiet enough to avoid being a nuisance, and how quiet is an attempt to avoid detection?

We must acknowledge that balancing the user's ability to see what's happening with the design and usability of the site is a difficult problem. This difficulty solidifies the point: default behavior is critical. Even invisible elements can be privacy-aware by the use of sensible default modes of behavior.

Implicitly places trust in Coremetrics

This approach relies on Coremetrics to continue to do the Right Thing with regard to its opt-out records and its handling of data internally. The nature of the HTTP cookies requires that if the system is enabled at all, the cookie in question will be sent along with the request to Coremetrics. Coremetrics cannot know whether it is to save the information sent until after it receives the information and looks at the value of the cookie. As a result, even those who have completely opted out of the system have their data reported; it's up to Coremetrics to honor the web surfer's request to have the information ignored. If Coremetrics changes its policy and begins to read data marked for opt-out, there's no way for anyone to tell.

Again, this is a side effect of the way that HTTP works; its statelessness makes it extremely difficult for the client to be able to say, "Hey, I have some stuff here, here's my cookie, should you get the contents of what I have?" It's technically possible, but solutions using available technology are inelegant.

Opt-out mechanisms fail

Building on the issue of default behavior is the recognition that opt-out systems are prone to failure, on several fronts. In this chapter alone, we've discussed how an opt-out mechanism failed on the server and another case of how client software behavior caused an opt-out system to fail. Finally, people who opt out of tracking mechanisms can have their activity tracked when using other computers, depending on their computing environments. In any of these cases, the opt out mechanism is defeated. As a result, those who have explicitly opted out are once again being tracked with extreme detail, often without their knowledge. We believe that reliance upon such an unpredictable mechanism is unworkable.

We return to the consideration of our data security principles from Chapter 6. Can an opt-out system really satisfy a design criterion like "fail safe default?"

No guarantee against future misuse

There is no guarantee about what will happen with the database that is built. What mechanisms are in place to prevent the data from falling into the wrong hands—perhaps those who would like to use the data for blackmail—or being used in ways completely unrelated to the original purpose—perhaps being stolen by someone trying to perpetrate fraud against unwitting consumers.

One such attack might go something like this. Alice buys some product from Bob's web site, which uses the *eLuminate* service. Mallory steals a copy of the *eLuminate* database, which she doesn't find very useful by itself. However, if she's able to see that Alice buys from Bob's web site, she can call Alice on the phone—since Alice's phone number is also in the database—and explain that there was a problem processing her VISA card—since the card type is also in the database. Mallory then explains that she wants to verify Alice's card number, and as she's talking, she stops mid-sentence to announce, "The computer shows your card number is all zeroes." This kind of transactional data—all available from the *eLuminate* database—might be enough to convince Alice that Mallory is legitimate and that it's safe to give Mallory her card number and expiration date.

Even if Coremetrics does take reasonable precautions to ensure the safety of the data and would fight such subpoenas, what happens if Coremetrics is bought by another company without the same convictions?

The primary difference between Coremetrics' possession of this information, and some other apparently related situations, is that Coremetrics, as a service provider to the vendor, does not own the data. Coremetrics doesn't have the option of selling that which is not theirs. Nevertheless, the potential for mishandling is present, as is the possibility of the data being stolen despite taking every reasonable precaution.

This is the tricky part about privacy: once private information is disclosed, there's no going back. There is no remedy against exposure of private information.

Unreliable data

The fifth problem is that data in the *eLuminate* database is likely to be taken as reliable. What is to prevent someone from creating a simple program that will constantly feed bogus information to the *eLuminate* data collector? We estimate that building such a program from scratch would take a web programmer no more than a few hours to create and to debug. Individuals could have a similar effect by adding a few lines of HTML on their web sites. For the purposes stated by Coremetrics, this margin of uncertainty isn't highly important. But considering this in the context of unintended use of the database, there could be very serious consequences.

Two of the online privacy principles we discussed in Chapter 4 had to do with the accuracy of data collected. The first is access, and the second is rectification. How can a user verify that the data in the *eLuminate* profile are correct? How can a user contest incorrect data in the profile? As just explained, anyone can write anything to a database that will accept anything from anywhere on the Web, as is the case with *eLuminate.*

Unnecessarily enables tracking across sites

Here we come right to the point. In answer to our remaining question about the privacy implications of this system—"What else does the system enable?"—we submit that the cookie used to identify users of the *eLuminate* system is persistent for all conversations with Coremetrics. This means that like ad servers, the *eLuminate* system is built in such a way that activity on one site can be correlated with that user's history on another Coremetrics' client site.

Descriptions of the *eLuminate* service seem to indicate that the tool is used only to identify visitors of a particular site, that demographic data provided to a given site operator is only data collected from his site. If this is true, there is only one imaginable reason for the *eLuminate* architecture to work as it does, that is, by having *everything* from *every eLuminate*-enabled site being reported to a single source. That reason is the ability for a global opt out of all *eLuminate* tracking, irrespective of the site that calls the *eLuminate* code.

Remedies

Were the *eLuminate* cookie different for each of its clients' sites, the risk posed to the Web user would be less significant, as multi-site profiling would be rendered much more difficult. However, it would require that an opt out take place on each of the sites that the user visits. Whether to make the cookie global or local is a key decision, one that we would have made differently.

Weighing in on the side of localization, a trivial solution to this problem is the placing of *eLuminate* data collectors in the domain name of the site using the service. So, if www.example.com is using *eLuminate*, instead of having all data reported to data.coremetrics.com, it could be reported to coremetrics.example.com. Thus, only example.com data would be collected with that cookie. Another site that uses *eLuminate* would have a different server, and a web user who visits both sites will have different cookies for each site that he visits.

As noted, this would break the global opt-out capability. Here is an interesting question: if Coremetrics is indeed merely a vendor providing a service for web sites, how is it that Coremetrics has the right to engage the web site's customer in a conversation that will hinder Coremetrics' ability to do its job? If the *eLuminate* system indeed is a "seamless plug-in" to the server, why is it that privacy preferences do not follow what the user has specified for that site?   *Surprise!*

Returning to the idea of localizing the reach of the cookie, this has a negative impact on the user: the user must specify privacy preferences in more places to get the same protection that would be offered by a single opt out on the Coremetrics site.

On either side of this debate, it must be acknowledged that the other side has valid objections. Neither position in the globalization versus localization of the cookie's reach is without undesirable side effects.

Management of opt-out systems can indeed become difficult. We're going to give this more thorough consideration in Chapter 10.

Case Study #5: The Struggle Between Convenience and Security

Bank One's online service provided a method for customers to retrieve account information via a web browser interface. While providing a convenience for customers via a secured (encrypted) page, we found a case where the mechanisms of the rest of the system were implemented such that the benefits of encryption were defeated for perhaps the most typical attacks. A customer was able to store his account number on the local machine. (The Bank One site referred to this as an "Access ID" which in some cases was the credit or debit card number of the account holder.) By failing to deselect the option, "Save Access ID on this computer for future logins," the user allowed the account number to be written in the cookies file of the web browser. In future transactions, the Access ID field of the web form was automatically populated with the account(s) of the customer.

Storage of this information on the client side was insecure and the cookie was inappropriately protected against accidental transmission in the clear.

Since the publication of the original report describing this problem, the system has been fixed. It's a useful case study, because it shows the struggle between user convenience and system security, perhaps the longest-running debate in the development of computer systems.

Potential Compromise of Customer Information

By choosing the convenient method of entering an account number, the customer inadvertently exposed a flaw in the Bank One Online system. There are two primary avenues of attack that threaten the secrecy of the private customer information. Which avenue is most dangerous will depend largely on the environment and behavior of the user.

Local disk access

Because the account number was stored in cleartext (i.e., not encrypted) in a cookie that resided on the client side, anyone with the ability to read the browser's cookies file could get ahold of sensitive account information that would be critical to gaining access to the account itself. In some cases, these users' cookies files could be readable by a relatively large set of users, thus providing the technical means by which many people could gather account numbers.

On machines where multiple users share the same browser profile, such access is trivial.

Another related attack works just like this, except instead of having access to the local disk, the attacker has access to the same network as the target and the user's cookies file is stored on a "network drive," or remote filesystem. In such a case, the sensitive information is likely to be transmitted across the network between the client and the remote filesystem's server in the clear. Thus, even though the cookie itself is transmitted over an encrypted channel (namely

TLS [52] or its predecessor, SSL [71]), the action of writing that cookie to disk causes the data to be transmitted across the local network in the clear.

Obviously, any user with administrative access to the filesystem (or its backups) would have the ability to read the sensitive information as well.

Remote access to cookies

Although there are some basic precautions implemented in browsers to prevent sites from reading each others' cookies, some bugs have caused these precautions to fail [128, 129, 85]. Thus, there are browsers that will improperly reveal private account information to sites programmed to steal users' cookies.

Additionally, one precaution that could have been used in the Bank One Online system was not. Cookies can be tagged as "secure," which means that the client will not transmit the cookie to the server unless the connection was encrypted. The cookie with this account information was clearly designed to operate only where the session was encrypted, so that the account number will not be sent over the Internet in the clear. However, the flag that would prevent the browser from sending the cookie in the clear was not set. Thus, any connection to any site in the bankoneonline.com domain where the URI started with the string /logon would cause the browser to send the cookie to the server, whether the session was encrypted or not.

Risks

The risks here are significant and important, but the information that is exposed is not all of the information that an attacker will need to login to or to abuse the credit card number. Nevertheless, very little additional work is necessary to perpetrate real abuses.

To use the cookie to impersonate the user, an attacker will also need to supply a personal identification number (PIN). PINs themselves don't provide much security. The security of using a PIN is that it is part of a two-factor authentication process. One step uses something you have (such as the ATM card) and the other uses something you know (the PIN). The card is a token that can be stolen, but the PIN has no physical token. Lockout mechanisms—where a certain number of unsuccessful attempts to enter the PIN will cause the account to be locked—ensure that brute-force attacks against a particular PIN will not be feasible. However, as discussed in the Least Privilege section of Chapter 6, an attacker can improve his odds of success quite significantly by attacking a set of accounts instead of a single account.

In the case where the account number is used as a credit card or debit card, an attacker has an even easier time, since the only other information that the attacker will need to abuse the card in many cases is an expiration date. (Some abuses can take place without knowing the correct expiration date, but in the general case, the correct expiration date will be needed to make a purchase.) If credit cards are only active for three years at a time and the granularity of expiration dates is one month, then the attacker has a one in 36 (12 months times three years) chance of guessing the correct expiration date on the first try. The more guesses he gets, the better his odds are.

Solutions

For the long term, user authentication for account information access must be made more robust. This almost certainly means decreased convenience, at the very least in the form of longer PINs. However, given the fact that the cost of fraud is borne by the financial system's customers, insistence on convenience far above security will result in higher costs and greater hassle in dealing with abuses of this information. Dismissing security concerns is only in the interest of attackers.

Cookies used to store state information must be made completely unusable outside of the scope of the application in which they're used. That is, a user ID token in a cookie should not be connected to information that can be used to impersonate the holder of that cookie.

Cookies intended to be transmitted only in an encrypted channel should be marked as "secure," which will prevent the client from sending the token in the clear. Although one could argue that the server is under the control of the issuer of the cookie and thus able to be guaranteed never to be transmitted in the clear, failing to take advantage of available precautions is poor security practice, particularly when this results in a single point of failure.

Finally, HTTP cookies should not be used for handling authentication tokens. HTTP provides mechanisms for authentication. Such mechanisms were designed for the specific purpose of solving the problems related to the security issues at hand. A great deal of benefit could be derived simply from using the right tool for the job.

What We've Learned

Consideration of these case studies is entirely appropriate because these were all problems that were found "in the wild." The problems that we saw in this chapter included:

- Failure to check return codes

- Failure to follow specification

- Unintended side effects of otherwise useful features

- Poor application of available security technology

No one has seriously suggested that any of these systems was built with malice in mind. These were systems that were designed and implemented by competent professionals. Yet, each one of these systems failed, in at least one way, resulting in some kind of unanticipated risk being foisted upon someone—always the user, and sometimes also the web site operator.

If security is the enforcement of policy, it's important for us to recognize that when we're building these systems, we need to do it in such a way that we're effectively supporting the articulated policy. Security and privacy isn't a simple question of putting some legalese on your web site that says, "Do not try to gain additional privileges, and we are allowed to collect information about you during your visit." Security and privacy are about giving careful thought to these issues, deciding what the system should and shouldn't do, and then building the system in such a way that it's not capable of doing what it shouldn't.

These cases should also help us to drive home another point: *never build systems with a single point of failure.* Violation of policy should require several of our policy enforcement mechanisms to fail. In general, the higher the cost of the failure, the more mechanisms we should have in place to mitigate the risk.

We're all human beings. We all make mistakes. Even the most brilliant and competent among us will err. We should design systems that recognize this fact. We build in tolerance for faults in the deployment environment, so why would we ever design systems without tolerance for faults in the development environment—the human mind?

There's no reason that our users should pay the price for our inability to design and to build system perfectly. Recognition of our own limitations and weaknesses is an important lesson that we can gain from studying other systems. If we design and build our systems correctly, not only will we reduce the likelihood of error, but we reduce its severity, and more successfully avoid forcing the cost of our mistakes on our unwitting end users.

Part III

The Cure

Learning from Failure

NO DOUBT ABOUT IT: TODAY'S systems are complex beasts. We have application software, sometimes running into millions of lines of code. We have software that uses third-party shared libraries, running atop operating systems, running atop all types of hardware. Hardware talks to the network in many different ways. A logical system can even be spread across many machines, separated by as little as a bit of Ethernet cable or as much as an ocean.

We have enough technical problems to overcome when putting these things together and trying to run them, but that, of course, isn't the whole story. On top of all of these complexities, we have all kinds of other issues weighing on us. There are market forces that influence our functional requirements, and scheduling and budgetary concerns that influence our design and implementation decisions.

In some sense, it's amazing that we ever get anything to work at all.

This chapter deals with failure, but from a different perspective: taking its inevitability as a given and incorporating it into a process for minimization of risk and improvement of our systems.

When we are confronted with security and privacy problems, it's easy to forget that we're really talking about system failure. There isn't anything magical about security problems; they're weaknesses that come from faults in design or implementation. Because of the consequences of leaving many of these problems unaddressed, they're given very high priority and tend to get addressed almost immediately. This has a tendency to underscore our inclination to forget that we're just dealing with defects. We might not even get to analyze problems and to produce patches with the same process for defect resolution that we'd get in dealing with defects that aren't specifically security-related.

For the remainder of this discussion, we're going to be dealing specifically with security-related failures, but in the context of a more general discussion about failure.

Types of Failure

When a system gets cracked, we're obviously dealing with a failure. There are several types of failures that occur. Often, only one failure type is necessary to leave the system vulnerable to exploit. Talking about the types of failures that can occur is helpful because from that discussion, we can get a better sense of how to recognize the inevitability of mistakes and take best advantage of that recognition. Specifically, what we want to do is increase the number of things that must "go wrong" before the system can be exploited.

Policy

Likely, the most common and most dangerous type of failure—the failure of policy—is perhaps the most difficult to detect. This is an especially good area for incorrect assumptions to be made.

One reason why policy is so critical to the safety of a system is because it is where safety starts: this is the definition of what is and what isn't allowed. Presumably, before such a policy is articulated, a risk analysis has been completed, verifying the organization's idea of "acceptable level of risk." That, along with the organization's high-level objectives, is the highest (and most general) statement of policy.

Moving down a layer, the high-level objectives have been balanced with the acceptable level of risk and turned into a specific list of practices that the organization will follow. A company might define at a high level that it will work to keep profits high by keeping its margins at a certain level and by keeping costs down. Once we move into a specific policy statement, we're dealing with practices that will help the organization achieve its high-level goals uniformly. So, if we want to keep profits high and costs low, we're going to tell people things like "don't run with scissors." The risk is just too high. The chance, however unlikely, that someone could get hurt, isn't the big issue: it's that running with scissors doesn't do anything to help us achieve our goals in the first place; there's nothing to be gained. Therefore, even something that's unlikely just isn't worth the risk. Things get much more complicated in most real-world cases, of course, particularly when what could be gained is of roughly the same value of what could be lost.

Policy covers everything from the highest-level statement of goals and objectives down to the specific nuts and bolts of the operation, how it should work in theory.

Management

Once policy is in place, execution of the plan falls into the category of management. Note that this isn't just about people who wear suits, can't figure out why *Dilbert* is so funny, and spend all day "leveraging value-add" over power lunches. Any operational functionality falls under this category, as one can manage systems on the network without being a manager.

It's a win–win, you know.

Management failures tend to center around people not following policy. Companies generally have fairly strict policies in place regarding the discussion of former employees (often restricted to mere confirmation of the employment and salary history), how to handle requests from law enforcement (usually sending such persons looking for information to an internal lawyer), and how equipment may be employed (typically along the lines of "use what you're given, don't work around it"). In the first two examples, these policies have arisen from expensive litigation or in an attempt to avoid it. The third example is of more interest to us in this context, because we're interested in computer security.

One example of a management problem that has been particularly difficult for many organizations to deal with is the use of modems. As dependence upon computing technology increased, both the use of laptop computers and internal networks has increased. Laptop machines have historically included built-in modems, and because they're often used from hotel rooms (which don't always have a convenient Ethernet outlet ready for you) they simply need to have them.

The problem is that machines in the company office are provided connectivity through a managed network, including protections against various types of attacks by outsiders. This is what is expected for internal machines. However, as long as people have modems, it will be possible for them to work around that managed network and the security services that it offers. If, for example, someone decides that he wants to check his AOL account and it's forbidden from work, he can simply dial out to AOL through his modem and do whatever he likes without going through the company firewall. Of course, it might also be true that he's connected both to both AOL and to the company's internal network.

This is interesting. The result of having these kinds of connections is that people might—without having any idea that they're doing it—be providing all of the connectivity necessary for an attacker to get into the company's network. Perhaps the company's firewall would catch some kind of malware attached to some email. That same email might flow straight through AOL. So the user is on both networks at once, he gets the mail through AOL, and then it starts to do its damage on the internal network, potentially doing anything that the user can do.

This isn't just random paranoia, these are the kinds of things that have happened in numerous environments, and have made it possible for attackers to work around the security systems that were keeping them out.

When an inside user goes against the stated policy, there's a failure in management. In many cases, this failure effectively makes whatever technology is in place useless.

Technology

Technology failures are the kind that tend to get all of the attention. Everything from buffer overruns to design failures that prevent the system from behaving as it's expected fall into this category. When looking at a system in deployment, what we might assume is a technology failure could actually be a policy failure. For example, if a firewall allows a particular type of packet to pass through in an unexpected way, it doesn't necessarily follow that the problem is technological. It might just be that there wasn't a sufficiently well-defined policy to prevent the action. If, on the other hand, the firewall were configured not to allow such a packet to pass but it did anyway, that would be a failure of technology.

Obviously, the more technology we throw at a problem, the more opportunities we have for a screwup someplace. Looking at the complexity present in modern Internet-based systems, it's easy to see that we have plenty of opportunity for technology failure. In Chapter 8, we considered several different failures in deployed systems, all of which were technology failures of one sort or another. What's especially interesting isn't that these systems *themselves* all had spectacular sorts of failure, but sometimes—such as the case with "The Struggle Between Convenience and Security"—in a particular deployment environment, the technology used to deliver the application interacted in unexpected ways and had unintended consequences.

Contributors to Failure

We've seen that some failure is just a part of the job in dealing with large, complicated systems. Better, we know a bit about the types of failure that we have and we know some things about how to deal with failure. The obvious question that gets raised at this point is, "What contributes to failure?"

This isn't merely an academic curiosity. Understanding what contributes to failure can help us to see when we're working with lots of these "failure contributors," which should help us to avoid some of the traps that are so common.

Lack of Expertise

This is probably a good time for us to face the reality that very few people *really* know what's happening in these systems that everyone relies on. Most people designing, implementing, and operating these systems work in their own little areas of expertise, either knowing a lot about a tiny piece of the puzzle or knowing generally how things fit together but not understanding the specifics of why various parts work as they do.

In general, the basis of most undergraduate computer science education is little more than a tour of computer science, exposure to many different areas in stints of 10 to 15 weeks. In that time, students are introduced to basic computing concepts, software, and hardware. Various universities have different ideas on what makes for core curriculum, but most will spend some time working with programming languages, software design and implementation, networking, and some areas of application like databases, operating systems, or artificial intelligence. Sadly, a lot of people finish their undergraduate education and suspect that they're now "programmers" or "engineers," ready to face the world's problems.

The fact is that after four or five years of education, people are just about ready to start learning. Over the course of the next four or five years, when the application of all of that education is being made, and when people learn how many different approaches there are to various problem domains, people develop into mature professionals.

Computing is a curious study, in no small part because people are always in such a hurry. Students want to get to their degree in as little time as possible, and people out in the workforce want to get through training without spending so much time that they get behind in their day-to-day jobs. People often find themselves in unfamiliar space thanks to the changes forced upon them and the need to get up to speed so they can respond to the demands placed upon them. So, while the boss is going on and on about the power of the Web, people are running out to buy books like *Learn How to Save the World by Programming the Web in 11 Hours.*

It's strange that libraries and stores aren't full of books that claim readers can become proficient in painting, Chinese, or playing an instrument in less than a month. On the other hand, maybe what's even more strange is the reality that libraries and stores are full of books claiming you can learn to program in less that a month.

Learning another language is a great point of reference for us because nobody would seriously argue that trying to learn a foreign language does not take effort and time. Sure, native English speakers might be able to hold a basic conversation in Spanish after studying it for a year. But what about speaking Russian? Reading Chinese? For native English speakers, these are things that are recognized to take a long time because they're so very different from what most native English speakers know. Note that we're talking about a competent speaker, someone with mastery over his own language needing to take years to reach a certain level of proficiency.

Exactly the same principle applies to the skills needed to build systems well: it takes years of study and practice to learn the art and to refine the skills needed.

Even with expertise and experience, no one is perfect. Very often, we'd write our systems differently if we were able to implement a solution again after we had solved the problem once. This curiosity isn't limited to programs. Ask anyone who has written a book for a list of changes he'd like to see and you'll likely get a fairly significant list of things the writer would do differently. The fact is that we rarely understand exactly how to do something until after we've already done it once.

So far, we have addressed only the matter of becoming skilled in general. Gaining expertise in specific disciplines requires more study and more practice to build on the basic skills. Even the most skillful programmer put to work in an area he doesn't know well is going to run into trouble because of lack of experience with the tools or the techniques of that specific discipline. Would, for example, a competent application developer ever know that using double encryption doesn't make a significant change on the effective key length of the system [127]?

It's true that with only so many hours in the day, only so much time to spend learning, it's impossible for everyone to know everything. For that matter, it's impossible for anyone to know everything. Even that gray-bearded guy you work with, the "know everything" guru, doesn't really know everything. What makes him different is that he knows the limits of his knowledge, knows where to look for more, and understands what he finds.

A better way to operate can be found in the guru's example. Rather than trying to impress one another with how much we know, showing off what we do and hiding what we don't, we would all do much better to recognize our own limitations—openly, if necessary—and to contribute what we can in the areas where we are strong. A well-orchestrated team will have members whose strengths offset others' deficiencies.

Tools

Many of our vulnerabilities are the result of very basic problems like incorrect handling of data received from untrusted sources. As mentioned way back in Chapter 1, buffer overflow and input formatting problems account for more than half of CERT's advisories some years. One might wonder why we're still being bitten by such a basic problem that has been understood for so long.

Q. Why is this so clumsy? A. The trick is to use Perl's strengths rather than its weaknesses.

—Larry Wall

The issue isn't often one that comes down to programmer competence or even external pressure to deliver code on the aggressive schedules set by employers. Reflecting on the idea of the protocol stack, we recognized that there was tremendous value in the ability to deal with the problem at hand, at the right layer of abstraction. Thanks to the protocol stack, when we're working on the semantics for a message that will be passed between two hosts, we don't need to worry about things like how to get the message from one host to another.

This lesson—appropriate abstraction—is one that we're a bit slow to learn when it comes to our programming languages and our development environments. Much of the code written today is written in unsafe languages using library functions that are unsafe.[1] I do not suggest that one cannot write safe code in such a language, but rather, that writing safe code requires greater understanding of the tools in question and of the problem of writing safe code. Instead of being able to concentrate on the task that's being addressed, programmers often find themselves confronted with the need to manage memory and to check the bounds of buffers before populating them with data.

A lengthy rant extolling the virtues of Common Lisp originally appeared here.

The point here is that the tools that we have today aren't doing much to help us avoid so many of the things that have historically given us problems. Of course, another significant part of this problem is that many programmers don't take advantage of the tools that are available, including syntax checkers, debuggers, and code analysis software. Some tools that programmers must use (like compilers) could also provide help (such as warnings), but programmers must see the warnings and respond to them.

When it comes to tools, most of the industry just isn't doing itself any favors. Our refusal to use tools that help and our refusal to accept the help that we do happen to encounter is significant. Incorrect or lacking use of good tools remains a significant contributing factor to failure.

---

[1] C readily springs to mind, but it's hardly the only language with unsafe functions in its library.

Project Management

Management is a big, complicated beast. Particularly when a project gets large and there are lots of people and lots of efforts to coordinate. When money starts to get tight and tradeoffs need to be made, things get even worse. It gets worse still when the project starts to run behind and someone decides that the way to solve the problem is to throw more people at it [69].

We've looked at failures. We've talked about the horrible tools we have to work with. We've seen all that stands in our way of getting things done. Yet, day in and day out, we continue to keep at it. This is an industry full of optimists. The upside of all of this optimism is that we undertake projects without even knowing whether they're possible. We invest heavily in the projects to the point that we simply must deliver something—anything—so we'll back off of some requirements often before canceling an entire project outright.

The downside of all of this optimism is that we underestimate how long it will take or how much it will cost to do just about anything. It's very difficult for us to predict how well we're going to do, how long anything of any complexity will take, or how much of anything we'll need to devote to a project to make it successful. Many of the first models for software engineering were based on the idea that building software is like manufacturing: you simply figure out how to make a given part and then you produce as many of those parts as you need, freely connecting them to others in order to build larger systems. The reality of software has turned out much differently from our first expectations.

So we wound up being too optimistic about the definition of how to build software that meets its specification and to deliver it on time.

Rapid Pace of Change

Change is just part of the deal when it comes to technology. We understand that pretty well even if we complain about it. For many of us, constant change is one of the big attractors to high technology; we just cannot imagine ourselves in a "stagnant" position, where we do basically the same thing from day to day.

Thus, we might think of change as our friend, something that keeps us going, something that keeps us interested in what we do. The problem with change, though, is that when it's frequent we have a severely limited period of time to get to know the system in any given state. The more parts that go into the making of a system, the more likely that some part will change and, therefore, the less time we'll have to work with and to understand how the system would work in any one state. The less time that we have to understand how the system works and how its pieces interact, the greater the risk that something we do will have an unintended consequence.

Change is a transition of state, moving from one state to another. Thus, we might be moving to a better state, but the process of getting there is seldom pleasant. Nations rarely get their independence merely by asserting it. Nations that declare themselves sovereign typically need to fight bloody wars to defend themselves and their sovereignty. So the new state (independence) is more desirable than the old (subjection), but moving from one to the other has a high cost (hardship and loss of human life).

Viewed in these terms, it's easy to understand that change is sometimes difficult, even devastating. Operating your business in a new location might be a nice idea, but if the process of moving your business will destroy it, the cost of change will be too high to make it worthwhile. On the other hand, if change means that your business cannot operate normally during some period of change—such as a major system upgrade—and that change can take place when it would affect the fewest number of people—such as 3 a.m. to 5 a.m. Sunday morning—it's likely to be worthwhile even if the new state isn't terribly different from the previous.

When it comes down to it, the question of whether the change is worthwhile will depend on the difference between the cost of the change and the amount of gain that would be achieved by the change. In an environment where change is frequent, the anxiety, instability, and other problems that come with the change are a part of standard operating procedure for a significant part of the time. In high technology, we spend a lot of time "between states"—even frequently enough that it could be called a state—because of the rapid pace of development and the frequency of changes in systems needed to keep up with development. This means that we spend a lot of time trying to get work done when it really isn't very conducive to doing so.

Subtlety

Problems that we confront aren't always a question of whether something is behaving correctly or incorrectly. We determine correct implementation by adherence to design. Design flaws are harder to identify and to correct. Sometimes these problems can arise from strange circumstances that are difficult to predict, to test, or to reproduce.

Even more difficult is the case of myopic design, where one system works perfectly according to its design and purpose, but interacts with another perfectly working system in ways that have unexpected side effects. These are problems that arise not from any particular issue with the systems in question, but rather how they work together. Good examples of these are included in Chapter 8, particularly in the cases of "Centralization Unexpectedly Erodes Privacy" and the "Service Model Creates Privacy Holes." The systems both did exactly what they were designed to do. Their implementations, however, wound up enabling tremendous additional functionality because of their implementation in an environment where a domain cookie would be used to identify system users. More directly stated, these systems were myopic because they were not designed in the large.

Many of the issues that we face are simply not questions of correctness. Questions like how systems will interact with others will depend a great deal on factors that might not even be identified in the design and implementation phases. How systems will influence each other, what kind of influence they'll accept, and the like, are all issues of great subtlety. It's hard to know what factors will come into play and even harder to know how they'll affect each other without actually seeing them in deployment.

Limited Understanding

Rapid pace of change, lack of expertise, and subtlety are contributors to a bigger, more general problem: limited understanding. Systems are so large, have so many parts, and cover so many problem domains that it's almost impossible for anyone to be fully aware of all of the issues involved. Even for people who are aware of all of the pieces in the puzzle, the question often becomes an issue of where the line is drawn between "things I can fix" and the "black box" upon which the application or operating system is built. Some could, for example, explain basically how the Apache web server works. Whether someone could discuss at a greater level of detail what's happening in the operating system through various states of the system will depend on whether the operating system is part of his "black box" or his area of expertise. Or, one could go a step lower, down into the hardware itself, watching the switches being turned on and off inside of the computer.

The point is that few people understand everything needed to build a system. Indeed, the entire history of computing shows that it's possible for us to accomplish great things with teams of people whose understanding is limited. It simply isn't necessary to know everything to be able to contribute usefully to a project.

It is, however, still a risk; something that needs to be managed. This is also a worthwhile area for consideration when it comes to identifying and mitigating risk in the design and development processes themselves. Our inability to get everyone to understand everything is a limit, but one that we can manage quite well if we have the honesty to evaluate our own performance and expertise.

Complexity

Closely associated with these other contributors to system failure is the issue of complexity. Part of the reason why we cannot understand how things work, or we cannot always see the subtle issues, is because of the number of variables that we have in the system. It's always amusing to hear non-programmers say things like, "It's just software, can't you add such-and-such?" Of course, it's "just software" and if we knew about the requirement from the beginning, we'd probably have very little difficulty adding it—though we might not have any idea just how long it would take.

Fools ignore complexity. Pragmatists suffer it. Some can avoid it. Geniuses remove it.

—Alan J. Perlis

Let's take a look at a typical network-based system. First of all, we have the hardware itself. Zillions[2] of transistors are packed into the CPU, which is connected to the rest of the motherboard, including other integrated circuits, memory units, buses, and all kinds of fun stuff. A little bit of static can cause complete system failure. Dust is the enemy, capable of causing all manner of problem. The system must be operated at a certain temperature or the risk of miscomputation is too high. Voltage must be regulated. All kinds of things can happen down in the hardware that make things go wacky.

$1 + 1$ can be 3 if it's hot enough.

Then there's the complexity of software. First of all, we have an operating system that we're running on the machine, which is software, and a foundation upon which other software runs. Just the operating system itself is doing all kinds of crazy things, talking to the hardware and dealing with all of the noise it makes, driving a window system, taking input from the keyboard and mouse, scheduling what runs when, and probably dozens of other things all at once.

On top of this mess, we put applications. Applications to do all kinds of stuff. Any particular user on the machine could be running many other additional processes, all of which are probably horribly complicated, with dozens of features and millions of lines of code.

The complexity of a system today is the product of the complexity of its hardware, its operating system, and its applications. We've significantly increased the complexity of the system twice—once, when we put an operating system on the hardware, and again when we put an application on the operating system—and we aren't even talking to the network yet.

This is essentially what's happening on any host on the network. Now, when we have hosts talking to each other, relying on each other to operate, we've brought the complexity of the system to another dimension: the sum of the complexity of every host that ours depends on. More concisely written,

---

[2] A zillion is technically defined as 10^n, where n is a positive integer greater than five.

$$C = \sum_{j \geq 1}^{N} \alpha_j \beta_j \gamma_j \delta_j,$$

where

C = complexity,

α = complexity of hardware,

β = complexity of operating system,

γ = complexity of applications,

δ = complexity of the network,

N = number of hosts involved.

(This equation just means that "the complexity of the system equals complexity times complexity times complexity times complexity for each of the hosts involved in the system.")

In practice, anything that we're working with now has a fairly large number of components, each of which probably has several layers of complexity. Nothing is simple.

Dealing with Failure

Several strategies exist for dealing with failure, but through all of the papers, proposals, and implementations, everything basically comes down to *avoiding failure* in the first place or building systems that are *fault-tolerant.*

Of course, when we're building systems, we want to design and to build them correctly. We want to do the very best job that we possibly can. Some systems have been especially interesting in the context of avoiding failure because they take a more strict view of correctness. Provably secure systems [38, 62, 145] and provably correct implementations [33] are on one extreme end of the scale. Using the certainty of mathematics, these systems strive to ensure that we have exactly what we think we have. Unfortunately, even a provably correct system is vulnerable to the problem of incorrect assumptions [80].

Another general approach to dealing with failure is recognizing it as an inevitability and making systems that will continue to operate in one form or another even in the face of failure. Examples of this approach are myriad, but one especially common design worth discussing is in the context of secure networking.

Zone Defense

Prevailing wisdom tells us to build in layers, using security "zones" to keep things logically together, requiring an attacker to break through several zones before getting to the really important stuff. Figure 9-1 illustrates this concept.

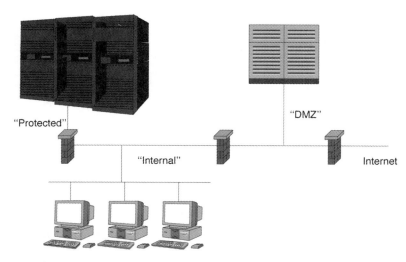

Figure 9-1. Three-Zone Network

In Figure 9-1, the outside Internet is completely untrusted. We'll talk to clients across that network, but we won't really believe anything they say by default. They'll need to prove to us who they are and we'll be sure to check their "papers" every step of the way. Just beyond one firewall is a *demilitarized zone* (DMZ), a network that is neither on the internal network nor external Internet. Hosts there will have some measure of protection, but not the same protection granted to internal hosts. Regular user machines and probably most servers for typical internal user activity will all reside somewhere on this large "internal zone." Then there's another network, a "protected zone," where there's an additional level of security to keep the insiders from accessing the area. Customer lists, sensitive databases (including things like HR and accounting functions), and other things that don't need to be directly available to the general internal user community are all especially good candidates for being put into special zones created for specific purposes.

If Mallory wants to attack this network, she's going to need to break through one level of protection to get from the Internet to the DMZ. From there, she'll need to get as much information she can so that she may effectively attack the next layer of security, which separates the DMZ from the internal network. If Mallory can get this far she's not going to find much of interest out there. The good stuff—stuff that could be useful for things like blackmail and extortion (and therefore easily converted into cash)—are behind yet another level of protection.

The beauty of this system is that no matter what kind of failures we have, no matter how bad the failure, we haven't lost everything in one fell swoop. A complete failure in the external firewall to restrict the traffic flow would allow an attacker to get unfettered connectivity to things in the DMZ. Of course, there are going to be host-based security mechanisms in place that will mean that Mallory has more work to do.

> **TIP** *The moral of the story here is that even though you're running systems behind firewalls, it's best to lock them down as much as possible. Don't run unused services and don't install unused software. The thing to do is to create many layers of security so that someone who wants to take advantage of some weakness is only going to find himself confronted with another layer of security that must be circumvented. Although especially good attackers will have the ability to work through many systems layer by layer, there are several things working to the advantage of the defender, including the expense of getting this target, by comparison to others. Folks looking for free disk space and bandwidth are going to move on to easier targets, thus eliminating a significant class of attackers. The other thing working in the favor of the defenders is that even very good attackers are going to take time to collect their intelligence and to plan a course of attack. This will give much more opportunity for other systems—like intrusion detection systems—to notice the strange behavior and to ring an appropriate alarm.*

Recall from our discussion of an attack from Chapter 1 that an attacker is first going to gain as much intelligence as he can about the target and then will look for weaknesses in the system which can be exploited. If we think of Figure 9-1 as a network under attack from an outsider, we can see that an attacker is going to need to peek through a firewall in order to understand what's happening in the DMZ network. In practice, this is a lot easier than a lot of people who rely on these systems are inclined to believe.

In any case, that DMZ network is an obvious target because it has some level of visibility to the outside world. Perhaps that's where web servers are kept for the company's corporate web site. Maybe the external email relays are kept there. The important thing about the DMZ from the company's perspective is that it is not a trusted network. Although the company owns the network and has staff to operate the network, it has only one layer of protection from the external Internet, so the network is not one that's trusted the same way that the internal network is trusted.

Also, because the DMZ is a network separate from the rest of the company, it's very convenient for the company to limit the kind of connectivity that would be allowed between the DMZ and the internal network.

When looking at the principles of secure systems design, including what we discussed in Chapter 6, it's important for us not to forget that these are general, high-level principles that apply in network design just as much as they do in software design. This concept of building networks that are fairly small and function-specific is an important application of the design principles of "separation of privilege" and "least privilege." The ability to interact across the network with specific hosts shouldn't be taken for granted—where two hosts have no need to communicate, why should we make the system capable of supporting communication between them?

Of course, much of what we're doing in building internetworked systems is about enabling communication. However, another principle that we discussed— "complete mediation"—gives us a clue about how to handle our high-level requirement without creating security problems for ourselves. Bob needs to get mail to Alice, Bob doesn't need to have the ability to write into Alice's mail spool. The infrastructure can work in small pieces, such that each does its job, with the end result being that something Bob sent from his mail user agent eventually winds up in Alice's mail user agent.

Much of what this comes down to is defining what is and isn't supposed to be flowing from one zone to another. Policy comes into play here. What's allowed and why, what its risks are, and how those risks will be mitigated are all issues for policy. Then we need to make sure that the policy is enforced. That's why the firewall is in place between the outside and the DMZ, and between the DMZ and the internal network.

When we build buildings, we put firewalls in place so that in the event of some failure that results in a fire, we limit the spread of the fire to the particular zone that's already burning. If a fire is in progress, we don't take down firewalls so that we can get in more easily to stop the burning. We recognize that the firewall draws a line, so that even if our efforts to stop the fire are not as successful as we hope, at least we won't lose the rest of the building.

In computer networks, firewalls aren't about "keeping the bad guys out" any more than firewalls in buildings are about "keeping the fires out." Firewalls are about enforcing separation between zones. Someone able to take advantage of a bug in a system in the DMZ might be able to cause a problem in that zone, possibly even taking administrative control of the zone. Keeping the firewalls in place, however, can go a long way toward preventing the spread of that compromise into our internal systems.

For the same kinds of reasons, we have a firewall between the internal network and a "protected" network. Perhaps the protected network is especially sensitive or important to the business because of the data that are kept on it.

Customer lists, employee databases, personnel and financial records could also be in there. For the most part, these are not needed by insiders. So, rather than putting them on the same network that the programmers are on, it's best to put them in a separate area of the network. Of course, in the process of doing this, we've just recognized that we needed to create another "zone" for the systems, based on what their intended and expected types of use happen to be. Accounting and software development groups are not going to have the same kinds of requirements for their network operations, so why treat them like they would?

Returning to the idea of Mallory attempting to gain access to sensitive company information from the outside, we can see from this architecture that it would be necessary to break into the DMZ, to break into the internal network, and from there, to break into the protected network.

Of course, if there's a hole in the firewall that allows a system in the DMZ to speak directly to the protected system, much of the benefit of having the firewalls in place will be lost. Sadly, this is a very common means for people to configure their systems.

Hard Crunchy Shell

Let's contrast this with the other extreme in network design, the "hard, crunchy shell and soft chewy inside" design, where a single network has all of the good stuff on it. Web servers visible to the outside, internal client machines, and the big, scary databases are all in the same zone—it's all "internal" stuff, as shown in Figure 9-2. The idea behind this philosophy is that it's "impossible" to break

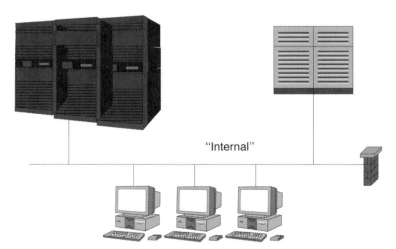

Figure 9-2. One Big "Internal" Zone

through the perimeter, but once you're in, you can do pretty much anything you like without being hassled.

The entire internal network in this case is subject to the same level of protection afforded by the DMZ in the case of the system with multiple zones.

This simple "two-zone" architecture—that's "inside" and "outside"—has several consequences, some more obvious than others.

- We've significantly reduced the number of obstacles presented to attackers.

- We've significantly increased the damage caused by a failure.

- We have not built the network so that a "fire" in one area will not easily spread to others.

Once again, look at some of our secure systems design principles from Chapter 6:

Consider the others, too, to see how they might apply.

Least common mechanism principle. By putting everything on the same network, we now have a system that's capable of going in for one purpose and "while it's at it," doing something else. Imagine a problem like a buffer overrun vulnerability in a web server, particularly one that allows stack smashing or another arbitrary command execution. Although the host is on the network for a specific purpose, it's now possible for an attacker to get the host to do something else. Were the web server on a separate network, a DMZ perhaps, the buffer overrun vulnerability would have less impact. Although it would still be possible to execute arbitrary instructions on the host, that wouldn't be a very useful mechanism for the attacker as he tries to find a way back to the big database servers.

Separation of privilege principle. There is no useful separation where there is only one privilege, the ability to communicate on the network. If, instead of having a simple Boolean answer to a very general question like, "Does the host need network access?" we would take the time to enumerate which networks the host must access and how, we could provide another means to ensure that faults in the host design, implementation, or management would have minimal impact. Returning again to our stack-smashing example, although the attacker can run arbitrary code on the vulnerable host, if the network will not allow the vulnerable host to do anything that it shouldn't, this kind of vulnerability can be a significantly smaller problem.

Least privilege principle. Once we've taken the time to enumerate all of the different kinds of privilege that we have in the system and how we're going to go about granting necessary access, we must go one step further to make best use of the work done so far. We must grant the absolute minimum set of privileges for that part of the system to do its job.

The issue of privilege is an important one and should be well understood. An example of good separation of privilege is in your key ring. If you have different keys for your house, car, office, and garage, you have good separation of privilege. If you go to dinner and give the valet your whole key ring, you have failed to enforce the concept of "least privilege." All of the separation in the world doesn't do you any good if you just deal with all of the privileges in one big group, like a huge key ring full of keys that gets handed over to anyone who needs any key on it for any occasion.

Zoning for Real

Following this line of argument makes it fairly easy to tell which approach makes more sense from a pure data security standpoint. Of course, there are operational issues that need to be managed, like how many separate zones and zone policies the staff can reasonably manage given the limitations in budget and staffing. When it comes to the matter of designing these networks, we need to remember that other principles like "psychological acceptability" also come into play. If we make the systems painful to use in our zeal to build them safely, we can easily undermine the value of the system we've created. As soon as the people we're trying to protect start looking for ways to work around the system, we're in trouble.

Another thing to think about in the context of zoning is how various software packages can affect what our zoning situation looks like. For example, if we return to the idea of the network with several zones enforced by firewalls, we can think of an easy way that the zoning we think we have might not really be there. That example is the case of a database server that has a built-in web dæmon so that instead of having to build your applications to run on some front-end machine, which then makes queries to the back-end, you can do everything you need right there on the machine that's running the database server.

Even though we have all of these firewalls and whatnot between the ultimate target and the source of the attack, if we built the front-end to our company on a database-driven web site that runs on the same machine as the back-end, we've effectively circumvented every layer of protection there. So, instead of an attacker having to break through firewalls in order to cross three zones, he's able to waltz right through every bit of protection until we get to the big target. One buffer overrun that allows him to smash the stack, and the game is up.

Firewall Technology

If we're going to know what firewalls can and can't do for us, we're going to need to understand some basic issues about how they work. This will, of course, be useful, because we are relying on these firewall systems to provide us some means of enforcing our policies.

We could go on and on about firewall technology here, but that won't be necessary because some really good books about firewalls have already been written [8, 198]. There is a basic issue of both philosophical and technical nature of firewall design and implementation with significant bearing on what we're doing when we use firewalls to enforce our zoning policies.

This point should be driven home: firewalls are generic policy-enforcement mechanisms; they're not meant to keep the bad guys out. If it's keeping bad guys out that you want, you'll need to define a policy that supports that objective. Firewalls can help you support that policy, just as we saw through examples earlier in this chapter. Whether you're using a packet filter, a proxy, or both, isn't as important as your understanding of what you're trying to accomplish and how the firewall will help you do that.

Minimizing the Impact of Failure

All right, so failure is going to happen at some point. We know what kinds of failure we're going to encounter, and we know what kinds of things contribute to failure, but the question remains, "What do we do about it?"

When designing and implementing our systems—this means building software, building networks, and even defining our policy—there are goals that we can place before ourselves that will complement our design principles from Chapter 6. These will help us to avoid many of the problems that we run into during the course of designing and building our systems. Perhaps more importantly, these will help us to reduce the impact of any component's failure.

Simplicity

No matter what we do in design and implementation, our systems are going to be complicated. Complexity makes understanding difficult, which leads to many problems. Do not contribute to complexity any more than necessary.

Simplicity has a tendency to propagate downward. That is, when requirements are simple, they can be satisfied by simple designs, which can be satisfied with simple implementations, which can be tested with simple test cases. The more straightforward we can make systems, the more time we can spend ensuring that they work well together and dealing with the complexity foisted upon us by the environment into which we're deploying these systems.

Elegance

Few new programmers recognize that style counts. Elegance is an important goal because it tends to lead to clarity and simplicity. Elegance is well-applied ingenuity. In programming, this means making every statement count. In networking, this means getting traffic from source to destination efficiently.

Elegant designs and implementations tend to stand on their own merit; they do not need to have a great deal of additional support from other things to make up their deficiencies.

Appropriate Abstraction

Abstraction is an important concept in computing. Abstraction allows us to work with spreadsheets and documents rather than bits aligned in memory and on disk. Abstraction allows us to work at a higher level than we'd be able if we had to deal with everything as it is literally represented in the computer.

A danger that can present itself when trying to reach abstraction is the tendency to try to make things *too* generic, *too* abstract. This is dangerous because getting too far away from the task at hand can cause us to forget what foundation we're using as the basis for our systems, and can cause us to design something that has very little hope of being implemented properly.

Return to the example of our protocol stack that's used in networking. The ISO OSI model is a nice way for us to be able to look at the problem at hand. Imagine the kind of complexity that would have to be built into web browsers and web servers if, instead of dealing with things strictly at the layers of application and presentation, they also had to worry about things like how to frame the message itself for transport across the network or how to route the data from one place to another.

If everyone had to deal with these problems in all of their applications, there would be a horrible redundancy of effort while everyone solved the same problem over and over again. We'd have tremendous opportunity to create many incompatible versions of the same thing, and it would be very difficult for us to get anything done, because we wouldn't be able to hire people to build applications who understand just the protocols that are involved for the job at hand. We'd also need people to be experts at every level of networking, including such relatively arcane things as routing or mapping IP addresses to physical interfaces.

Appropriate abstraction is neither too concrete nor too abstract. It identifies the problem and allows us to deal with the problem at hand in such a way that the solution can be used by other applications that might face the same problem.

Early Identification and Mitigation of Risks

As already discussed, the entire industry is one of optimists. We just don't have any idea when to quit putting features into things. Our motto seems to be, "If it ain't broke, it doesn't have enough features!" Of course, in the process of doing all of this, we take on impossible tasks with ridiculous deadlines, and then we work 20 hours per day to get everything implemented. We do this because we're changing the world, we're in a big hurry, and we're working in Internet Time.

Our motto will make both the security expert and the grammarian shudder.

Although things are getting more reasonable in the aftermath of the dot-com bubble burst, we're still taking on incredibly huge tasks and failing to deliver on many of the promises that we're making. A large part of the reason for this is that we do not appropriately manage the amount of risk that we're taking on. We just don't know what things are risky, putting things we don't know how to do off so that we can do all of the stuff that we do know how to do up front, because that lets us get 80% finished in less than half of the allotted time. We can show all of the whizbang features to the boss and they can take them out and show them to people who might be inclined to throw money in our general direction.

We can get things up and running in a hurry this way, but it's a terrible way for us to manage risk. All of the risk in the project is in the stuff that we don't know how to do. So we end up putting that off to the very end, and yet that's the very thing that could hold up the whole project, the very thing that could make the project infeasible. If we identified that from the beginning and tried to work on that first, we could have figured out whether it was worth doing the rest.

Constrained Languages

Another way to reduce the amount of complexity in a system is to reduce the number of options available. In configurations, place limits on what the system can be allowed to do. In languages, keep the programs within well-defined constraints.

There are downsides to this, of course. Making system configuration and programmability too restrictive will interfere with elegance. This is the same basic question of large programming language compared to small programming languages.

Small programming languages are easier to learn. A small programming language reduces the amount of variability in programs written in that language, thus increasing readability. These are the points that advocates of small languages will tend to raise.

Advocates of larger programming languages typically point out that "small programming languages make for big programs," obviously also meaning that "large programming languages make for small programs."

Naturally, both camps are right. The question then becomes one of optimization: what are the criteria that you're trying to meet, and how do you prioritize them? There's no single formula that applies in all cases, no standard that can be universally applied. Understanding the tradeoffs, however, is important because it will allow us to make the correct decisions about just how much programmability and flexibility we build into our systems for each application.

Failure Anticipation

Let's just start out assuming that failure is going to happen. If we start with that assumption, we have the ability to plan for it and to evaluate how it will impact the operation of our system. Spreadsheets allow financial people to play "what if" games to understand the risks and the rewards of each course of action, understanding how various factors will impact the financial health of the organization. Managers of investment funds recognize that not everything will always perform well. They manage their funds such that the fund will have a net gain over a period of time, where the wins outpace the losses.

If we do the same thing in our systems, we can recognize that it's possible for certain aspects of the system to perform in suboptimal ways. We can play similar "what if" games with our systems, understanding how various types of failure in our systems' components will impact the overall functionality and safety of these systems.

When we think in these terms, it becomes clear why such things as single points of failure are so bad. Don't assume that because you have a firewall, you're safe. The question isn't what happens if it fails, but what happens when it fails? If you've considered the question and planned for the event, your whole system's security won't come crashing down when someone discovers that there's a bug in the particular product that you're using.

Peer Review

Just this week-end, I was saying to Monica, "I hope there's a document review this week!"

—Lee Ayres

One of the most important aspects of science is the concept of peer review. Any scientist can make any claim that he likes and can probably get some kind of an audience for it. However, it's the process of peer review, the writing of formal papers, and the presentation of research findings that actually persuades others. Critical review and commentary isn't designed to damage the egos or the careers of the researchers: it's designed to ensure that mistakes have been avoided and that findings can be duplicated. This provides a basis for us to believe that we're not dealing with some crackpot who made some things up and has a few equations "to prove" the findings.

Applying the same kind of "healthy skepticism" to our designs and implementations should help us to improve the quality of our offerings. We're all human and we're all going to make mistakes. Having our peers analyze our work and provide commentary will help us to ensure that we've eliminated mistakes that could be easily eliminated. This also provides a means for the less experienced to benefit from the knowledge of the more experienced.

When done with an eye to creating a better system, critical commentary and review can be one of the strongest allies that we have in building trustworthy systems.

Sidebar: Reading Code

When thinking about code reviews, most programmers quickly come up with long lists of other things they'd rather do, like go to the mall, clean fish tanks, and fill out long forms for bureaucrats. Shockingly few programmers spend time reading source code.

Writing well requires a lot of reading. Whether you're writing English or Common Lisp doesn't matter: a writer unfamiliar with the literature of the language is going to be faced with significant hindrance when it comes to learning new vocabulary and seeing others' usage.

There are several points worth keeping in mind about reading code:

- Reading code is the single best way to learn how something *really* works. Documentation can be absent or wrong. Descriptions by analogy can be flawed. But source code, the implementation, is definitive.

- Just as we learn to speak and to write by listening to others and reading their work, we can learn more about our craft by seeing how others approach the same problems that we do. Look for differences. What are the advantages and drawbacks to the offered implementations?

- Code reviews need not be painful experiences where 20 people get crammed into a meeting room, looking at some bit of code overhead while someone shouts, "Any comments for lines 14 through 17?" Individual reviewers and very small teams can be tremendously helpful and productive.

- Not every line needs to be read by every programmer on the project. It's often best to identify the modules that are most heavily used, focusing review efforts on the code that will be called the most.

- Discussion that arises in such reviews about the relative merits of different approaches is likely the stuff of good comments. Remember, comments don't say what's happening, they say why we're doing what we are doing.

Many of the benefits that peer review provides code can be found elsewhere in the development process, including in the review of documentation. Peer review has worked for centuries throughout the sciences; it will serve us well in computing, if we're willing to try it.

We've seen that failure is a part of the process of creation. If we succeed in making something, it's going to be the result of many small victories and losses. Understanding the types of failures that we'll encounter, what contributes to failure, how we are able to deal with the failure, and how we can minimize risk of future failures should help us to see system failures in a different light. At least if we can use failure as learning experiences, our efforts in dealing with them won't be completely wasted. Let's shift gears a bit and look at a very general policy-based solution offered to offset privacy concerns: opt-out systems.

Why Opt-Out Systems Cannot Protect Privacy

SO FAR, WE'VE SPENT A lot of time talking about privacy from different angles. We have considered what privacy is, how we can build systems that are privacy aware, and how secure system design principles apply. Now we're ready to come to examine a specific point, a practice widely in use, to understand whether we as an industry are approaching the problem with any hope of mastering it. Privacy advocates have long decried personal data being put into databases without their knowledge. The developers and maintainers of such database systems have tried to relieve the pressure put upon them by offering *opt-out* mechanisms.

The essence of opt out is that individuals whose data would be stored in some system and reported may assert their desire to stay out of such systems and the operators of such systems would obey those wishes. The opposite of opt out is *opt in*, where the system's default mode of operation is not to collect such information, but for persons who specifically state their desire to participate, such information collection will take place. What all of this comes down to is the simple question of default behavior.

Here, we're going to discuss opt-out systems in the specific context of the Web, to understand how the design and implementation of these systems affect privacy, and how effective opt-out systems can be in this environment. The same sort of test can be applied to other kinds of systems to see whether opt-out mechanisms can work in those environments.

Our consideration of this topic is especially important now, as we're moving past the first generation of commercial, networked systems built for widespread public use. Although we have been building and using these information systems for several years, we must not forget that they are still in their infancy. Ten, twenty, or even fifty years of work in this area is nothing to the thousands of years of civilization.

Let's keep a little perspective, eh?

How we address matters like default behavior will affect systems well into the future. Decisions we make now might limit our available options in the future. When we're building systems, we need to give serious consideration to what we're doing, to ensure that mechanisms we're using for protecting privacy actually will protect privacy. If we say that we're interested in protecting privacy but we rely on mechanisms that simply cannot work, we threaten to undermine confidence in our systems and to damage our own professional reputations.

To gain a complete understanding of the problem, we need to give consideration to three primary issues. First is the matter of the components that make up these systems, their properties, and what they mean for privacy. The next is how today's information systems collect data and how opt-out systems are implemented. The final issue that we consider is policy. Once we understand these areas, we'll be able to recognize how subtleties of each play off of the others.

Relevant Components

First, we're going to have to narrow the scope of our consideration significantly. Rather than looking at everything that might or might not be involved in the operation of a Web transaction, we're going to consider which architectural components come into play and focus on the most relevant.

We covered much of the relevant architecture in Chapter 7, but we're going to review some of the key parts here.

HTTP: Pushing Data Around the Web

HTTP is a simple, stateless protocol. Rather than trying to solve many problems all at once, it just defines a message format and a simple data exchange. This isn't unreasonable. Remember the protocol stack? That shows us how layering protocol on top of protocol can give us the functionality we need in the end without requiring that everyone deal with all of the complexity of all problems at once.

HTTP does not solve basic problems like moving data from one host to another. Strangely enough, HTTP also does not take advantage of a feature provided by the TCP protocol that carries HTTP—the concept of a session. Nothing is built on top of that transport layer to make a session layer. The client simply asks for what it wants in an HTTP message to the server and the server replies to the request in the form of an HTTP message.

HTTP messages have two parts: a header and a body. Client HTTP messages, such as shown in Listing 10-1, start with the requested URI and the version of HTTP. Following that URI are the rest of the HTTP headers, which include things like the preferred order of languages for the response, the MIME types that are accepted, the type and version of client software in use, and any cookies present. Following a blank line after the headers is the HTTP body. File uploads are contained in the body of the message.

Listing 10-1. HTTP Client Message

```
GET / HTTP/1.0
Host: animal.interhack.net:2345
Accept: text/xml, application/xml, application/xhtml+xml,
  text/html;q=0.9, image/png, image/jpeg, image/gif;q=0.2,
  text/plain;q=0.8, text/css, */*;q=0.1
Connection: open
Accept-Language: en-us
User-Agent: Mozilla/5.0 (X11; U; FreeBSD i386; en-US;
  rv:0.9.4) Gecko/20011010
Keep-Alive: 300
Accept-Charset: ISO-8859-1, utf-8;q=0.66, *;q=0.66
Accept-Encoding: gzip, deflate, compress;q=0.9
```

There are two primary mechanisms for clients to submit data to the server: the usual method is GET, which puts all of the requested data in the URI itself. The other is POST, which will not modify the URI, but will submit all of the data in the body part of the message.

Server HTTP messages, like the one shown in Listing 10-2, start with an HTTP status code, which would indicate success or failure of the request, could direct the client elsewhere to find the requested data, or could tell the client to send more data with the request, such as authentication credentials. Following the status code are HTTP headers, which would include things like the language of the response, its MIME type, the setting of cookies, and other data. After a blank line at the end of the headers, the HTTP body follows. The HTTP body contains the requested data.

Listing 10-2. HTTP Server Message

```
HTTP/1.1 200 OK
Date: Mon, 15 Oct 2001 13:47:59 GMT
Server: Apache/1.3.12 (Unix)
Connection: close
Content-Type: text/html

<!DOCTYPE HTML PUBLIC "-//W3C//DTD HTML 4.0 Transitional//EN">
<html>
  <head>
    <title>An HTML Document</title>
  </head>
  <body>
    <h1>Heading</h1>
    <p>A paragraph!
  </body>
</html>
```

We have discussed URIs in detail already, but let's consider some of the more significant privacy issues connected with URIs.

URI: Addressing Data on the Web

A URI is simply an address, indicating a globally unique location for any given resource. URIs work just like pathnames work on filesystems, but they have more properties. Recall that in Chapter 7, we discussed the following sample URI:

```
http://user:password@foo.example.com:80/bar?baz=quux&lang=en#blarg
```

To refresh your memory, note the parts of the URI above.

- The protocol (`http`)

- Optional authentication credentials (`user:password`)

- A hostname (`foo.example.com`)

- An optional service port number (`80`)

- The requested resource (`/bar`)

- An optional query string, the means by which data are uploaded to the server using the `GET` method (`?baz=quux&lang=en`)

- An optional section, identifying a specific point in the page (`#blarg`)

Because URIs are addresses, they'll show up in client history files, proxy logs, and server logs. In a nutshell, URIs appear in many places and should never be assumed to be private. URIs are no more private than a street address. It is important to recognize that, although URIs are effectively public, likely to be logged in many different places, there are provisions for putting sensitive data in the URI.

Putting authentication credentials in the URI itself is bad idea all the way around. The whole point of authentication credentials is to identify the user and to prove the identity of the user. In password-based systems (which is what we're dealing with in the case of the credentials that can be put into URIs), the security of the system is completely dependent upon the secrecy of the authentication credentials. Putting credentials that depend on secrecy in a token, which is effectively public because it's reproduced so many times, is a horrible idea.

If you're going to publish secret credentials, you might as well not use authentication at all.

Another issue is the matter of form submission data. In some cases, it's useful to have the result of a form be a part of a URI. For example, if you want a search engine's results to have the ability to be sent from one person to another, putting the search terms into the URI would make it possible for one person to forward the URI to another to see the same thing. There are side effects, however, in that the search itself is then effectively public. Because of this, there are significant downsides to this approach, not the least of which is that it could become possible for such things as content-based profiling of user behavior. Instead of just seeing that a user is going to Google n times every day, you could build up a list of what the user is searching for, based on the content of the transaction between the client and the server. Analogously, the difference between the two is like knowing how many times a given person has gone to a library in the former case and knowing what searches the user performed in the catalogs while there in the latter case. Few people would not find the latter behavior invasive.

> **NOTE** *Libraries have record retention policies that dictate the destruction of borrowing records after a short period of time—one year in many cases. Contrast this with the 30-year lifespan on many marketers' cookies and their multi-decade log retention policies.*

Marketers' interest in context-based advertising—serving advertising based on your specific activity or what you are viewing—is also noteworthy. Specific context, like search terms, rather than being treated as especially sensitive, are being seen as especially relevant, fair game for analysis.

The point behind all of this is that the Web, thanks in no small part to URIs, is a very *leaky* medium. Not much about a transaction will stay private unless the system is designed with an awareness of the lack of inherent privacy in URIs and care is taken to evaluate what the URIs will tell others who might be analyzing logs where URIs can be found.

These logs can be analyzed on the client side, on the server side, and also in the middle by operators of proxies. These are probably not the most disturbing log analysis options, however. What's more concerning is the ability for third parties, potentially unknown to the user, to be able to analyze such content data. A particular HTTP header is responsible for this, the referrer.

Referrals: Who Links to Whom

Before version 1.1 of HTTP, a header known as Referer—yes, it's actually misspelled in the standard and therefore in all standards-compliant software—was mandatory. This header simply shows who is linking to whom, or how the client found out that the requested URI exists. The Referer contains a full URI, including any authentication credentials and query string data present. Thus, the operator of a web site can see which URIs are causing clients to request various objects from their sites.

Redirection: Not Knowing the Answer but Knowing Who Does

Sometimes a requested document is no longer at the requested URI. Instead of simply telling the client that the requested object cannot be found, the server has the ability to tell the client where to go to find the object. This process of telling the client where to go to find the requested object is called *redirection*. There are two basic types of redirection: permanent and temporary.

> **NOTE** *HTTP 1.1 includes a new type of redirection, the 303 "See Other." Although this is intended to be used for cases where the developer wants to provide a constant URI that will redirect the client to the correct location for that moment, we have yet to see widespread use of this form of redirection. It would seem that the decisions made early on to make use of the temporary redirect for this purpose are still with us. Thus, we have a good example of how a simple hack, used to work around a problem, can remain in place much longer than the workaround is necessary.*

Our biggest concern with redirection in this context is that it puts the URI of the object the user is requesting in the hands of yet another site. If the user requests an object from FOO, but it's now at BAR, the browser will make a request to both sites. The user won't even know that BAR has been contacted until after it has taken place. In certain situations, the user won't know at all, such as in the case of an invisible dependency, made possible by HTML.

HTML: Telling Your Browser How to Display Text

HTML is the the application-layer language of the Web, the means by which a document's structure is defined. In addition to defining such things as which level of heading a particular string is or the fact that some part of the text is a paragraph, it can include such things as which objects need to be fetched in order to be able to render the page as it was intended to be seen.

Objects can be specified from any point on the Web; there is no restriction that a document's dependencies must come from the same server as the document itself. The specification for the dependent objects—be they JavaScript source files, images, text for frame sets, or anything else—is the same as for all other objects on the Web: a URI. Some objects are put on a page for the purpose of adding content and some are put on the page for the specific purpose of introducing a third party to the conversation. The latter are typically invisible images, which Richard Smith of the Privacy Foundation first called *web bugs* [179].

This property of HTML makes it possible for a document to be created such that the client pulls content in from many different sources in order to render the page. Although this is an important feature of HTML, it has some significant consequences. Now, instead of the user knowing that he's making a request from a given server, he could also be having many other conversations with other servers of whose existence he's completely unaware behind the scenes. This has an important consequence: log entries are being made not only on the client and the known server, but also on every unknown server and all intermediaries between the client and each of the servers. Because so many clients report the referrer, content from the transaction will also then be sent to those third parties. Given the amount of personal and transactional information that can be present in URIs, it is thus possible for extremely detailed records of a given transaction to be put into the hands of many different parties.

This is especially interesting in the case of redirection. It's possible to construct a page in HTML such that it requests an image from another party, even one completely unknown to the user. Now, if you factor in things like redirection—where the third party can introduce another third party—you can quickly see how transactional data included in the URI will quickly fall out of the control of any of the parties involved in the transaction.

Cookies: Solving the Stateless Problem

The final part of this puzzle is the matter of HTTP's statelessness. All of these leaks of transactional data are important to understand, but it's unlikely that any single transaction itself is very damaging. Because HTTP is stateless, there really isn't any good way to link all of the leaks together, to turn them into a bunch of records that can be associated. Consider the following facts:

- I'm a lumberjack.

- I'm the kind of guy

- I'm okay.

- I'm the great pretender.

- Who'll never settle down

- I sleep all night.

- I work all day.

- I cut down trees.

- I eat my lunch.

Now, tag them with a name and we see how much more useful the stuff is.

- I'm a lumberjack. (Lumberjack)

- I'm the kind of guy (Wanderer)

- I'm okay. (Lumberjack)

- I'm the great pretender. (Pretender)

- Who'll never settle down (Wanderer)

- I sleep all night. (Lumberjack)

- I work all day. (Lumberjack)

- I cut down trees. (Lumberjack)

- I eat my lunch. (Lumberjack)

We've only added one additional datum per transaction, some kind of persistent identifier, a nym. Now that we have that, we can look at the data in different ways in order to build a more complete picture of each one of the clients in the system. Notice, for example, what happens if we format things slightly differently, like we see in Table 10-1.

Table 10-1. Profile Database

Nym	Fact
Lumberjack	I'm a lumberjack. I'm okay. I sleep all night. I work all day. I cut down trees. I eat my lunch.
Wanderer	I'm the kind of guy who'll never settle down.
Pretender	I'm the great pretender.

We see some very brief histories, small reputations in this system: we only know two facts about the Wanderer and one fact about the Pretender. On the other hand, we know quite a few things about the Lumberjack. First of all, he tells us his occupation. We find out about his work schedule and he tells us a few things that he does.

Because we have added a name, clients now have the ability to build up reputation, a history. Individual clients are tagged, user patterns can be identified, and even used to predict future behavior.

In a nutshell, we can now put everything that we know about a client into a single profile of all activity in the system. It's true that we only learned one fact, one datum per transaction. How much we learn per transaction, however, is irrelevant because we have the ability to put it all together. Giving someone your life history all at once or one factoid at a time doesn't matter when you're telling a computer. Computers generally have remarkably good memories.

When we're talking to people, we have a basic assumption that they're not going to remember every little detail of our conversation. People will write down things they need to remember. After they're finished, they can easily throw away the paper. They might even lose it before they're finished. We assume that they're not going to go around comparing notes with others. Returning again to the question of default behavior, when we're dealing with people, they'll tend to forget things by default.

With computers, the default behavior is to remember. Computer systems very easily can compare notes and build up more detailed pictures of the people in the databases. By doing exactly the same thing, but changing our environment from dealing with people and pieces of paper to freely copied electrons stored in computers, we have made a fundamental shift in default behavior. That fundamental shift results in a net loss of privacy.

Understanding precisely why we're looking at a net loss in privacy when we're using computers to store data about people is much easier with a specific example. We'll do that now.

Systems for Data Collection

Turning our attention back to web systems specifically, let's consider some properties of data collection systems built for that environment. The model of delivering online advertisements is fairly convenient for us to consider, so we'll do that at a high level to review what exactly we're dealing with.

Logging Web Activity

Listing 10-3 shows a fairly standard web server log entry, one that would be typical for any type of web server, including the servers used for serving banner ads. We've split it into a few lines to make it easy to read in print, but in the native form, there's one long line for each record.

Listing 10-3. Web Server Access Log Entry

```
192.168.24.162 - - [17/Aug/2001:15:44:21 -0400]
"GET /pubs/fwfaq/ HTTP/1.0" 200 123451
"http://www.linuxsecurity.com/docs/colsfaq.html#3.1"
"Mozilla/4.77 [en] (X11; U; Linux 2.4.3-12 i686)"
```

This might not seem to make very much sense at first glance, but by looking at the contents of the entry in more detail, we can get a clear understanding of just what is (and what isn't) included in typical log file entries. We'll first identify each of the fields and then discuss them.

192.168.24.162 is the IP address of the requesting client. Note that as far as the server can tell, a requesting client is a proxy.

— (dash) is the remote "logname," or user ID. Generally, this is determined by a protocol for user identification [95], but some other means have been tried as well, including Kerberos user IDs.

— (dash) is the remote user ID, as determined by HTTP authentication.

[17/Aug/2001:15:44:21 -0400] is the time of the request, including offset from UTC.[1]

"GET /pubs/fwfaq/ HTTP/1.0" is the request itself. This will include the query string and section identifier if present.

200 is the HTTP status code the server returned to the client in response to its request.

123451 is the bytecount in the response to the client.

"http://www.linuxsecurity.com/docs/colsfaq.html#3.1" is the HTTP referrer. Note it's a complete URI, and will include as much detail as the original URI. Query strings, document sections, etc., will all be passed.

"Mozilla/4.77 [en] (X11; U; Linux 2.4.3-12 i686)" shows the contents of the User-Agent HTTP header.

We have considered the most common web log format, generally called the "combined" log. Of course, any part of the transaction can be logged, but it's worth noting just how much information about the transaction is preserved in the typical log file.

Even without a persistent name in the system, we can see that users with typical web browsers do not enjoy much in the way of strong anonymity. If I see a bunch of requests from the same client in a short period of time—particularly if the User-Agent string is consistent and any referral data sent make sense—I can assign the user a name inferred from what data I do have available. For example, combining IP address, User-Agent data, and the current date and time (on a sliding window of, say, 30 minutes), I can probably identify the user pseudonymously. If the user's agent is sending the HTTP referrer, I have an even easier time than that, since a user surfing the logging site will have the Referer show how the user moves from page to page through the logging site.

For a very large class of users, this kind of identification mechanism provides a level of nymity somewhere between strong anonymity and long-term pseudonymity. The reputation and history of the pseudonymous user is very

---

[1] UTC is Coordinated Universal Time, a disambiguated and more accurate version of Greenwich Mean Time. Loosely, this refers to time kept on the Greenwich meridian (longitude zero), which is five hours ahead of Eastern Standard Time.

short-lived. Users for whom this would be true would include folks behind proxies (as would likely be the case in very large ISPs and companies) and on dialup modems, whose IP addresses tend to be dynamically generated and to change often. Broadband users often have dynamically generated addresses, but have the same IP address for a much longer period of time—sometimes even months—so the same argument applies in their case, but less strongly on the side of anonymity.

Unix is a fine operating system, but I prefer XEmacs.

We can even infer a pseudonym based on anomalous behavior or very rare User-Agent strings. For example, the class of users browsing the Web with Emacs-W3 isn't very large by comparison to the Web's population. If you find someone using that browser visiting your site on a regular basis, that might well stand out enough that you're able to give that user a weak pseudonym: "the Emacs-W3 guy."

The same can be used for anomalous behavior. If a server gets a bunch of hits on a certain part of its web site at the same time of day every day, always from various IP addresses in the same network, that might well indicate a fan (or a robot). A weak pseudonym might be useful in this case as well: "the guy crawling all over the publications area at 3pm every day."

Let's take the example of a fairly typical web site, one that issues cookies to its clients, such that each has a unique identifier. Now we've dramatically increased the strength (and probably the lifespan) of the pseudonym. Simply add to our "combined-format" log file a single field: cookie ID.

At first, this might not seem like much more than we had in the case of the weak pseudonyms. In most cases, it won't be, when seen side-by-side. Once we back up a bit and look at what things are possible in the cookie-based pseudonym by comparison with the inferred pseudonym, things begin to change rapidly. For example, changes in browser versions, behavior, or ISPs would destroy our ability to infer the pseudonymous user. If any of the elements used to identify the user changes, we'll likely identify the user as a new user that appeared in roughly the same period of time that the old disappeared. On an even moderately busy site, connecting old profiles to new just isn't feasible.

With a persistent identifier, instead of using data like IP address and browser type to identify the user, we can use such data to infer more things about the user. Now that we can key the profiles from the cookie numbers, we can begin to see things like:

- How many ISPs does this person use?
- How often does this person change ISPs?
- From where (geographically) does this user connect to our server?
- How often does this user upgrade his browser?

Getting answers to these questions would be trivial: all of the data needed to answer them are now present. Once we know the answers to these questions, we can begin to infer all kinds of things about the user, including how often he travels, where he travels, and how much he fools around with his environment (e.g., is this someone who upgrades to the latest and greatest version, someone who prefers to upgrade only after a major release has been out for a while and tested by everyone else, or someone who upgrades only when forced?).

All of a sudden, things look very different, and we haven't even taken into account things like what kinds of data could be used to link the person in the Real World to the activity found in logs.

It would seem that we have a privacy problem here: our users have completely lost control over their ability to maintain or not to maintain reputations with us. To address these problems, we might offer privacy-sensitive users the ability to opt out of the system. Let's see just how we'd do that.

Opt Out Implementation

Opt-out systems are systems that tag people and include them by default. This is important, because it means that if you don't have an identifier in the system, as soon as you're seen, you'll be given one. If you want to get out of the system, your choices are few. Your best option is to refuse to accept the tag in the first place. In most opt-out systems, however, this isn't feasible.

Consider the case of credit reporting agencies. After thinking about the risks present with having your credit history online and in the hands of an organization that you don't know, you've decided that you don't want to participate. No one is *making* you borrow money to buy a house; nonparticipation is arguably an option. Thinking the matter all the way through, however, reveals another problem. Not only will you find it impossible to get a loan to purchase a property without revealing your Social Security number and other data needed to retrieve a credit report, but no one will even *rent* you a property without these data. After all, if you decide to skip town without paying your rent, the landlord is going to want to have some means of retribution, an identifier that can be used to track you down, or at the very least, a way to have your nonpayment reflect upon your reputation.

So it turns out that unless you've been born into enough money to pay cash for everything you need from the very beginning, nonparticipation isn't really an option.

If nonparticipation isn't feasible, your other option is to request that you be excluded. This is an interesting paradox, however, since if you're excluded from the system, you'll simply be tagged and re-added the next time that you come in contact with it.

Direct marketers use huge databases to target their offerings to recipients likely to respond favorably. If you don't particularly care to be called on the phone every time you're trying to enjoy a few moments of private time with your family, you can opt out of the marketers' calling lists. It's important to note that you're opting out of the target lists, not opting out of the database. They still have your name, address, phone number, Social Security number, and just about anything else that anyone ever compiled about you. But now instead of being in *one* database: the list of known consumers, you're actually in *two:* the known consumers database and the consumers not to call database.

So we're opting in to the opt-out list.

So much for opting out.

Things are a bit better online. Instead of having a verinymous profile, online marketers start with no data about you. That quickly changes as your online surfing begins to include them, thanks to the banner ads and other elements that they're serving on the sites that you visit. Each time that you're exposed to an object served by their ad servers, your cookie ID is noted. If you don't have a cookie for that ad server, the ad server will give you one.

The reason why this is better than what we have offline is because the opt-out process is slightly more meaningful. In online opt-out systems, you actually exchange your unique identifier for an identifier shared by all users who do not wish to be identified in the system uniquely. There are still problems with online opt-out systems, of course. Some of the problems with these systems include the fact that they're still getting the data even if the cookie isn't useful to them.

Reflecting on the discussion we had just a few pages earlier about short-term identifiers and inference, we haven't really been able to opt out of the system. We've merely been able to opt out of the persistent identification. Other than the cookie, we're still sending just as much data to the data collectors as we were before.

Finally, the very elements that data collectors will cite as reason not to be concerned about privacy where cookies are involved—particularly the fragility of cookies—make failure of opt-out systems rife. As we showed in several of our case studies, people who believe that they have opted out of these systems can be just as much a part of the system as everyone else due to no fault of their own.

Knowing the Unknowable

The biggest problem of all with the implementation of opt-out systems is that they place the burden of action on the end users, who often have no way to know who is collecting data about them.

This is a tricky problem. How, exactly, do you tell everyone who has your phone number not to call it? The same problem exists in opt-out systems. You need to tell everyone who has put you into a database to remove you from the database. In the case of some databases, this isn't feasible and you need to settle for "the best" they can do.

I have a great idea for a business model. Let's compile a huge database of over 100 million Americans. Let's make it a standard reference guide, such that anyone offering credit will want to check this list to be sure that nobody known not to pay his bills will be granted credit. Now let's say that we don't warrant the accuracy of the data and let it be vulnerable to essentially every sort of character assassination. We'll run this way for a few years until it becomes impossible for anyone to do anything without being in the database. Somewhere in this "few years," people will learn that we exist. Now we'll tell people that the best way to prevent their reputations from being sullied is to have their own report pulled at least annually. It won't cost that much to do it, so we won't make much money from it, but if we get even half of the people in the database doing it, that's 50 million people ensuring us income.

We'd be providing great value in the marketplace, but at what cost to consumers? On average, they'll be happy with the side effects that our system will have: easy access to credit and reduced hassle in getting loans and establishing new service. What about those folks that don't like it? What do we do about them?

If we can establish a critical mass who do accept and promote it, the rest simply won't matter. If they don't like it, they can pay cash.

Does any of this sound familiar? Try getting new phone service without divulging your Social Security number. Try getting an apartment. Try buying a car. Try buying a house. Try starting a business. In any of these cases, you'll find that your Social Security number is "needed" for "credit checks" and that you "have nothing to worry about if you're credit-worthy."

Establish critical mass and there's no way to get out of the system. The best you can do is *to get on another list* of people whose data shouldn't be shared.

Looking back at our secure system design principles, it's clear that this sort of system leaves quite a lot to be desired.

Policy, Policy, Policy

We're now back to this question of policy. How do we enforce the policy?

One of the reasons that the question of policy enforcement is so problematic is because most people think immediately of the law as an example of policy. Of course, the law in most lands isn't about taking precautionary steps to avoid policy breach. The law basically spells out the boundaries and enumerates what will happen to its violators.

When we're dealing with private systems, this model works only when the consequences directly affect the potential violators. If a marketing, credit, or health care database is somehow exposed or exploited, the greatest danger isn't posed to the operator of the database—though there will certainly be some cost, potentially very serious cost. Those who will suffer the greatest loss (or the greatest risk of loss) are the people whose data have been exposed. Thus, the law as a model of handling policy enforcement in these systems fails.

We have the means to manage risk. Though firewalls, cryptography, and other technical tools are helpful, they are not the solution. The solution is a much more simple matter of up-front policy, one that has been argued in information science for decades.

Fail-Safe Defaults and Least Privilege are two important design principles that tell us opt-out systems cannot work in theory. The credit reporting and direct marketing industries demonstrate how opt-out systems are infeasible in practice.

So, now what?

We still need to begin with sensible policy. The difference is that in privacy-friendly policy, we must recognize some basic realities of our environment. Instead of working in a forget-by-default Real World, the computer systems that we build are working in a remember-by-default world of electrons. Instead of having extreme difficulty comparing notes, systems online can very easily put their profiles together to form much more detailed profiles. Instead of having users work without names, the Web makes it possible to tag users with unique names, without users knowing that they've been tagged and named.

Sensible policy means that we need to define just what it is that we need in order to perform the requested task. If there are other requirements that have an impact on how we tag users and monitor their activity, we need to ensure that such considerations are recognized as system requirements. Finally, if we're working in an area where legislation or regulation impact our requirements, we need to know about those requirements as well.

Once we understand our requirements, we're now ready to go about the process of building our policy. We need to specify what we'll collect, how we'll collect it, what we'll do with it, and all that good stuff from Chapter 3 and Chapter 4.

Developing systems so carefully, taking such great pains to ensure user affirmation before proceeding with data collection and management, and placing explicit limits on functionality so we can deal with identified risk aren't typically the kinds of things that are going to make us popular with our management. Even some of our users might not initially understand why proceeding this way is so important. All of what we're doing when we're building systems with privacy and security requirements is really about a single objective: earning the trust of our users. There is good reason for us to pursue this objective, though, as we consider next.

CHAPTER 11

Earning Trust

TRUST IS EARNED. OUR SYSTEMS can earn the trust of our customers—whether they're external buyers of our products or internal users of systems we implement—by recognizing the need to win customers' confidence. Instead of saying, "Trust us, we know what we're doing," we should have our customers see what we've done and conclude for themselves that our systems are worthy of trust and that we know what we're doing.

This is a much harder problem than we might imagine at first.

It means that instead of looking strictly at functional requirements of the system, we also must consider side effects. It means that we need to recognize

In God we trust, all others we monitor.

—NSA [50]

the boundaries that our systems must respect. It means that we need to deal with these issues from the beginning and to include maintenance as part of our plan for the system's deployment and operation.

The Business Case for Privacy

Talking about and encouraging developers to do the Right Thing is fine and dandy, but when we're building these systems in a commercial context, we cannot ignore the fact that if we're going to be able to build systems that way, it needs to make business sense. It's a basic fact of economics that if we want to stay in business we're going to have to put less into our systems than we get out of them. We cannot spend one million dollars to make one thousand dollars if we're going to stay in business for long.

This basic fact of economics, combined with increasing pressure for return on the investment in ever-shorter periods of time, is largely responsible for the way that systems are most typically run. We can see examples of this all around, but I'll tell you about one.

A Familiar Tale

We tanked before tanking was cool.

Very early in the rise of the Web—before the dot-com bubble—I worked at a company that had a product whose client integrated tightly with web browsers. We weren't really sure just how much we could or couldn't do with the paradigm, or even whether the kind of architecture that we were talking about was the one that would make the most sense in the long term.

To find definitive answers to our questions, we built prototypes for ourselves and demonstrations for management to see how things might be able to work together. Prototyping was a sensible thing to do—we learned a great deal about the limitations of the systems we needed to use as a foundation and were thus able to focus our energy on solving the problems that we could solve. Some of the problems we thought we wanted to address just couldn't be addressed with available technology. Knowing that we didn't have the time or budget to build the missing foundation, we could properly prioritize what we were doing and make best use of what resources we had.

Everything changed the day that an excited manager called our demo a "beta."

Despite all of our objections, we suddenly had a preliminary version of a product that customers would actually use, instead of a collection of experiments. By all accounts, we had a phenomenal group of developers; I was often amazed how such a small company could have such a group of hotshots and how well everyone could work together. To this day, I still have tremendous respect and admiration for each member of that development team. So, instead of having the talent being used to solve Hard Problems, it was applied to make product miraculously appear from what should have been throw-away code. And version 1.0 flew out the door.

So why wouldn't anyone wait for us to finish the product before selling it? There was no single reason, but many small reasons that all basically boiled down to the issue of getting maximum return on minimum investment in a relatively small period of time. The idea, of course, was to get something out there in the market that would bring in some money which would be used to fund additional development, to address deficiencies in the offering, and to get some feedback from folks actually trying to use the stuff, rather than just on our in-house tests.

Developers know this drill. We see it all the time. If we are going to be able to address the problems of privacy and security, we're going to need to convince our management and our customers that we need to put this stuff in from the very beginning. At the very least, we need to provide the foundation for these things so we can use them later, without having everything become an add-on. Security by add-on is no good because it almost always leads to increased complexity.

Increased complexity comes in many forms. It could have a major impact on compatibility which, if security had been designed in, may not otherwise have been an issue. Imagine trying to redesign the flush valve mechanism after shipping the toilet. Trying to add something so fundamental after the system is deployed has repercussions all the way back to the user interface. Security in computer systems is not much different.

Plumbing is always a good example.

Complexity is our enemy, so we want to avoid add-ons. We want to think about as many of these problems as early as we can. Thinking our designs all the way through will help us to avoid painting ourselves into the proverbial corner.

What If . . .

Managers love to play "what if" games. It's the ability to play such games that is largely responsible for the success of the spreadsheet. The fact that I don't have to explain what a spreadsheet is, despite the fact that few readers are financial types, is testimony to the widespread recognition of the spreadsheet's power and utility.

If we can play such games with finances, why not with designs?

- What if someone other than the user of our system sees a URI that was a part of a session on our site?

    - Did we expose his name?
    - Address?
    - Salary?
    - Social Security number?

- What if an attacker has broken into another machine on our end user's network and can sniff things flying across the wire?

- What if an attacker is a cryptography expert? Is that encrypted channel we created still safe?

- What if the access control list on our router fails?

- What if our firewall bastion host is running a web server with an input buffer overrun problem?

- What if we just throw a bunch of garbage at a server instead of a properly formatted request?

- What if someone cracks a user account on our server? Will all of our private data be readable?

- What if someone poses as a law enforcement official and convinces our system administrator to provide access to the system?

- What if our vendor's code has a back door?

We can ask an almost endless series of questions about our designs that will help us to understand how our systems behave when they're in various modes of failure.

Systems fail. People make mistakes. This is the environment in which we're deploying our applications. Recognizing these facts might even move us not to ask, "What if?" but, "When?"

Spending to Save

Banks are in the business of buying and selling money. It's their inventory, they move it from one place to another, they use it to buy goods and services, and they provide various services to get more of it. They need access to huge sums of money, both in physical access to cash and in electronic access to various accounts.

Some banks are *really* big, with thousands and thousands of employees. Anything that stands in the way of people getting their jobs done impacts productivity and, therefore, costs the bank money it wouldn't otherwise have had to spend. Multiply that by a few thousand, and all of a sudden, little annoyances that impact productivity can turn into big expenses that will impact profitability or result in higher costs to customers.

Office space can get expensive pretty quickly. Of course, banks can't work in just any old office space. Branches where they deal with cash are big buildings with all kinds of security gizmos, including a vault. All of this can get pretty expensive. Again, lots of expense weighs against profitability.

So why do banks build all of these obstacles to getting to their inventory and moving it around from one place to another within the system? Imagine all of the money that some huge bank would save if it didn't have to pay its people to authenticate against a bunch of systems as they went about their work from day to day. Imagine if, instead of needing people to manage the cash to be sure they had enough to last before the vault opened again, they just kept a big pile of cash right there next to every employee. "Need $100? Just give me your account number and I'll hand you a $100 bill from this stack right here." Wouldn't that be easier? Sure would be faster. Just think of all of the money that the bank would save not goofing around with making customers prove who they are.

How about instead of having some big expensive truck with a bunch of armed guards drive the cash around town, they just stuffed it into a FedEx envelope and sent it overnight? It sure would be easy to get cash moved around that way. It'll even be there by 10:30 the next morning. How's that for convenience?

And instead of making employees be physically present on-site to get everything done, wouldn't it be nice if employees could just use a Web interface to perform all of their work from the Internet? Then they could even work at home, and it wouldn't be nearly as problematic for them to work different schedules, or even longer days—spending their time helping customers instead of driving through traffic to and from the bank.

It's true that this sort of thing would make many things much easier and would make it possible to increase productivity significantly. However, when it comes to knocking down barriers and providing easy access to the things people need to serve their customers, we must raise the question, "Easy for whom?" Employees of the bank would be able to get better access to money for their customers. So would outsiders have an easier time getting access to money that isn't theirs.

If banks were careless and too heavily focused on providing easy access to money, they could be spending their money to build an infrastructure that others could abuse. At some point, the amount of risk presented outweighs the amount of benefit expected.

Even if the losses themselves that arise from theft and error do not endanger the operation, having daily reports of bank robberies could undermine confidence in the banking system. If confidence in the system is undermined, people might be inclined to put their money under the mattress for safekeeping instead of depositing it with the bank. Banks without customers depositing their money there simply cannot continue to exist.

Thus, banks invest a great deal of money in building an image of trustworthiness. Their branches are large, strong structures. The employees are intelligent, competent, and well-dressed. Locks can be found on the doors between rooms. Cameras record the faces of all who enter, move about, and leave the premises. A sticker bearing the logo of the Federal Deposit Insurance Corporation tells grandma that her first $100,000 is insured, so even if Bonnie and Clyde get through all of this security, her savings account is safe.

Considering how much a bank's visible security is used to deter theft, to recover from theft, and to make customers feel safe might prove interesting. Knowing the exact proportions isn't as important to our discussion as realizing that the end result of all of this security—both perceived and real—is that it exists to make people trust the system and to have reason for such trust.

Today, many companies' most valuable and important asset is information. Without access to information, many people within the company cannot do their jobs well. The more information they have, the better they can serve the goals of the business. The more easily they can work through the raw data to extract higher-level knowledge, the more efficiently they can work. This results in competitive advantage, more profitability, and could even make it feasible for the company to offer its customers services that would otherwise be prohibitively expensive.

Access to information is obviously important. However, if access to information is too easy, the information will fall out of the control of its holder. Informational self-determination—privacy—will be impossible to maintain. Without the ability to maintain control over the flow of information, abuse will happen, and such abuse will undermine trust in the system.

Putting considerations like up-front cost and time to market too far ahead of trustworthiness is certain to place limits on the success that our systems will enjoy. If we want our systems to be universally accepted, trustworthiness isn't optional. Trustworthiness is a necessity. When information is your inventory, trustworthiness means enforced privacy. If we want to make our systems trustworthy, we must be willing to make the necessary investment; slapping a few "security features" to the list of the system's benefits won't cut it.

Prevention versus Cleanup

When confronted with the reality of break-ins, pragmatists will ask just how big of a problem a break-in really is. Just how much does it matter? Maybe instead of spending all of this money on trying to keep everything up to date and doing all of these expensive reviews of our work, we should just go about our business and if someone gets in, we'll deal with it then, lock them out, and go on our way.

Many organizations operate this way, even if they don't come right out and say that's how they're going to operate. Ironically, these organizations would be better off coming out and saying that they're going to work like that, if that's what's going to happen. At least in that case, employees would know exactly what to do in the event of a break-in and wouldn't have to waste a lot of time standing around looking at each other, trying to figure out what to do, only to conclude that nothing else *can* be done.

Because so many people are so hesitant to get into specifics when talking about problems that they have encountered and how they're going to be able to deal with them, it's difficult for us to be able to cite a large body of work that shows the difference between prevention and cleanup.

One example worth considering is that of a company that wanted its web site evaluated for security. The person responsible for the safety of the site was ready to go, but could not get a budget approved for even a few thousand dollars for an external assessment of the system's configuration. More than six months after asking my firm for a quote for a simple, high-level assessment, the site was attacked, and the content was deleted. Subsequent investigation showed that the site was vulnerable to at least a half-dozen different avenues of attack that would grant complete control over the filesystem where the web server's content was stored. The same system that didn't warrant a few thousand dollars' worth of assessment, was repaired and eventually replaced at a cost that ran well into the tens of thousands of dollars.

In many cases, organizations have very little idea how much their information is worth to them. Part of a break-in typically involves downtime, which can be difficult to measure if employees are able to do some work. Nevertheless, if we let folks fudge their figures a little bit, we can probably get at least some ballpark idea of how much a break-in costs in terms of hard costs. The total cost of a break-in is even harder to measure, though, since that would include intangible and otherwise difficult-to-quantify things like damaged reputation. Damaged reputation might not have a dollar value today, but if it hinders your ability to attract new customers or to retain your old ones, that's certain to have real dollar value.

Anecdotal evidence like that of the break-in just mentioned suggests that for every dollar spent in prevention, a victim would have to spend ten in cleanup. Many will argue that even spending ten times the money doesn't really get you back to the place where you started, since no amount of money will make customers forget that you mishandled their information.

Good Privacy Is Good Policy

Whether you think that a good figure for the cost of prevention compared to the cost of recovery is one-to-ten, one-to-three, or one-to-100 doesn't matter. If reputation is a concern, it's easier to work to prevent having the problem than it is to try to ensure everyone that the problem won't ever happen again. This is especially so since if you didn't do anything to prevent it from happening the first time, you have quite a long way to go before getting to the point where you can say that the problem that was exploited simply cannot be exploited again.

Early in the book, we discussed what privacy means to organizations, to individuals, and to societies. Everyone has some vested interest in privacy.

Your organization's privacy

As we discussed earlier, your organization has an interest in privacy. Failure to control the flow of information about the organization and what it's doing can result in loss of competitive advantage, loss of intellectual property, and even inability to engage in any kind of planning. Imagine that every time someone went into any kind of meeting, minutes were taken and published in the newspaper.

The equivalent of publishing everything could happen if the organization isn't careful.

Many people believe that because they work on intranets, behind firewalls, "safe" from the outside world, they have no reason to fear. Only persons in the company would be able to see what they have, and no one would be interested, right? This might be true in many cases, but considering that the vast majority of attacks against firewalls and internal networks originate from inside the organization [70]—think of the number of contractors, temporary employees, or disgruntled employees that might be lurking behind the firewall—there seems to be a fairly compelling reason to question that logic.

Of course, this view of "inside and outside" with no greater granularity fails on the test of secure design principles. Even in this case, privilege comes into play. Separation of privilege means that we take a granular approach to finding what needs to be done for various job functions. If data entry personnel do not need to be able to pull files down from the research area's file server, we need to be able to build the system in such a way that data entry folks can do what they need to do without having access to everything.

Least privilege means that having the separation isn't enough—we must take advantage of it to specify at a granular level exactly what is and isn't allowed by policy. Having a zillion options for connectivity throughout the organization does us no good if we're just turning everything on for everyone.

Competitors want to know what's happening inside of your network. Vandals want to play with the numbers in your spreadsheets. Enemies of the company or of its nation want to destroy it. Throughout most of human history, there has been little opportunity for these attacks to be perpetrated against many targets. It's simply too expensive to mobilize a unit even to gather intelligence about a target. It's cost prohibitive.

Just as the Internet has made business able to overcome obstacles, the Internet can help attackers to overcome the obstacles that prevent them from carrying out their "business." Now an attacker doesn't need to bear the expense of mobilizing a unit of reconnaissance experts to find out what's happening inside an organization. An attacker simply needs to get ahold of some cheap computer hardware and someone with some expertise. Other basic economic facts—like world superpowers running out of money and being unable to pay their agents—create significant opportunities for unethical competitors and rogue states to hire well-trained experts. Worst of all, thanks to computers' programmability, this model scales pretty well.

While stopping short of predicting the end of Life As We Know It, I feel quite safe in predicting that we have only seen the tip of the iceberg when it comes to the dangers of connecting everyone in the world to everyone else.

Your personal privacy

When it comes to personal privacy, the most common example that we see today is the crime of identity theft. This is becoming a serious problem in the U.S. As noted, identity theft is a crime that is perpetrated by someone with enough information to engage in an action—especially a financial transaction—as another. So the criminal gets the goods and the victim gets stuck with the bill.

Irrespective of the limits placed on credit cards and the other "safety measures" that are put in place, creditors tend not to be terribly sympathetic. Victims' credit records are still seriously impacted by identity theft and it takes years for the bogus entries in the record to expire.

As we see greater convergence of the Real World and computer systems, the need for personal privacy extends much further than to electronic records whose misuse could have electronic damage.

Consider the case of knowing someone's schedule. An attacker who is able to predict his prey's whereabouts can greatly increase his chances for success, being sure to attack when the target is most vulnerable. A campus rapist who wants to find likely victims can watch a dormitory to see who would make easy targets, but in his attempts to watch the targets, runs a serious risk of drawing attention to himself. Numerous logistical obstacles complicate an attacker's ability to gather data on targets.

Now consider that such a college dormitory, as a security measure, implements electronic locks, where student ID cards are used to grant access. This solves several important problems, including what to do about lost or stolen keys. In the case of student ID cards, new cards (with new numbers) can be issued, and the old cards can be tagged as "stolen," so that any attempts to use them will trigger an alarm. Such electronic lock systems often advertise the feature of being able to tell who is and isn't in the building at the time when a crime was committed—a feature that requires an audit trail, or electronic record of activity.

Our attacker now doesn't need to risk being caught sitting outside of a dormitory late at night, trying to establish when potential targets are most vulnerable. If our attacker can get ahold of the audit trail of the electronic lock system, he could simply search the data for anything he likes, greatly increasing the efficiency of his target selection process, possibly even allowing him to do so for multiple dormitories simultaneously.

The moral of this story is that a security feature presents a privacy risk. Risk of abuse of such data isn't about a blemish on an electronic record. This kind of risk isn't abstract. Failure to recognize or to administer privacy in an era of digital convergence can have very real consequences, even to the personal safety of people who might not even understand that a computer system is keeping a record of their activity.

Don't think for a moment that personal privacy isn't important. It's the first—and often, the most successful—line of defense against attack, whether online or in the real world.

Your customers' privacy

Although customer privacy could be covered by the privacy considerations for an organization, it's worth using a separate category. Considerations tend to be different, because instead of having direct impact on the health and even viability of the custodian of the information—the organization—problems with respect to customer privacy can have a much wider reach.

Now, instead of harming merely the organization that's responsible for the loss of privacy, we're talking about the harm that will come to people who bear little or no responsibility for the problems being foisted upon them. Imagine if it's the information collected from your records that made it possible to perpetrate identity theft against one of your customers. Imagine if it's the information on your computer systems that told the world that one of your customers is taking a drug for a serious disease.

Failure to control the flow of information about customers can be embarrassing for the organization. The information the organization lost control of can materially damage and even destroy the reputations and lives of the persons described by the data. Remember, we're not talking about a single transaction, a single datum that ran out of control—it's information, the sorts of things that can be extrapolated from that datum, and the kinds of things that can be learned when that datum is compared with other data that might be available, even from other sources.

What this tells us is that protecting data about our customers is imperative. We're not "safe" in doing anything we like simply because the data aren't "medical," "financial," or even "personally identifiable." Data are the building blocks of information, so if we want to avoid causing problems for our customers, we need to recognize our responsibility toward them. The best way to keep people from getting ahold of information that could be used against our customers is to prevent them from being able to get ahold of data that can be used to learn such information.

Policy

In software, we measure bugs as deviations from design. If we do not separate the design and implementation phases of building systems, classifying and correcting defects can become quite a bit more difficult. Doing it effectively could even become impossible.

Building systems that are secure and properly enforce data privacy will similarly mean that we must consider what should and should not happen ahead of time.

Policy, if it has any hope of being effective, must be enforceable.

Privacy Policies

Talking about privacy and policy together tends to make people think about the "privacy policies" that appear on various web sites, starting out by saying how the site's operators "think your privacy is important" and then going on to describe—in dense legalese—why exactly you can't sue them for doing anything they want with any data collected about you or your visit. Those aren't privacy policies. They're "don't sue us" policies.

Generally speaking, privacy policies are about what data are collected, how they will be handled, and how long they'll be maintained. Online, particularly with web sites, these are an attempt to quell the fears of consumers who are concerned about what might happen if they decide to use a particular web site. This is an interesting problem. Privacy hasn't historically been a problem for people who use computers. Throughout the earliest days of the Web, very little attention had been paid to privacy, despite the very serious privacy implications of what was being enabled and the comparatively little attention that was being paid to the privacy problem.

One can then ask the question, "Why did privacy become an issue online?" The answer is because of the sorts of tracking mechanisms that were not only enabled because of the technology, but actually used by the people building commercial systems. Suddenly, this "one-to-one marketing" that has been talked about in marketing circles for years became a real possibility, and the ability to profile user behavior, along with the widespread acceptance of the underlying technology, made doing so on an unprecedented scale, feasible.

People implicitly placed some degree of trust in the infrastructure until how that trust was being handled came to light. Then, instead of fixing the problems—unsafe data handling and a lackadaisical attitude about the importance of consumer privacy—we saw a rush to document existing practice behind a facade of concern for user privacy.

In some sense, the situation is better now than it was, because we now have the ability to see what the sites with which we're interacting are theoretically doing with the data collected. In many other ways, the situation is actually worse: the descriptions of what's happening are not written to inform readers, but to put them at ease. We see meaningless phrases like "personally identifiable information" being used as the foundation for many discussions of privacy.

Effective policy must state its reason for existing. At a very high level, we need to understand what it is that the policy hopes to accomplish. When we understand this, we'll have a metric by which to judge the specifics of the policy and its implementation: whether we have come closer to achieving our high-level objective.

Our privacy policies can be important tools in building the trust and confidence of our users. Through such policies, we can tell users exactly what they can expect us to do. We can explain why we need such data and what we'll do with it. Being armed with an understanding of our intentions, they can then decide just how much they're going to interact with us and how.

If we're clear and reasonable about what we're doing, leaving our users' data ultimately under their control, we can demonstrate that we're sensitive to their privacy concerns, and give them reason to trust us. That's the kind of basis on which a productive long-term relationship can be built.

Security Policies

The security policy is where we want to specify what we have determined is our acceptable level of risk. We need to be able to understand—and to have the policy's audience understand—what we're trying to accomplish. Furthermore, if they don't buy into the policy (for example, if they think it's a Draconian, one-sided document crafted by lawyers in an attempt to turn employees into drones without rights), the audience will not respect it, and might even be challenged to find ways to circumvent it.

Effective security policies have several important parts, which we now consider.

- **Scope:** What is and isn't covered by the policy.

- **Assets:** We need to understand what we're trying to protect if we're going to be able to circle the proverbial wagons around it.

- **Value:** Knowing the value of what we're protecting will also help us to know the line between fighting to retain control of it and just giving up. We don't want to spend a million dollars trying to protect one thousand.

- **Risks:** At a high level, we need readers of the policy to understand what risks the policy is attempting to address. Are we talking about a risk of exposure? A risk of modification?

- **Threats:** Who are our likely attackers? It isn't necessary to enumerate them, but readers should have some idea when they're reading something that is going to keep the organization resistant from disgruntled ex-employees and what is designed to foil the attempts of corporate spies.

- **Practices:** Once we know who our attackers are and what they're after, we need to know how we're going to address these concerns. This shouldn't be a rigid list of things that employees should not do, but rather a guideline that will help them to understand what to do when they're confronted with a choice which would be in line with the policy. Specific practices and limits on who may do what should also be included in most cases. The point is to help people understand what they should and shouldn't be doing to get their jobs done, and to make that consistent with the organization's picture of acceptable level of risk.

The *Site Security Handbook* [68] does a good job of defining the role of policy and what it should contain. Many other references are available as well.

Practice

All of the policy in the world isn't going to do us any good if we don't follow it. We're concerned here with earning trust. Ultimately, if we're going to be successful in earning trust, we need to show by our actions that we're worthy of that trust.

What to Do

We have discussed privacy theory and practice at length. But when it comes down to it, how do we apply all that we've covered in the operation of our systems online? Particularly when we're building systems for the Internet-using public, how do we build systems that are worthy of the trust we want the public to have? One could enumerate many, many practices, but we're going to focus on nine that seem especially worthy of consideration, given the state of Internet systems today.

Stating policy and intent

One of the biggest ways to get on the hotseat is to collect data without having a policy for handling it or spelling out your intentions. Particularly if you're running a system that works seamlessly in other systems—as is the case with banner advertisement servers and hit counters—intentions need to be spelled out. Many people, particularly when online, have become increasingly skeptical of others' actions.

Thanks to better cookie handling in browsers, when seeing that the server is trying to set a cookie, more people than ever will notice. A larger number than ever will ask, "Why are you setting a cookie?" If you have a clear statement of your intentions—*why* you're doing what you're doing—and a clear statement of your policy—*how* you're going to do what you say you want to do—your users are going to be significantly more comfortable in using the system that you've put before them.

When offering statefulness—the ability to remember you from one visit to another—in systems intended for use by the general public, an important factor of the statement of intention is the benefit to the users that will come from the system's design and implementation. For example, if building an online store, it might be convenient for the end user to be able to make purchases without needing to specify which card to use for payment, which address to use for billing, and which address to use for shipping.

Of course, to a retailer, these are important data for being able to understand with greater detail which customers are using the system and how they are using the system. Customers once won are worth keeping, so making customers want to return to the site is important. Perhaps discounts could be offered based on historical buying patterns. Perhaps certain discounts might be offered to shoppers who spend over a certain threshold on the site. These are side effects that are possible thanks to the ability to build statefulness into the transaction.

If this is what you'd like to do, it's best to state exactly what it is that you're doing. If benefits to shoppers are spelled out, they're going to be much more likely to do their shopping at the site. If, on the other hand, the site seems to know everything about them without any indication of how or why, this might present a certain negative response, at least from the more privacy-conscious consumers.

We're going to return to this example of Internet shopping several times throughout our discussion of practice.

Following policy and intent

That's "Caveat emptor" for our Latin-speaking readers.

Today's Internet-using public understands the maxim, "Let the buyer beware." Looking at the public's reaction to some of the case studies here when they were originally revealed, we can be sure that the public does care deeply about privacy online and does react favorably when apparent violations of policy are brought to light.

Statement of policy is useless if it is not followed. Statement of intent is useless if intention changes. On the other hand, the public can easily see whether such statements of intention and policy are being followed. Independent research groups, hobbyists, and auditors are likely to find infractions and are likely to report them.

Although infractions aren't necessarily fatal, they can seriously undermine the public's ability to trust the vendor. If, on the other hand, some relatively obscure problem causes an unintended consequence, a vendor's swift reaction to correct the problem and to right any wrongs that might have been committed through the problem, can actually help to build additional trust in the vendor. A dismissive "this isn't a problem" message is much more damaging to credibility than an honest admission of an oversight and a fulfilled promise to rectify it.

If you should find yourself in such a position, avoid the temptation to try both reactions simultaneously. "This isn't a problem, but we're going to fix it anyway," tends to make people wonder, "If it's not a problem, what's there to fix?" Indeed, some have tried this, with mixed results.

Many sites online today attempt to follow many online privacy principles, such as those discussed in Chapter 4. These principles themselves are good in theory. We must take great care in implementation not to paint ourselves into a corner using these concepts. Additionally, we mustn't think that because privacy principles from some privacy group or another are addressed, that the "privacy problem" is somehow "solved" once and for all.

A quick review of these principles is in order. There are three categories of privacy principles, each of which has several complementary principles. We'll briefly consider these before we discuss the practices that will help us to build systems that earn trust.

Data collection and handling practices that ensure that the risks we're taking are the risks that we have evaluated. The specific principles in this category include notice, choice, minimization, usage, classification, and security. These principles all complement each other well, contributing to a comprehensive strategy for responsibly collecting and handling data entrusted to our care. Taken together, our systems will not collect data without users knowing what's happening and having meaningful choice about the data collection.[1] If the user grants us the privilege of collecting data, we would then collect as little as we need to accomplish the task at hand and use the data in accordance with our stated purpose. Finally, we'll note the kind of data we have and be sure to give the data appropriate levels of protection.

Data correctness practices will help us to maintain the quality of the data we manage. We'll need to grant appropriate access to the data we've collected. Particularly when maintaining data about people, we must recognize

---

[1] Interestingly, sites that post the most complicated policies tend to be more likely to use persistent cookies. Such sites could keep track of when a user last read the privacy policy. A user visiting the site after the policy has been changed could then be notified, and changes could even be highlighted with changebars or a different color text. If the notice is hopelessly complicated, and available technology isn't being used to manage it, that's not useful notice at all.

that we're not dealing just with data, but we have in our hands the basis for someone else's reputation. Such persons should be able to see what data we have about them and be granted the ability rectify any erroneous data. This is a principle that can sometimes prove problematic, especially in pseudonymous systems, unless great care is taken in the first place to manage the problems presented. Very simple steps, including strict formatting requirements to the use of checksums and even cryptographic hashing algorithms, can go a long way toward enforcing correctness in our data. Our systems are more useful with high quality data, making this principle an easy sell.

Policy compliance practices that keep our implementations in agreement with our policies. Designing systems whose behavior can easily be verified will greatly simplify our attempts to ensure policy compliance. Verifiability also plays off of our data handling practices. For example, the principle of minimization guides us to collect as little data as we need. Minimization can be implemented in a system by having it throw away data it doesn't need or by having the system avoid receiving the data in the first place. Verifiability points us toward the latter option, since a user watching how our system works will be able to see what data we're collecting. If we're not collecting the data at all, the user can see that. If we're collecting the data and throwing away what we don't need, the user cannot verify our compliance to stated policy without getting into the system itself. If our systems claim to do one thing—through our policy statements—while appearing to do another—through implementations that would allow much more—we run the risk of raising the suspicions of our users. Of course, policy compliance is assisted by providing remedy and recourse for serious failures in policy.

Audits

Regular assessment of practices in light of policy is a useful tool to help system managers ensure that they continue to be well-positioned to deliver on the promises made to their customers. A system can easily go into production being perfectly compliant to policy. As changes in the system occur, undesired side effects might be introduced that make the system fall out of compliance with its policy. An example would be of a web site that includes a policy statement advising users that no third parties are involved in the delivery of content. The site might specify that it does not use cookies to identify users uniquely.

At some point later, however, in response to some business requirement, the site might opt to include a hit counter or some other service-based model of maintaining site usage statistics. Such statistics are necessary for maintenance of the site, understanding what is and is not useful to its visitors, and ensuring that the site is being used as it was intended. Using a service model for such statistical collection is well within the rights of the site operators; not all site operators have the ability or the desire to handle this sort of thing in-house.

The problem with introducing a service-based mechanism for usage reporting is that it could make the system violate its own privacy policy. Typical implementations of service-based usage facilities include the delivery of some "content"—sometimes visible content, sometimes merely an image, and sometimes an invisible web bug—by the third party. This will allow the third party to record transactional data that will be used to deliver the usage statistics to the site operator. This third party, in addition to collecting transactional data, might also tag users uniquely, perhaps with an HTTP cookie. Does such a case make the site violate its own privacy policy? At the most technical level, probably not. The site still does not identify users uniquely, and if the object placed on the site is merely an invisible web bug, one might stand behind the definition of "content" and say that web bugs are not site content. Users of the system, however, are unlikely to interpret these matters the same way, since it's ultimately the site's inclusion of the code necessary for the service-based site usage reporter that made third-party identification of users and possibly even tracking possible.

Regular assessment of system policy, implementation, and practice can ensure that if any such discrepancies do occur, they will be discovered and resolved quickly. On the public Web, if we don't audit our own systems, we can be sure that others will. Some will do so to assess online practice. Others will do so out of curiosity. Others will do so out of malice. Better to do the work yourself and to correct problems before others discover them, than to explain to the customers how policy and practice got out of sync.

Recognizing the environment

The position that we're advocating is simple: let people be people. We all make mistakes and no matter how many case studies we examine, no matter how many classes we take, and no matter how many systems we implement, we're going to make errors. Build systems that let people be people and recognize that mistakes will occur, so when they do, they won't undermine the system's safety and security.

Furthermore, because the people that design computer systems are imperfect, the systems themselves will fail from time to time. Do not place complete trust in any single mechanism for mitigating a risk. Assuming that because one sits behind a packet filter or even a "full-fledged firewall" that one is impervious to attack. Do not assume that because the connection between the web server and the customer database is write-only that an attacker cannot ever read out of the database.

You can't trust code that you did not totally create yourself.

—Ken Thompson [182]

The more things—human and technical—that must simultaneously fail, to create the situation necessary for the system to violate its policy, the better the system will be able to handle the failures that are sure to happen. Systems that are able to operate successfully despite the failure of individual pieces around it are the kinds of systems that are more worthy of users' trust.

Avoiding centralization

Counting eggs can be a chore if they're spread all around and one needs to search to find them all. Putting them all in one place will make counting them and maintaining them much easier. Some might then reason that the solution to the Problem of Egg Management can be thus described: Put all your eggs in one basket.

Even mom knows that's not how to mitigate risk.

Centralization is problematic for privacy, partially because putting all data together in a single place makes it possible to examine the data to learn more than the data themselves. Information useful for a wide variety of purposes can be gleaned from sufficiently large quantities of data. If your requirements do not dictate the use of such data to extrapolate information, there is little argument in favor of centralization and the arguments against it, from the perspective of risk management, are myriad.

Centralization also makes each target for attackers more worthwhile. If we want to avoid significant damage coming from any single successful penetration, we do well to limit the amount of damage that could be caused. Instead, for example, of putting everything that the attacker could possibly want directly in the same place, we spread the data such that our systems may draw from the various sources to use them, while making it necessary to go through significant hoops to find the raw data outside of the system and to be able to piece them all together to form the same picture that would normally be had by looking through the application's interface.

An example of how this might be implemented in practice would be an internal intranet application that would need to make use of data available through an employee directory, but would also need additional information about user roles within the application itself in order to do its job. One might reason that it is preferable to duplicate the data from the directory into a local directory or database that is specific to the application, adding to it all of the data necessary to support the application.

Such a design, however, creates a large problem with centralization that would not exist in a design where the system would get what it needs from the employee directory and the additional data it needs from the local database. In this sort of design, a compromise of the database would not result in the exposure of data from the employee directory. Compromise of the employee directory would similarly have no effect on the integrity or privacy of the data in the application's own database.

Compromise of the application itself would result in the exposure of such data; however, it would be limited to the data the application uses, which is unlikely to be a full copy of the employee directory.

Considered in these terms, it's clear that the issue of decentralization is really just an architectural mask for the secure design principle of separation of privilege.

Avoiding linkability

Creating a consistent identifier, or key, that can be used to tag data is often necessary for making use of large sets of raw data. Therefore, in privacy-aware systems, we want to take care to avoid creating such linkability where there is no such need for it.

How do we know when linkability is necessary? Our statement of policy and intent will tell us what we need to do with the data and how we'll handle them. If we do not have an immediate need for linkability as stated in the policy, we should not make such data linkable.

Should a need arise as the system's design evolves, restatement of policy and intention is necessary. Once such restatement has taken place, we can reevaluate our practices to see just how we can link data and for what purpose. Again, we should take care that when making data linkable, we link only what is necessary and avoid linking what doesn't need to be linked.

Avoiding too much information

The phrase "need to know" is often used in connection with especially sensitive information. As it turns out, this is also an important philosophy for us when we're designing systems that make use of data, particularly of data about people. If we need to know someone's location to give accurate weather reports, we only need to determine which station is the closest and to forward the report of that station. The most common mechanism for finding location in the U.S. is using the U.S. Postal Service's ZIP code. Although an effective means of identifying location for the purpose of serving weather, it's also an effective means of gaining additional demographic data, such as average household income, how that income compares with the nearby communities, and how that compares with the nation.

Such data can be used to infer a great deal more than is necessary for the purpose of serving the weather. In practice, sites that serve weather often do so by putting the ZIP code in the URI of the document with the information. URIs, being essentially public, are certain to be leaked to numerous third parties.

Another excellent case of a mechanism for data collection is the collection of birthdays to deliver horoscopes. Though officially only "for fun," such services are taken seriously by many. By giving very specific horoscopes—which is to say "more of the same vagueness"—providers of horoscopes argue the necessity for a specific date and year of birth, rather than just the sign of the Zodiac. Interestingly, date of birth is commonly used in conjunction with other data to identify people uniquely in databases.

Thus, data collected "for fun" online could result in getting enough data to identify people uniquely in marketing databases. This possibility could be avoided if the data collected would provide only enough information to serve its immediate purpose.

Avoiding secondary uses

Closely related to the issue of having too much information is the issue of reusing it. In the case of our online store, we might have customers provide billing and shipping addresses. Obviously, when purchases are made, we'll send receipts and goods to the appropriate addresses. If, however, we add to that the building of a customer database by reading all customers' billing addresses, some might feel that their privacy has been violated, since it was provided for one purpose—to which the customer agreed—and used for another—to which the customer did not agree. Using the technical definition of privacy, this view is justified. An even larger number of customers would believe their privacy violated if such a mailing were to be built and rented or sold to third parties, a common practice in many industries.

Perhaps the most common example of secondary uses would be the magazine subscription. The greater the proportion of copies for each issue that will be sold by subscription, the greater the level of demand that can be predicted ahead of time, thus reducing losses that would stem from excesses in printing and reduced earnings that would stem from failing to produce enough copies to meet the demand. With the ability to predict demand reliably, profitability increases, even greater than the costs associated with mailing each issue separately.

Prices for magazines delivered to the home are generally lower, giving sometimes significant financial incentive to readers to subscribe. Collecting and maintaining mailing lists for magazine delivery comes with an additional opportunity for increasing profitability: renting and selling the list to marketers.

Though disclosures and opportunities to exempt oneself from such lists are fairly commonplace now, such has not always been the case.

Avoiding leaky channels

Certain channels of communication are "leakier"—more likely to cause exposure to unexpected third parties—than others. Where possible, the avoidance of channels that are very leaky is preferable to finding ways to overcome the tendency for such data to leak.

Although HTTP can itself be thought of as a fairly leaky channel, it's worth noting that there are multiple mechanisms available within HTTP for communication between the clients and servers. The most obvious case of the distinction is in the use of the GET method as opposed to the POST method of sending data to the server. Particularly when uploading form data, the use of POST is much to be preferred for preventing accidental exposure of certain data that might be used by parties other than the intended recipient.

Tools

Numerous tools are available to implementors of systems to specify and to enforce policy. None is a silver bullet—all systems must be well-designed and follow privacy-aware practice if they're to be privacy-aware. However, good implementation of the designs can go a long way to achieving the trustworthiness that we seek in the construction of such systems.

The biggest hurdle standing in the way of secure systems is often not one of available technology, but of attitude in the design and implementation of our systems. Throughout this book, we have discussed why we should care about building in privacy, how we can understand the nature of privacy in electronic computing systems, and how we can avoid undermining our systems' security by accident.

There are a few areas that are worthy of particular mention in the discussion of tools, however.

P3P

The W3C has specified a standard for the specification of machine-readable privacy policies, called the Platform for Privacy Preferences (P3P) [189]. P3P is useful because it allows clients and servers to specify their privacy expectations. This will allow, in a much more automated way, clients to decide whether, and to what degree, they wish to interact with particular servers online. Despite its original and far-reaching plans, P3P 1.0 is nothing more than a language for privacy policies.

Although P3P developers, and some supporters, rightly and honestly acknowledge the limitations of P3P, some vendors have made grandiose promises about what P3P can do to solve online privacy problems. Misplaced belief in vendor promises is dangerous because it can result in deploying P3P with the hope of solving problems that P3P was never designed to solve.

Whether P3P is adopted remains to be seen. As technology like P3P comes and goes, we must always remember to evaluate these tools critically. Before we make use of tools that will help us in our quest to make privacy-aware systems, we need to understand what problems they're trying to solve and how well they actually address the problems.

Configuration

Modern operating systems, though lacking many of the security features present in earlier operating systems, possess a wide variety of mechanisms for access control. These mechanisms can be employed to support policy. For example, if an application needs to read from a Java properties file in order to get the necessary data to make a connection to a back-end database, that properties file can easily be set to be readable only by the user ID under which the Java application runs. Taking that simple step of using file permission options can go a long way to enforce the policy of preventing local users from accessing the database without going through the application.

Because most operating systems today support the concept of a "superuser" that's essentially able to do anything, there is, of course, less protection than there can be in such an environment. A step as trivial as putting tokens in a file readable only by one user can be defeated by an attacker able to achieve access to that user ID or that of the superuser. Nevertheless, the concept is still important, and would require that an attacker of this system circumvent yet another obstacle to achieve his goal of access to the database.

Cryptography

Cryptography is one of the most useful and important tools available in modern computing for the enforcement of privacy and security policy. Cryptography can be used to enhance the privacy of data by making it readable only by the intended recipients. Cryptography can be used to help in the authentication of users and agents in the system. Finally, cryptography can also be used to ensure the integrity of data.

As is true with many highly technical mechanisms, there are many opportunities for error in both design and implementation of cryptosystems. Though a useful tool, cryptography will not eliminate these problems. Care must be taken in the use of and reliance upon cryptography.

Maintaining Trust

No part of security is "fire and forget." Privacy, reputation, integrity, and trustworthiness are hard problems. With the right mindset going into it, the technology can help. Understanding and evaluating risk, mitigating risk widely, and being determined to maintain the trustworthiness of our systems will help us to operate systems that are worthy of the trust we want our customers to be able to place in them.

In the next chapter, we consider an example. We have criticized ad traffickers and marketers a lot throughout the text, so let's consider the problems they face and see whether such castigation is deserved. We discuss the design and implementation of a privacy-friendly system for delivering third-party content, *Napersnik.*

CHAPTER 12
Your First Assignment

BECAUSE A LARGE PART OF the privacy debate has been connected to the Web's ability to present a customized view of content online, such as news, weather, stocks, and advertising, we're going consider how to build a system that will allow users such customization without sacrificing their privacy.

We have covered a lot of information about the problems of privacy and security. We have discussed secure design principles, the Internet as a deployment environment, and have considered five case studies that should help us to understand more clearly how subtle problems can arise in our designs. In this chapter, we're going to put your newfound knowledge to work. Your job is to design a system that can deliver third-party content (like a news ticker, advertising, or a hit counting service) without invading the privacy of site users.

Implementation is left as an exercise for the reader.

We start with system requirements and discuss some approaches that we might try. We then move on to design, specifying how we can satisfy our requirements, all the while keeping privacy in mind. Our goal here is to focus on concepts, particularly the privacy and security-sensitive concepts. To avoid getting distracted from this goal, we're going to leave many questions of detailed-level design unanswered. Were we actually describing this system for development, we would obviously need to make a more complete statement of design.

So, the question now is, "What exactly are we doing?" This is a reasonable question to ask after we hear the one-sentence version of the task at hand. It's precisely what we demand—or should demand—of our customers when we're building systems for them. As we consider these requirements, you might think about what other requirements you would impose on such a system. As we resolve the requirements while going through the design, think about how you would address the requirements and how you would think about applying what we've considered throughout this book.

People are generally loathe to add still more client software to their environments. Much of the promise of the Web was that such relevant data could be retrieved from anywhere that a browser could be found. Thus, although we would be able to address many of these problems more effectively in a system that would require client-side software, or at the very least some sort of software in the middle to act as a broker between users and the content providers, we take a different route. We focus specifically on the problem of providing customized views of content on today's Web in a completely server-side solution, or more correctly stated, without requiring any additional client software than that which is already available. This includes not only common desktop-based web browsers, but also more lightweight clients like those found in web-enabled phones.

Delivery of customized content turns out to be a much more difficult problem than many people realize. The need to be able to sort through huge amounts of data and to determine which to present is key in providing content that is most wanted. Providing links to relevant content is critical for the success of the system; people will not use the system if they can visually sort through data and find items of interest more easily than the system.

The question of deciding when to show particular content isn't just a question of "what space is available" and getting the right amount of content to fill the allocated amount of space. In traditional print media, in addition to such things as space available, there are questions like which page you want, which section the page should be in, which issue the content should be in, and many other factors. When we work online, we have many of the same considerations that exist in print media. However, it's not quite the same; instead of trying to understand the audience as a group so that we know which content to place in a given spot for printing, we have the ability to render the page at the time that the reader is making the request. Thus, instead of making the page work for most of the members of the group—by identifying what things that group has in common, and effectively leaving out the rest—we have the ability to build the page such that it will work for the user as an individual. This is an important difference between what we deal with in traditional one-to-many media and the sort of one-to-one media that gets marketers all excited.

Of course, the obvious thing to do—and the route which apparently everyone working in the space today has taken—is to tag each user uniquely and to let that user's activity online create a history, or reputation, inside of the system that can be used to predict interests and future behavior. Figure 12-1 illustrates how such a system works.

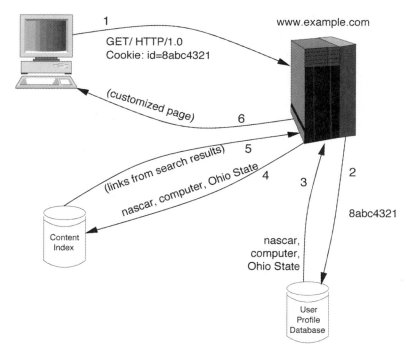

Figure 12-1. Finding Content Using a Pseudonym

The order of events shown here is:

1. The Client initiates the request, including nym in the cookie, which the server receives and extracts.

2. The web server looks up the profile for nym.

3. The web server receives the profile for nym.

4. The web server searches the content index for matches.

5. The web server receives links to the matching content.

6. The web server generates the page including matching links and serves to the requesting client.

This model does work. The problem is that it does everything pseudonymously. Although probably not a problem in the cases where users know that they're initiating a connection to the content server in question, this has significant privacy implications when users do not realize they're talking to such a content server. On today's Web, content often comes from sites that users don't realize that their clients involve, particularly in cases like hit counters and advertising content.

We're interested in solving the problem without resorting to forcing users to surrender their anonymity.

Our attempt to solve this problem is a system I call *Napersnik*.[1]

Functional Requirements

So we don't like the model that's often used. But we can't just say, "Don't do that." We need to figure out what problems "that" solves and be sure that we can also solve those problems. We now consider a more complete list of requirements so we can understand exactly what we're trying to accomplish, and we include our anonymity-by-default requirement. We're going to focus on the key components of a system for delivering content as a third party.

Table 12-1 summarizes the list of our requirements. The format is fairly standard: each requirement is assigned a unique number, in the format of *system.type.number*. This is a particularly useful way to specify requirements, since we can have higher-level requirements specified by our legal departments, groups responsible for specifying strategic position, and the like.

The first field is the highest-level namespace. This is likely the name of the specifier. Our legal counsel might specify some requirements with regard to data handling and document retention policies. Requirements from legal counsel would be in the prefix LAW. Requirements from our internal audit group might have the prefix AUD. Requirements specific to the *Napersnik* system would be identified with NAP.

The second field would specify the type of requirement we're facing. Functional requirements could be identified as FUN, privacy requirements as PRI, security requirements as SEC, and operational requirements as OPS. The final field is simply a number that identifies each type of requirement uniquely.

Now that we've seen the overview of our requirements, we need to consider each one. We're not trying to resolve each of these requirements yet; we're

---

[1] *Napersnik* is Russian for "confidant." The idea is that this is a system you can trust with information about yourself and your preferences.

Table 12-1. Key Napersnik Functional Requirements

Number	Description
NAP.FUN.001	Transparent Third-Party Operation
NAP.FUN.002	Identify Location for Content
NAP.FUN.003	Series
NAP.FUN.004	Promote From Anonymous to Pseudonymous
NAP.FUN.005	Promote From Pseudonymous to Verinymous
NAP.FUN.006	Resume Nym
NAP.FUN.007	Target by Source Network
NAP.FUN.008	Target by Profile Data
NAP.PRI.001	Client Anonymity by Default
NAP.PRI.002	Review and Comment on Profile
NAP.PRI.003	Allow Cookieless Operation
NAP.PRI.004	Allow Profileless Operation
NAP.PRI.005	Maintain Profile Secrecy
NAP.PRI.006	Maintain Transaction Log Secrecy
NAP.SEC.001	Prevent Insertion of Bogus Transactions
NAP.SEC.002	Minimize Server Exposure
NAP.SEC.003	Minimize Local Access
LAW.PRI.001	Data Handling and Sharing
LAW.PRI.002	Document Retention
LAW.OPS.001	Conspicuously Posted Privacy Policy
AUD.OPS.001	System Accounting
AUD.OPS.002	Network Accounting

elaborating on the needs that each proposes and discussing what issues are at hand. Questions about how to solve specific requirements will come later, in the section on design.

Transparent Third-Party Operation

We need *Napersnik* to operate as a third party, to be able to serve content to users of another site. For example, *Napersnik* should make it possible for a web site to include calls to itself for the inclusion of images, HTML, or any other type of object. *Napersnik* should work completely transparently, not requiring the user to jump through any hoops to get to the content that comes from it.

Although this ability is a built-in where HTML is involved, we're specifically concerned with the ability to serve content that's specific to the site using our service. Thus, if we use *Napersnik* to offer web site operators a fee-based service—for example, a news ticker—we should be able to give our customers code that will direct their users' clients to include our content. When we receive and process these requests from clients, we should know which of our customers directed the client to fetch our content.

In addition to being able to use this datum—the site causing the client's request—for monitoring use of our system, we might want to use it as input to our algorithm for deciding which content to serve.

Identify Location for Content

If *Napersnik* is used as a third party to augment content from a site, we need the request to specify where the content is to appear. Very large sites are likely to have diverse readership. In such cases, knowing the site causing the request won't be very useful for determining whether a particular piece of content is on-target. Just as newspapers offer advertisers space by section, we should have the ability to offer our customers the ability to tell us where the requested content will appear from the perspective of the user. Thus, when we're choosing the content, we'll have the ability to choose content that will make sense in the context where it will appear.

For example, if *Napersnik* is offering a news ticker service to web sites, we might have a portal site of some sort as a client. The portal site, rather than following its own news and serving it directly, has contracted us to provide the service. From the user's perspective, this means that along the right side of every page on the site, a narrow column of news items appears.

When we're choosing which news items to include in that column, we want to know the context for the request. So if we're on the top page of the portal site, we might not have much context about the types of content that we can use. If, however, we're down in a section related to job hunting, that's useful to know. If we have space for one news item on that page and our choice is between a story about unusual weather patterns sweeping the nation or the latest unemployment figures, the preferred option is pretty clear. The reverse is also true—given such a choice, we'd make the opposite decision if we're on the weather page. Without knowing what context into which we're providing our content, we cannot make a good decision about what should appear.

We thus need to be able to have the request specify the site, the page, and perhaps even the part of the page where the content is needed.

Series

Some types of content are best presented in a series, or should be seen a specified number of times.

For example, if we want to offer on our news service the ability for clients to follow a particular developing story—instead of just showing the most recent news item at the top—we can place the articles about the story into a series. Then, instead of having several stories that are part of a series competing for space or providing the need for a teaser to a subsequent page that lists all of the stories in the series, we can simply designate one story—perhaps the first—as the "top," which will be shown. After the top story has been seen, we'll then be able to replace it in the lineup with a followup story.

Another option would be to avoid displaying items already read in the ticker.

Client Anonymity by Default

Because *Napersnik* is a system to be trustworthy, people to whom it's showing content must be anonymous by default. By definition, privacy isn't something that we can manage for them—they must determine for themselves what is and isn't alright to do with data about them. That must include naming the data, even if the name we give it doesn't have anything to do with their True Names.

Client anonymity is something that makes *Napersnik* different from other offerings in this problem domain—others falsely claim that end users are anonymous. *Napersnik* will offer them anonymity by default.

Because of the intended deployment environment—the public Web—there are going to be some complications to anonymity. Indeed, such things as IP address and browser type and configuration will be reported to us even though we're not asking for it. In the case of the former, it's necessary to be able to return requested content. In the case of the latter, it's a consequence of using software that wants servers to know what it is, in hopes of having content providers build sites to work specifically with them.

We're requiring that the system itself provide end users anonymity but we must acknowledge that we're providing it on top of an architecture that presents obstacles to the maintenance of strong anonymity. Our objective is not to exacerbate these problems. We're not attempting to fix the privacy problems already present in the architecture. Thus, our anonymity is real anonymity, as anonymous as one can be on the Web without taking additional steps to undermine the anonymity-eroding side effects of the architecture itself. It's also as anonymous as we can offer clients. The problems that we are not solving are not problems that can be solved on the server side.

Promote from Anonymous to Pseudonymous

Anonymity is going to present us with certain limitations in identifying what would be of interest and predicting user behavior. Our basic assertion here is that most of what's being done today can be done anonymously. We acknowledge that more can be done pseudonymously.

Users wishing to gain additional features available through the use of pseudonyms should have the ability to "promote" their nymity from anonymous to pseudonymous. Doing so would grant the server the ability to build up a history of usage and would allow the server not only to use data for that particular transaction, but would enable the server to analyze activity after the fact.

This promotion should not be exclusively one-way; pseudonymous users wishing to return to anonymity should have the ability to do so.

Promote from Pseudonymous to Verinymous

Even greater ability to determine relevance and interest would be available in a verinymous profile. Again, we have never asserted that verinymity is *bad*. If a user wishes to accept the benefits and risks of being known verinymously by a *Napersnik* installation, that user should have the ability to do so.

Users should then be able to add data to their profiles that would promote them from pseudonymous to verinymous. Verinymous users wishing to revert to pseudonymity should be able to do so. It is worth pointing out that once the profile has been made verinymous, demoting it to pseudonymous presents a certain risk that not all verinymous data would be removed from the profile or that some transaction performed with the verinymous profile wouldn't cause the system's pseudonymous identifier to be linked with the user's True Name.

Users concerned about these risks—or wanting to return to pseudonymity in such a way that the linking of the pseudonym to a True Name isn't feasible—would be better off abandoning the profile altogether and starting a new one under a completely different pseudonym. Of course, if that new pseudonymous profile were ever made verinymous, it would be possible to link the old verinymous profile with the new.

Resume Nym

Sometimes proper identification of the user will not be possible. If, for example, the client no longer maintains the credentials necessary to identify the user to *Napersnik* (e.g., if the token is stored in a cookie which was deleted) or if the tokens are not available on that client (e.g., the user is on a different or new client), the user should be able to identify himself so that he can take advantage of *Napersnik*'s knowledge of his profile in selecting relevant content.

One possible way to resume a nym would be to login to *Napersnik*. Since client anonymity is the default mode of operation here, at the time when a user creates a pseudonymous or verinymous profile, one of the fields could be for a password of some sort that would provide a very basic means for users to prove that they're the legitimate user of the nym. Of course, verinymous users who opt to provide an email address to the system could have a password or a hint that will remind them of their passwords sent to them by email. Pseudonymous users who forget their passwords would not be able to recover.

Review and Comment on Profile

The ability for a person to review and to contest data maintained about him is a well-established need for privacy-aware systems, particularly in such contexts as financial records. Because of the potential for inaccurate data to find its way into the profile and the risk of unintended consequences of such data being taken at face value, the ability to review and to comment is one well worth providing online.

Target by Source Network

The source of our client's request, networkologically speaking, could prove to be a useful datum to include in the algorithm for determining relevance of content. It should be noted that there are many cases where the source IP address will *not* indicate geography. There are many cases where geography could be roughly determined with an IP address, but due primarily to the rise of large, national Internet Service Providers and the use of HTTP object caches, IP addresses are decreasing reliable means of identifying where the client is physically or geographically located.

This isn't to say that source network isn't useful. For most users on today's Web, we can use the IP address to determine at least which ISP someone is using. Other things might be inferred from the source network, such as whether we're dealing with a home, a business, or an academic user. These issues might well be worth considering when serving content.

Anonymizing proxies and other privacy-enhancing software, of course, will even further interfere with our ability to glean any useful information about the source of the client.

Target by Profile Data

Of course, if we're providing a means for users to identify their interests to the server building content, we're going to want to take advantage of that ability. Whether we're dealing with anonymous, pseudonymous, or verinymous users, we need to take advantage of any announcement of interests being made by the client.

Allow Tokenless Operation

We know that we're going to need to exchange some kind of metadata between each client and the server in order to be able to make decisions on which content will be most relevant to the requesting client. Metadata will need to be exchanged in the form of some kind of token. In the context of the Web, this usually means an HTTP cookie, but we're not yet holding ourselves to specifics on design and implementation. If, for example, it turns out that we have something else that works for our purposes in this context, we might decide to use that instead. It's best to specify the requirement generically so that when we get into specifics, our requirement will fit, whether we're using traditional cookies or something else that is not known by the writers of the requirements.

Some folks are going to be uncomfortable with the concept of using any kind of mechanism to maintain persistent state, even though we're able to offer real anonymity. The fact is that many providers of various types of content have claimed to provide end-users anonymity without really understanding the nature of anonymity or even knowing that there are many shades of gray between anonymity and verinymity. It also must be recognized that in this system, if the number of variables we're tracking anonymously is high enough, it is technically feasible to perform data mining on the logs that could be generated from transactions with anonymous users, such that we could make our anonymous users pseudonymous. Given enough data, we could probably even turn them into verinymous. In any case, we're going to need to proceed thoughtfully in order to build up enough good reputation that people will be comfortable with our system maintaining state.

Although probably not a very large part of our likely user population, we must recognize that some persons will exercise their right to refuse to accept the risks posed by the way we intend to customize content for them. Our system should not refuse service to such persons.

Allow Profileless Operation

Some users simply don't want to accept the risks present with any system offering personalized content. Some might opt not to disable the state maintenance mechanisms in their clients altogether because they visit some sites with which they do want to allow state maintenance.

So, for persons who do not want to configure their browsers to reject our state management tokens, we should offer the ability to keep a blank profile. Operation in this mode would be the same as tokenless, except that a blank token would be included in the transactions.

Maintain Profile Secrecy

Pseudonymous and verinymous profiles can contain sensitive data; therefore, we should keep them safe from outsiders. Such profiles are likely to be the target of subpoenas, discovery orders related to litigation, and all types of attackers. We have an obligation to end users of this system to make every effort to keep these data private.

Maintain Transaction Log Secrecy

Although not usually as attractive a target as normalized databases and polished profiles, even transaction logs are a worthwhile target. Also, because these tend to reside on the servers that have direct connections to Internet-reachable hosts, there is considerably greater risk of exposure when compared with systems that store databases.

Nevertheless, we need to address these risks to prevent the exposure of data to attackers.

Prevent Insertion of Bogus Transactions

At the very least, we should be able to detect clients that are providing us bogus identifiers and to prevent such records from filling our access logs or making entries in our databases. The strength of this mechanism need not be to protect against dedicated attackers with sufficient sophistication to reverse-engineer a network-based system. However, identifiers should have some sort of mechanism that will allow us to determine whether the token is likely to be genuine.

Minimize Server Exposure

In an effort to manage the risk that will be present from exposing our systems to the Internet, we want to keep such exposure as minimal as possible. For example, we would not want to run an NFS server and to expose it to the Internet if we're not going to use it. We need to identify just what needs to be exposed, and how much it needs to be exposed in order to support system functionality. Anything beyond must be denied.

Minimize Local Access

Just as we want to avoid giving remote Internet users free reign of the system by providing unrestricted access, we want to prevent local users from being able to get all of the goods on any of our servers. There are several reasons for this. If there are any legitimate uses for local users, for example, these local users' privileges should be restricted to the minimum set necessary to perform their jobs. We don't want to have our backup tape flippers being granted direct access to the user profiles, for example.

This will also allow us a greater level of safety in the event that a system is compromised. If we have some kind of problem on the system that allows the compromise of the host as a particular local user, if that user's access is limited, another security failure will be necessary to achieve the level of privilege needed to read the data that we're especially interested in protecting.

Data Handling and Sharing

We must articulate what data we're going to collect, how we're going to handle them, and how we share them. We have similar procedures in place for the handling of all of our inventory and supplies. In a system such as this, our inventory is data, and we should give the same level of thought and care to its handling that we do to more concrete types of inventory.

Document Retention

Our legal department has specified a document retention policy. That policy should include electronic records, as well. We should be sure that our system is compliant with the policy, as this reduces the burden of record maintenance—it's easier to keep track of things if we're only worrying about what's actively being used—and reduces the level of exposure if the organization should be pulled into some kind of legal proceedings.

Specific concerns with this system and document retention policies will be in the area of profile expiration and log retention.

Conspicuously Posted Privacy Policy

Once our system is up and running, we must ensure that we're providing a conspicuously posted privacy policy. That is, folks who want to know what we're doing and how we're doing it should have no problems finding or understanding the policy.

The most obvious solution to the problem of understanding the policy would be in the simplicity of policy. No matter how simple the policy's words are, if we have 18.4×10^{14} different ways of dealing with the data we collect, we'll have a huge policy. Clarity in policy is often indication of clarity of procedure. Clear procedures are less prone to error.

Recall that this is a real privacy policy, not a you-cannot-sue-us policy. The idea is for users to be able to see and to understand what we're doing so they can decide just how much they're willing to let us know.

If we're performing any state management (whether anonymous, pseudonymous, or verinymous), we should have the ability to recognize the last version of the privacy policy that the user read, and present the policy in such a way that changes are immediately visible. At the very least, the system can tell that the user has not seen the most recent version of the privacy policy.

System Accounting

As part of our ability to audit the system's operation and use, we need to provide accounting records that show who was using each of our servers, when each one was being used. This functionality should be provided by the operating system.

Note that we're not talking about remote end users, but use of the server outside of the context of *Napersnik*.

Network Accounting

As part of our ability to audit the network's operation and to plan for future capacity needs, we need to know how much bandwidth we're using and we need to identify the kinds of traffic patterns we have in the system. This functionality should be provided by our access router, and may be augmented with additional tools.

Having considered each of these requirements, we can see that we're being faced with a significant technical challenge. Although our proposed system is intended to accomplish a task that's well understood, security and privacy requirements will necessitate finding more original solutions.

Understanding what we're now challenged to do, we can move on to the next phase of our development—design—wherein we actually try to address these problems.

Design

Because the focus of *Napersnik* is on the issue of nymity, we need first to determine how we're going to handle the naming of clients.

As we have discussed in detail earlier, the most convenient mechanism we have for storing state data—including client names—is the HTTP cookie [113]. We support four modes of operation:

Tokenless operation uses no cookie. Useful for when the client refuses cookies or does not support them. If the client does not support cookies or uses them in connection with *Napersnik*, we lack the ability to offer customized content on any user preference data.

Anonymous operation is where all state data are stored in the cookie itself and no unique name is in effect for the client.

Pseudonymous operation is where the cookie stores a unique name, a persistent identifier for the client. The actual profile is stored on the server. No information about the user's true name or other real-world identifier is stored in the profile.

Verinymous operation is where the cookie stores a unique name, but included in the server-based profile are data that identify the user's true name, address, phone number, or other real-world identifiers.

So let's take a look at a design that tries to address our requirements. We're going to consider an architectural design, how those components will interact, and the formats of the tokens we'll use to support this system's operation.

Architecture

Several architectural components are needed to support the operation of *Napersnik*.

Client originates the request. This would be a user's browser, a web robot, or some other program that initiates requests by talking to the HTTP server.

HTTP Server will be the front-line interface to the world. All clients will send their requests for content to this server.

Profile Server will contain all of the appropriate data for pseudonymous and verinymous profiles.

Content Index is an easily (and quickly) searchable index of the content available for serving. (The index isn't the complete content; it's merely a list of URIs and appropriate tags used to determine which content to serve, as described below.) Note that the algorithm for choosing the appropriate content is implemented here.

It's worth noting that we have not specified the interfaces to the profile server or content server. There is no requirement for them to be HTTP. In fact, there is potentially a significant advantage if they're not.

In keeping with our secure design principles, each of these servers should be able to perform only the minimum necessary functions to perform their roles successfully. The web server will, by far, have the greatest variety of possible input because of its need to support full HTTP.

Cookie Formats

A *Napersnik* cookie has one of two formats: anonymous and named. In the cookie format itself, we make no distinction between pseudonymous and verinymous cookies. The difference in pseudonymity and verinymity is in the profile server, and what data are contained in the profile.

Named cookies

The named cookie is straightforward. We simply define a user ID that's unique to the system. We have many options for the creation of this number. My favorite is to view the number as a string of individual digits that must conform to a specific standard.

User IDs are 15-digit numbers, as shown in Figure 12-2. The actual user ID is composed of 12 of the 15 digits, leaving three digits for parity, to assist in the assurance of the cookie's correctness.

A simple parity algorithm we could use would be to add each group of identifier digits and to place the last digit of that sum into the parity digit. For example, if the first four identifier digits are 0123, the sum of those digits is 6. The final—indeed, the only—digit in the sum is 6, which we would then place into the fifth digit of the cookie value. We do that for each of the groups of four identifier digits, resulting in a 15-digit number.

If our ID assignments are sequential, our first cookie would then be 000000000000011. Our second would be 000000000000022. The tenth would be 000000000000101. The eleventh would be 000000000000112. You get the idea.

Not that I would do such a thing, of course.

We don't need the parity digits to ensure that the data were transferred correctly from the client to the server. We need the parity digits to protect the system against certain jokers out there on the Internet who might be inclined to edit their cookies' values manually, thus assigning themselves user IDs instead of using the ones given them by *Napersnik*. Of course, this system isn't really *secure*. We just get an additional level of comfort about the likelihood that the cookie we've been given back is actually the one we assigned. Our ability to trust our parity data to protect us from jokers on the Internet is limited to the secrecy of our parity mechanism. The problem we're trying to solve here is the occasional random goofing around that will be done; dedicated attackers are going to be able to forge cookies that we'll accept as correct. This is why the HTTP state management standard [113] points out that cookies are not intended to hold authentication data.

If we wish to save some space in the representation of these user ID numbers, we can convert them from decimal to a more compact form, such as base 36. That would save us a bit of space; instead of being represented as 100010000000112, the cookie's value would instead indicate the user ID as ZG7YJTGMO. This would provide another layer of protection against manual tampering with the user ID.

We can safely call our user IDs "tamper resistant," but it would be generous to describe the IDs as "secure" for use on the public Internet.

Armed with this understanding of the simple mode of cookie handling, we should be ready to consider *Napersnik*'s anonymous cookie format.

Anonymous cookies

Because the named cookie needs only to store the key into the profile database, its job is dramatically easier than that of anonymous cookies. The anonymous cookies must be used to store the entire profile.

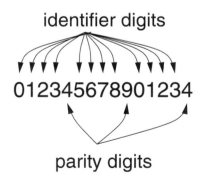

Figure 12-2. Napersnik Named Cookie ID Format

By defining a format for the named cookie, we were able to provide a tamper-resistant user ID. By defining a format for anonymous cookies, we'll be able to maintain flexible, client-side databases of sorts.

For the anonymous profile cookie, several record types would need to be defined. Indeed, which record types would be used will vary among uses of the *Napersnik* design. Rather than trying to anticipate all of the possible needs, we'll provide a more flexible system of addressing such needs now as well as future needs.

HTTP cookies are nothing more than strings of data that have some properties. We'll therefore use a few conventions that will allow us to store many independent data in a single string of text. Figure 12-3 shows our solution.

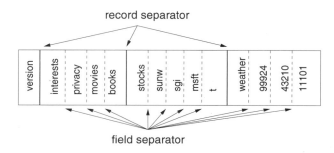

Figure 12-3. Napersnik Anonymous Profile Cookie Format

A second cookie will maintain the status of the client, while still allowing the user to remain anonymous. Data needed to keep track of what has and what hasn't been seen will be stored in that status cookie. Thus, when we're deciding which content to display, if we're looking at limited-run content, we'll know if the requesting client has seen a particular piece of content the specified number of times or whether it should be shown to the client again.

This status cookie is a dramatically simpler format: after a ten-digit serial number for the cookie, one digit corresponds to one piece of content. The serial number will be used not to tag clients uniquely, but to tell the server reading the cookie which digit-to-content map to use. Assuming that we change the map of what content we're tracking once per day, we might simply use a number like 2001090100, following the format of yyyymmddxx, where xx is a two-digit number that can be incremented if necessary to define multiple maps in the same day.

In practice, we can count on cookies providing us four kilobytes of data, which will then allow us to keep track of over 4,000 separate pieces of content. As we keep track of what content we have in the system, we'll just assign a particular digit in the cookie to represent it for the entire time that we're tracking that piece of content.

For example, in our news ticker implementation, if we have specified that we're going to show a particular headline to each client until it's been seen four times or has been selected, we'll assign it an available digit, one that's not being used to track another piece of content at the time. We might define that slot to show a number of times that the client has seen the headline, perhaps representing the number in base 36 so that we can have the option to show the headline 35 times, instead of nine. A lowercase r will be used to mark an item as "read."

On the server, we'll maintain a table for mapping particular stories to digits in the cookie. That table might be represented like Table 12-2. In reality, instead of having headlines or descriptions in the "item" field, we'd have either URIs or keys into the content index mentioned earlier.

Table 12-2. Table for Mapping Content to Status Cookie Digits

Slot	Value	Item
0	2001090100	This slot shows that this is the first table to be issued on September 1, 2001.
1	2	"Squad Helps Dog Bite Victim"
2	r	"Red Tape Holds Up New Bridge"
3	1	"Yet Another Online Security Gaffe"
4	A	"Email Users Long For 'Good Times' "

The user of the client in this system would have a status cookie that starts out with 20010901002r1A. If serving exactly the same set of headlines, the server would increment the counters on all content tags, using Set-Cookie to overwrite the old status cookie with the new, whose value would begin with 20010901003r2B.

Later in the day, if we stop tracking the story "Email Users Long For 'Good Times' " and we replace that slot with a new story, "Disney To Buy Apple Rumors Persist," we'll need to create a new version of the map, 2001090101.

One of the critical pieces of the online privacy association's guidelines is access to data. This problem can easily be solved by keeping all data about the user's history and activity in the hands of the user. If the user wishes to see exactly what we've stored, he can simply look. Of course, with all that we've done in order to ensure parity of the data and to make access fast by storing only keys into indices, if we want to provide useful access, we'll need to provide a tool for dissection of the cookie.

Somewhere on our web site, we might then offer users the ability to see what their cookies mean. By ensuring that the domain name and the cookies' Path elements match, we'll be able to get all of the cookies that *Napersnik* has set for the user. Dissecting the cookies and turning them into human-readable form will allow the user to understand exactly what it is that we're doing, and will allow us to address the problem of access.

Interaction Diagrams

Seeing how the architectural components will interact with one another will help us to understand what follows. The important thing to recognize at this point is that *Napersnik* clients able to receive customized and targeted content fall into two categories: named (including both pseudonymous and verinymous) and unnamed (anonymous).

Figure 12-4 shows the named clients' interaction with other components of the system.

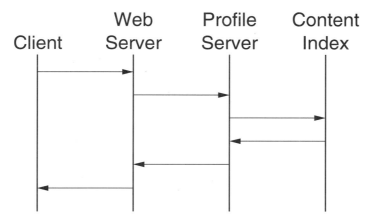

Figure 12-4. Napersnik Serving Content to Named Clients

In this configuration, the steps are:

1. The client sends a request to the web server, including a cookie if one is present. This cookie contains a nym, which identifies the user uniquely.

2. The web server parses the client's request and then sends the request for the content type to the profile server, along with the client's nym.

3. The content index uses the profile server's input to choose the appropriate content, returning it to the profile server.

4. The profile server returns the result to the requesting client.

In the anonymous client configuration, the steps are:

1. The client makes a request to the web server, including the profile cookie and the status cookie.

2. The web server parses the profile cookie to determine the profile.

3. The web server parses the status cookie.

4. The web server passes the request to the content server.

5. The content server returns the result to the web server.

6. The web server returns the result to the client.

The only real difference between these two is in the location of the profile. Anonymous clients have their profiles stored completely client-side. Named clients have their profiles kept in a centralized profile server. The difference isn't that great architecturally, but there are very serious differences between anonymous and named clients. Most significantly, clients with nyms will be able to build up reputations for potentially long periods of time. This will also enable a wider variety of secondary uses (particularly where raw HTTP dæmon log files are involved), including such things as data mining that could have implications on individual nyms within the system.

Figure 12-5 shows the anonymous clients' interaction with other system components.

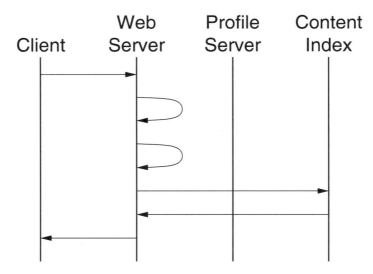

Figure 12-5. Napersnik Serving Content to Anonymous Clients

Deployment

As is always true, our deployment environment will be significant in our ability to enforce our security and privacy policies. We therefore want to give it some specific consideration.

Our deployment environment is illustrated in Figure 12-6.

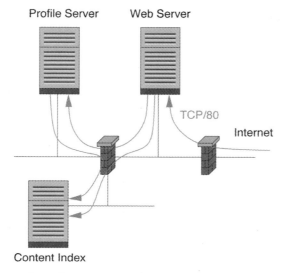

Figure 12-6. Napersnik Deployment Environment

There are several key issues that we want to observe. Our system is built such that it will allow only these connections:

- Internet to the web server's TCP port 80

- The web server to the profile server's TCP port 2800

- The profile server to the content index's TCP port 2801

- The web server to the content index's TCP Port 2801

Enforcement of this policy is in several forms:

- The hosts themselves do not listen on any other service ports.

- The firewalls perform egress filtering.

- The firewalls perform ingress filtering.

- The external firewall allows traffic only to the web server's TCP port 80 and reply packets.

- The internal firewall allows traffic from the web server to the profile server's TCP port 2800.

- The internal firewall allows traffic from the web server to the content index's TCP port 2801.

- The internal firewall allows traffic from the profile server to the content index's TCP port 2801.

Depending on administrative requirements, we might allow such things as certain types of ICMP traffic. We should take care to avoid such things as in-band administration channels that would allow direct contact between these hosts. A common practice is to leave remote terminal access services (like Telnet and rsh) enabled, despite security problems with these services. Even "secure" remote access service is a bad idea in many cases.

Sidebar: Plaintext Remote Access Considered Harmful

Telnet is generally unencrypted, which means that the sessions can be watched in transit. Combined with weak user authentication—such as reusable passwords—this provides a highly effective avenue of attack for persons able to watch network traffic in transit. Rsh has very weak authentication, allowing users to extend trust relationships, usually in insecure ways. Both are vulnerable to TCP session hijacking [7, 139].

An encrypted, remote-access interface is far better for most classes of attack, but remember that there are also risks there. Even if we're not vulnerable to things like sniffing reusable tokens or being able to hijack usable sessions, we still have done nothing to prevent an attacker who has achieved access to one of the machines that supports our system from gaining access to others. Of course, if passwords are not floating around, passwords vary from host to host, and other good authentication mechanisms are enforced, it's not like breaking into one system in the target will result in administrative control of all of them. It is worth pointing out, though, that this kind of authentication isn't common and that we do provide an avenue of attack against other systems that simply wasn't possible before. Any time we're providing administrative access over the same interfaces that are used to provide other services, we're creating a risk of one type of access being used to gain another.

A much more sensible practice is to have host access out-of-band. One such possibility would be direct console access. Another possibility would be to use serial consoles and a "console server" that would allow administrators to login to the console server and then to connect to the consoles of hosts they need to administer. Still another possibility would be to put a second network interface on each of the hosts and to allow administrative access over that interface.

When using any of these options, remember that the point of our network configuration is to provide as little access to other hosts and other networks as possible. Never would we want to think that we're safe simply because we put a firewall in front of a network of these servers and then allow all of the internal hosts unrestricted access to each other. Never would we want to restrict access between hosts on one network and then on a second network provide direct host to host access. An attacker who has taken over a machine should be stopped dead in his tracks, unable to penetrate the system further. Not thinking through the system in terms of failure modes is a sure way to build the system in such a way that the only thing slowing down an attacker's penetration is trying to determine which of the bewildering number of avenues into the system he should take.

In keeping with our secure design principle of least privilege, all traffic that is not explicitly allowed by policy—that includes both security and operational requirements—will be denied. In keeping with our secure design principle of compromise recording, logs will be generated for any denied packets, and the logs should be analyzed. Even if we have additional components in the system like automated intrusion detection systems, we should be sure that we're paying attention. There isn't anything to stop an attacker from deciding to attack the intrusion detection system first to keep any alarms on future activity from alerting administrators to his presence.

Operation

Operation of *Napersnik* is relatively straightforward. Rather than needing our system to manage campaigns aimed at consumer awareness and giving them ample opportunity to object to data collection and sharing practices, we simply provide a default state of anonymity. Users must go out of their way in order to become pseudonymous or verinymous in *Napersnik*. It is noteworthy that this philosophy is itself derived from one of our secure design principles: fail-safe defaults.

Various mechanisms can be used to entice users into "upgrading" their profiles to pseudonymous or verinymous. Some additional features of convenience can be offered to users with nyms in the system, and there are people who will find the value of convenience worth the additional amount of data collection and use that having a unique nym would offer. One such convenience might be the ability to continue to work in the system with the old profile, even if working from a different machine or local user account where the cookies are not the same. Describing such mechanisms in detail is beyond the present scope—we're concerned with the technical details of making such a system work. Convincing users to provide greater information about themselves and making good use of those available options is largely a question for our marketing and management groups.

Privacy is informational self-determination. Users who decide for themselves to tell their vendors their habits, their names, their addresses, and any other data are perfectly free to do so. The services that we as system developers and operators will be able to offer these users will be greater than the services that we can offer to anonymous users.

By building our system with anonymity—real anonymity, as strong as is feasible by the implementation environment—as the default, we'll provide a good basis for our customers to trust us.

Next Steps

Hopefully you have enjoyed this foray into the realm of privacy and security. Much has been covered here, but much more has been missed. I urge you, dear reader, to make immediate application of your newfound knowledge. Our aim with our information systems, be they web sites, application software, operating systems, or special-purpose devices, should be trustworthiness. Trustworthiness is largely the result of doing what we say and saying what we do.

Seeing this, or any other, book as the final word on security or privacy would be foolhardy.

A great deal of progress has been made in our understanding of the design and construction of modern computers since our first attempts to build programmable computing devices. Much has been written about security and privacy. One lesson through all of this is clear: there are no easy answers to such complicated problems. No one can know everything, but everyone can know something. We would do well to ensure that we have acquainted ourselves with the problems, that we understand how the systems we're building will behave, and that we foresee how our systems will interact with others. A tremendous source of wisdom on how we can understand and approach the many aspects of building trustworthy systems can be found in the research literature. I cannot emphasize enough the need to be familiar with the literature of our craft. This book's references should serve as a good starting point for further reading.

Nevertheless, if we spend all of our time looking to the past, perhaps in admiration of how far we have come, and how much better things are now than they were in years past, we will never progress. We do not progress by ignoring the lessons of the past; we move forward by building on them.

Take these lessons with you and be on the lookout for new ones as you go forward, designing, implementing, and operating systems of your own. By developing our systems to recognize users' rights to privacy and securing data about them, we can provide systems finally worthy of the trust that such systems tend to get.

For this, indeed, is the source of our ignorance—the fact that our knowledge can only be finite, while our ignorance must necessarily be infinite.

—Sir Karl Popper [153]

References

[1] ALBITZ, P., AND LIU, C. *DNS and BIND*, 4th ed. O'Reilly & Associates, Inc., April 2001.

[2] ALVESTRAND, H., KILLE, S., MILES, R., ROSE, M., AND THOMPSON, S. RFC 1495: Mapping between X.400 and RFC-822 message bodies, Aug. 1993. Obsoleted by RFC2156 [98]. Obsoletes RFC987, RFC1026, RFC1138, RFC1148, RFC1327 [99, 100, 101, 102, 82]. Status: Proposed Standard.

[3] ANDREWS, M. RFC 2308: Negative caching of DNS queries (DNS NCACHE), Mar. 1998. Updates RFC1034, RFC1035 [135, 136]. Status: Proposed Standard.

[4] ANKLESARIA, F., MCCAHILL, M., LINDNER, P., JOHNSON, D., TORREY, D., AND ALBERT, B. RFC 1436: The Internet Gopher Protocol (a distributed document search and retrieval protocol), Mar. 1993. Status: Informational.

[5] AUTOMATIC EXECUTION OF EMBEDDED MIME TYPES. CERT Advisory CA-2001-06, April 2001. [online] http://www.cert.org/advisories/CA-2001-06.html.

[6] BACKBYTES. Computing, 11 March 1999.

[7] BELLOVIN, S. M. Security problems in the tcp/ip protocol suite. *Computer Communication Review 19*, 2 (April 1989), 32–48. [online] http://www.research.att.com/~smb/papers/ipext.ps.

[8] BELLOVIN, S. M., AND CHESWICK, W. R. *Firewalls and Internet Security: Repelling the Wily Hacker: The Addison-Wesley Professional Computing Series*. Addison-Wesley, 1994.

[9] BERNERS-LEE, T., AND CONNOLLY, D. RFC 1866: Hypertext Markup Language — 2.0, Nov. 1995. Status: Proposed Standard.

[10] BERNERS-LEE, T., ET AL. *Weaving the Web: The Original Design and Ultimate Destiny of the World Wide Web by its Inventor*. Harper, September 1999.

[11] BERNERS-LEE, T., FIELDING, R., AND MASINTER, L. RFC 2396: Uniform Resource Identifiers (URI): Generic syntax, Aug. 1998. Status: Draft Standard.

[12] BERNERS-LEE, T., MASINTER, L., AND MCCAHILL, M. RFC 1738: Uniform resource locators (URL), Dec. 1994. Updated by RFC1808, RFC2368 [64, 86]. Status: Proposed Standard.

[13] BHUSHAN, A., BRADEN, B., CROWTHER, W., HARSLEM, E., HEAFNER, J., MCKENZIE, A., MELVIN, J., SUNDBERG, B., WATSON, D., AND WHITE, J. RFC 172: The file transfer protocol, June 1971. Obsoleted by RFC0265 [16]. Updates RFC0114 [17]. Updated by RFC0238 [23]. Status: Unknown.

[14] BHUSHAN, A., BRADEN, B., CROWTHER, W., HARSLEM, E., HEAFNER, J., MCKENZIE, A., SUNDBERG, B., WATSON, D., AND WHITE, J. RFC 264: The data transfer protocol, Jan. 1972. Obsoleted by RFC0354 [19]. Obsoletes RFC0171 [15]. Status: Unknown. Not online.

[15] BHUSHAN, A., BRADEN, R., CROWTHER, W., HARSLEM, E., HEAFNER, J., MCKENZIE, A., MELVIN, J., SUNDBERG, B., WATSON, D., AND WHITE, J. RFC 171: The Data Transfer Protocol, June 1971. Obsoleted by RFC0264 [14]. Updates RFC0114 [17]. Updated by RFC0238 [23]. Not online. Status: Unknown.

[16] BHUSHAN, A., BRADEN, R., CROWTHER, W., HARSLEM, E., HEAFNER, J. F., MCKENZIE, A. M., MELVIN, J. T., SUNDBERG, R. L., WATSON, R. W., AND WHITE, J. E. RFC 265: The File Transfer Protocol, Dec. 1971. Obsoleted by RFC0354 [19]. Obsoletes RFC0172 [13]. Updated by RFC0294 [18]. Status: Unknown.

[17] BHUSHAN, A. K. RFC 114: File transfer protocol, Apr. 1971. Updated by RFC0141, RFC0172, RFC0171 [83, 13, 15]. Status: Unknown. Not online.

[18] BHUSHAN, A. K. RFC 294: The use of "set data type" transaction in file transfer protocol, Jan. 1972. Updates RFC0265 [16]. Status: Unknown.

[19] BHUSHAN, A. K. RFC 354: File transfer protocol, July 1972. Obsoleted by RFC0542 [142]. Obsoletes RFC0264, RFC0265 [14, 16]. Updated by RFC0385 [20]. Status: Unknown. Format: TXT=58074 bytes.

[20] BHUSHAN, A. K. RFC 385: Comments on the file transfer protocol, Aug. 1972. Updates RFC0354 [19]. Updated by RFC0414 [21]. Status: Unknown.

[21] BHUSHAN, A. K. RFC 414: File transfer protocol (FTP) status and further comments, Dec. 1972. Updates RFC0385 [20]. Status: Unknown. Not online.

[22] BRADEN, R. STD 3: Host requirements, Oct. 1989. See also RFC1122, RFC1123 [24, 25].

[23] BRADEN, R. T. RFC 238: Comments on DTP and FTP proposals, Sept. 1971. Updates RFC0171, RFC0172 [15, 13]. Updated by RFC0269 [27]. Status: Unknown.

[24] BRADEN, R. T. RFC 1122: Requirements for Internet hosts — communication layers, Oct. 1989. See also STD0003 [22]. Status: Standard.

[25] BRADEN, R. T. RFC 1123: Requirements for Internet hosts — application and support, Oct. 1989. See also STD0003 [22]. Updates RFC0822 [42]. Updated by RFC2181 [58]. Status: Standard.

[26] BRANDEIS, L. Olmstead v. U.S., 277 U.S. 438, 48 S.Ct. 564, 1928.

[27] BRODIE, H. RFC 269: Some experience with file transfer, Dec. 1971. Updates RFC0122, RFC0238 [193, 23]. Status: Unknown. Format: TXT=5961 bytes.

[28] BRUNNER, J. *The Shockwave Rider*. Del Rey Books, 1975.

[29] BUGTRAQ MAILING LIST. [online] http://www.securityfocus.com/.

[30] CERT Coordination Center. [online] http://www.cert.org/.

[31] CERT Coordination Center FAQ, 2001.

[32] CHRISTIANSEN, T. What's the plural of 'virus'?, June. [online] http://language.perl.com/misc/virus.html.

[33] COGLIO, A., GOLDBERG, A., AND QIAN, Z. Toward a provably-correct implementation of the JVM bytecode verifier, 1998.

[34] COMPUTER INCIDENT ADVISORY CAPABILITY. [online] http://www.ciac.org/.

[35] CORBATÓ, F. J. On building systems that will fail. *Communications of the ACM* **34**, 9 (1991), 72–81.

[36] COSELL, B., AND WALDEN, D. C. RFC 435: Telnet issues, Jan. 1973. Updates RFC0318 [154]. Status: Unknown. Not online.

[37] COUNCIL OF EUROPE. Convention for the protection of individuals with regard to automatic processing of personal data. European Treaty Series No. 108, January 1981. [online] http://www.privacy.org/pi/intl_orgs/coe/dp_convention_108.txt.

[38] CRAMER, R., AND SHOUP, V. A practical public key cryptosystem provably secure against adaptive chosen ciphertext attack. In *CRYPTO* (1998), 13–25.

[39] CRISPIN, M. RFC 1730: Internet Message Access Protocol — Version 4, Dec. 1994. Obsoleted by RFC2060, RFC2061 [40, 41]. Status: Proposed Standard.

[40] CRISPIN, M. RFC 2060: Internet Message Access Protocol — Version 4rev1, Dec. 1996. Obsoletes RFC1730 [39]. Status: Proposed Standard.

[41] CRISPIN, M. RFC 2061: IMAP4 Compatibility with IMAP2BIS, Dec. 1996. Obsoletes RFC1730 [39]. Status: Informational.

[42] CROCKER, D. RFC 822: Standard for the format of ARPA Internet text messages, Aug. 1982. See also STD0011 [43]. Obsoletes RFC0733 [45]. Updated by RFC1123, RFC1138, RFC1148, RFC1327, RFC2156 [25, 101, 102, 82, 98]. Status: Standard.

[43] CROCKER, D. STD 11: Standard for the format of ARPA Internet text messages, Aug. 1982. Obsoletes RFC1653 [103]. See also RFC0822 [42].

[44] CROCKER, D., POGRAN, K. T., VITTAL, J., AND HENDERSON, D. A. RFC 724: Proposed official standard for the format of ARPA network messages, May 1977. Obsoleted by RFC0733 [45]. Status: Unknown. Not online.

[45] CROCKER, D., VITTAL, J., POGRAN, K. T., AND HENDERSON, D. A. RFC 733: Standard for the format of ARPA network text messages, Nov. 1977. Obsoleted by RFC0822 [42]. Obsoletes RFC0724 [44]. Status: Unknown.

[46] CURTIN, M., AND DOLSKE, J. A brute force search of DES keyspace. In *;login:*, vol. 23. USENIX, May 1998, 54–59.

[47] CURTIN, M., ELLISON, G., AND MONROE, D. Internet privacy project.

[48] CURTIN, M., ELLISON, G., AND MONROE, D. "What's Related?" Everything but Your Privacy. Tech. rep., The Ohio State University, Department of Computer and Information Science, October 1998.

[49] DAVIS, C., VIXIE, P., GOODWIN, T., AND DICKINSON, I. RFC 1876: A means for expressing location information in the domain name system, Jan. 1996. Updates RFC1034, RFC1035 [135, 136]. Status: Experimental.

[50] DEADLY TRANSMISSIONS. NSA Study, December 1970.

[51] DENNING, D. *Information Warfare and Security*. Addison-Wesley, 1999.

[52] DIERKS, T., AND ALLEN, C. The TLS protocol version 1.0. IETF, January 1999. RFC 2246.

[53] DIETRICH, S., LONG, N., AND DITTRICH, D. Analyzing distributed denial of service tools: The shaft case. In *Proceedings of 14th Systems Administration Conference (LISA 2000)* (December 2000), USENIX, 329–339.

[54] EASTLAKE, D. RFC 2137: Secure domain name system dynamic update, Apr. 1997. Updates RFC1035 [136]. Status: Proposed Standard.

[55] EASTLAKE, D., 3RD, AND KAUFMAN, C. RFC 2065: Domain name system security extensions, Jan. 1997. Updates RFC1034, RFC1035 [135, 136]. Status: Proposed Standard.

[56] EICHIN, M. W., AND ROCHLIS, J. A. With microscope and tweezers: An analysis of the Internet worm of 1988. In *IEEE Symposium on Research in Security and Privacy* (1989).

[57] ELZ, R., AND BUSH, R. RFC 1982: Serial number arithmetic, Aug. 1996. Updates RFC1034, RFC1035 [135, 136]. Status: Proposed Standard.

[58] ELZ, R., AND BUSH, R. RFC 2181: Clarifications to the DNS specification, July 1997. Updates RFC1034, RFC1035, RFC1123 [135, 136, 25]. Status: Proposed Standard.

[59] EUROPEAN UNION Charter of fundamental rights, December 2000. [online] http://www.europarl.eu.int/charter/pdf/text_en.pdf.

[60] EVERHART, C. F., MAMAKOS, L. A., ULLMANN, R., AND MOCKAPETRIS, P. V. RFC 1183: New DNS RR definitions, Oct. 1990. Updates RFC1034, RFC1035 [135, 136]. Status: Experimental.

[61] EXPLOREZIP TROJAN HORSE PROGRAM. CERT Advisory CA-1999-06, June 1999. [online] http://www.cert.org/advisories/CA-1999-06.html.

[62] FEIERTAG, R., AND NEUMANN, P. The foundations of a provably secure operating system (PSOS). In *AFIPS Conference Proceedings (NCC 79)* (New York, NY, June 1979), 329–334.

[63] FERRAIOLO, D., AND KUHN, R. Role-based access controls. In *15th NIST-NCSC National Computer Security Conference* (1992), 554–563.

[64] FIELDING, R. RFC 1808: Relative uniform resource locators, June 1995. Updates RFC1738 [12]. Updated by RFC2368 [86]. Status: Proposed Standard.

[65] FIELDING, R., GETTYS, J., MOGUL, J., FRYSTYK, H., MASINTER, L., LEACH, P., AND BERNERS-LEE, T. RFC 2616: Hypertext Transfer Protocol — HTTP/1.1, June 1999.

[66] FIELDING, R., GETTYS, J., MOGUL, J., FRYSTYK, H., MASINTER, L., LEACH, P., AND BERNERS-LEE, T. Hypertext transfer protocol — HTTP/1.1. RFC 2616, June 1999. [online] http://www.ietf.org/rfc/rfc2616.txt.

[67] FRANKS, J., HALLAM-BAKER, P., , HOSTETLER, J., LAWRENCE, S., LEACH, P., LUOTONEN, A., AND STEWART, L. Http authentication: Basic and digest access authentication, June 1999.

[68] FRASER, B. RFC 2196: Site security handbook, Sept. 1997. See also FYI0008 [87]. Obsoletes RFC1244 [88]. Status: Informational.

[69] FREDERICK P. BROOKS, J. *The Mythical Man-Month: Essays on Software Engineering*, anniversary ed. Addison Wesley, 1995.

[70] FREEH, L. J. Cybercrime. Statement for the Record Before the Senate Committee on Judiciary Subcommittee for the Technology, Terrorism, and Government Information, March 2000. [online] http://www.fbi.gov/congress/congress00/cyber032800.htm.

[71] FREIER, A. O., KARLTON, P., AND KOCHER, P. C. The SSL protocol version 3.0, November 1996. [online] http://home.netscape.com/eng/ssl3/draft302.txt.

[72] FYODOR. The art of port scanning. *Phrack Magazine*, September 1997.

[73] FYODOR. Remote OS detection via TCP/IP stack fingerprinting, April 1999.

[74] GARFINKEL, S. *Database Nation: The Death of Privacy in the 21st Century*, softcover ed. O'Reilly & Associates, Inc., January 2001.

[75] GELLENS, R. RFC 2384: POP URL scheme, Aug. 1998. Status: Proposed Standard.

[76] (GERMANY), F. C. C. Decision on national census, December 12, 1983.

[77] GOLDBERG, I. A. *A Pseudonymous Communications Infrastructure for the Internet*. Ph.D. thesis, University of California at Berkeley, 2000. [online] http://www.isaac.cs.berkeley.edu/ iang/thesis-final.pdf.

[78] GOLDSCHLAG, D. M., REED, M. G., AND SYVERSON, P. F. Hiding routing information. In *Information Hiding*, R. Anderson, ed., no. 1174 in LLNCS. Springer-Verlag, 1996, 137–150.

[79] GRAHAM, P. Ten e-commerce mistakes, 2001.

[80] HALL, C., GOLDBERG, I., AND SCHNEIER, B. Reaction attacks against several public-key cryptosystems. In *Proceedings of Information and Communication Security, ICICS'99*, (1999), Springer-Verlag, 2–12. [online] http://www.counterpane.com/reaction_attacks.html.

[81] HAPPY99.EXE TROJAN HORSE. CERT Incident Note IN-99-02, March 1999. [online] http://www.cert.org/incident_notes/IN-99-02.html.

[82] HARDCASTLE-KILLE, S. RFC 1327: Mapping between X.400(1988) /ISO 10021 and RFC 822, May 1992. Obsoleted by RFC1495, RFC2156 [2, 98]. Obsoletes RFC987, RFC1026, RFC1138, RFC1148 [99, 100, 101, 102]. Updates RFC0822, RFC0822 [42, 42]. Status: Proposed Standard.

[83] HARSLEM, E., AND HEAFNER, J. F. RFC 141: Comments on RFC 114: A file transfer protocol, Apr. 1971. Updates RFC0114 [17]. Status: Unknown.

[84] HARSLEM, E., AND STOUGHTON, R. RFC 225: Rand/UCSB network graphics experiment, Sept. 1971. Updates RFC0074 [191]. Status: Unknown. Not online.

[85] HASELTON, B., AND MCCARTHY, J. Internet Explorer "open cookie jar," May 2000. [online] http://www.peacefire.org/security/iecookies/.

[86] HOFFMAN, P., MASINTER, L., AND ZAWINSKI, J. RFC 2368: The mailto URL scheme, July 1998. Updates RFC1738, RFC1808 [12, 64]. Status: Proposed Standard.

[87] HOLBROOK, J. P., AND REYNOLDS, J. K. FYI 8: Site Security Handbook, July 1991. See also RFC1244 [88]. Updates FYI0008 [87]. Updated by FYI0008 [87].

[88] HOLBROOK, J. P., AND REYNOLDS, J. K. RFC 1244: Site security handbook, July 1991. See also FYI0008 [87]. Obsoleted by RFC2196, FYI0008 [68, 87]. Status: Informational.

[89] HOROWITZ, M., AND LUNT, S. RFC 2228: FTP security extensions, Oct. 1997. Updates RFC0959 [161]. Status: Proposed Standard.

[90] INFRAGARD. [online] http://www.infragard.net/.

[91] INTERNET MESSAGE FORMAT, 2001.

[92] JAGIELSKA, I., AND JAWORSKI, J. Neural network for predicting the performance of credit card accounts, 1996.

[93] JOHNS, M. S. RFC 912: Authentication service, Sept. 1984. Obsoleted by RFC0931 [94]. Status: Unknown.

[94] JOHNS, M. S. RFC 931: Authentication server, Jan. 1985. Obsoleted by RFC1413 [95]. Obsoletes RFC0912 [93]. Status: Unknown.

[95] JOHNS, M. S. RFC 1413: Identification protocol, Jan. 1993. Obsoletes RFC0931 [94]. Status: Proposed Standard.

[96] JONES, L. Good Times Virus Hoax FAQ, December 1998. [online] http://www.public.usit.net/lesjones/goodtimes.html.

[97] KARGER, P. A., AND SCHELL, R. R. Multics security evaluation, volume II: Vulnerability analysis. Tech. Rep. ESD-TR-74-193, Vol. II, ESD/AFSC, Electronic Systems Division, Air Force Systems Command, Hanscom Field, Bedford, MA 01731, June 1974.

[98] KILLE, S. RFC 2156: MIXER (Mime Internet X.400 Enhanced Relay): Mapping between X.400 and RFC 822/MIME, Jan. 1998. Obsoletes RFC0987, RFC1026, RFC1138, RFC1148, RFC1327, RFC1495 [99, 100, 101, 102, 82, 2]. Updates RFC0822 [42]. Status: Proposed Standard.

[99] KILLE, S. E. RFC 987: Mapping between X.400 and RFC 822, June 1986. Obsoleted by RFC2156 [98]. Updated by RFC1026, RFC1138, RFC1148 [100, 101, 102]. Status: Unknown.

[100] KILLE, S. E. RFC 1026: Addendum to RFC 987: (mapping between X.400 and RFC-822), Sept. 1987. Obsoleted by RFC1327, RFC1495, RFC2156 [82, 2, 98].

Updates RFC0987 [99]. Updated by RFC1138, RFC1148 [101, 102]. Status: Unknown.

[101] KILLE, S. E. RFC 1138: Mapping between X.400(1988) /ISO 10021 and RFC 822, Dec. 1989. Obsoleted by RFC1327, RFC1495, RFC2156 [82, 2, 98]. Updates RFC0822, RFC0987, RFC1026 [42, 99, 100]. Updated by RFC1148 [102]. Status: Experimental.

[102] KILLE, S. E. RFC 1148: Mapping between X.400(1988) /ISO 10021 and RFC 822, Mar. 1990. Obsoleted by RFC1327, RFC1495, RFC2156 [82, 2, 98]. Updates RFC0822, RFC0987, RFC1026, RFC1138 [42, 99, 100, 101]. Status: Experimental.

[103] KLENSIN, J., FREED, N., AND MOORE, K. RFC 1653: SMTP service extension for message size declaration, July 1994. See also STD0011 [43]. Obsoleted by RFC1870, STD0011 [104, 43]. Obsoletes RFC1427 [108]. Status: Draft Standard.

[104] KLENSIN, J., FREED, N., AND MOORE, K. RFC 1870: SMTP service extension for message size declaration, Nov. 1995. See also STD0010 [107]. Obsoletes RFC1653 [103]. Status: Standard.

[105] KLENSIN, J., FREED, N., ROSE, M., STEFFERUD, E., AND CROCKER, D. RFC 1651: SMTP service extensions, July 1994. Obsoleted by RFC1869, STD0010 [106, 107]. Obsoletes RFC1425 [109]. Status: Draft Standard.

[106] KLENSIN, J., FREED, N., ROSE, M., STEFFERUD, E., AND CROCKER, D. RFC 1869: SMTP service extensions, Nov. 1995. See also STD0010 [107]. Obsoletes RFC1651 [105]. Status: Standard.

[107] KLENSIN, J., FREED, N., ROSE, M., STEFFERUD, E., AND CROCKER, D. STD 10: SMTP Service Extensions, Nov. 1995. See also RFC821, RFC1869 [160, 106]. Obsoletes RFC1651 [105].

[108] KLENSIN, WG CHAIR, J., FREED, N., AND MOORE, K. RFC 1427: SMTP service extension for message size declaration, Feb. 1993. Obsoleted by RFC1653 [103]. Status: Proposed Standard.

[109] KLENSIN, WG CHAIR, J., FREED, N., ROSE, M., STEFFERUD, E., AND CROCKER, D. RFC 1425: SMTP service extensions, Feb. 1993. Obsoleted by RFC1651 [105]. Status: Proposed Standard.

[110] KORMANN, D. P., AND RUBIN, A. D. Risks of the passport single signon protocol. *Computer Networks, Elsevier Science Press 33* (2000), 51–58. [online] http://avirubin.com/passport.html.

[111] KRILANOVICH, M. RFC 399: SMFS login and logout, Sept. 1972. Obsoleted by RFC0431 [112]. Updates RFC0122 [193]. Status: Unknown.

[112] KRILANOVICH, M. RFC 431: Update on SMFS login and logout, Dec. 1972. Obsoletes RFC0399 [111]. Updates RFC0122 [193]. Status: Unknown.

[113] KRISTOL, D., AND MONTULLI, L. HTTP state management mechanism. RFC 2965, October 2000. [online] http://www.ietf.org/rfc/rfc2965.txt.

[114] KUBISZYN, M. S. Emerging legal guidance on "deep linking." GigaLaw.com, May 2000. [online] http://www.gigalaw.com/articles/kubiszyn-2000-05b-p1.html.

[115] KUDLICK, M. D., AND FEINLER, E. J. RFC 627: ASCII text file of hostnames, Mar. 1974. Status: Unknown. Not online.

[116] LEAR, E., FAIR, E., CROCKER, D., AND KESSLER, T. RFC 1627: Network 10 considered harmful (some practices shouldn't be codified), June 1994. Obsoleted by BCP0005, RFC1918 [165]. Status: Informational.

[117] LEYDEN, J. Code red bug hits Microsoft security update site. The Register, July 2001. [online] http://www.theregister.co.uk/content/56/20545.html.

[118] MANNING, B. RFC 1348: DNS NSAP RRs, July 1992. Obsoleted by RFC1637 [119]. Updates RFC1034, RFC1035 [135, 136]. Updated by RFC1637 [119]. Status: Experimental.

[119] MANNING, B., AND COLELLA, R. RFC 1637: DNS NSAP resource records, June 1994. Obsoleted by RFC1706 [120]. Obsoletes RFC1348 [118]. Updates RFC1348 [118]. Status: Experimental.

[120] MANNING, B., AND COLELLA, R. RFC 1706: DNS NSAP resource records, Oct. 1994. Obsoletes RFC1637 [119]. Status: Informational.

[121] MARKOFF, J. U.S. data-scrambling code cracked with home-made equipment. New York Times, July 17 1998. [online] http://www.nytimes.com/library/tech/98/07/biztech/articles/17encrypt.html.

[122] MASINTER, L. RFC 2397: The "data" URL scheme, Aug. 1998. Status: Proposed Standard.

[123] MCKENZIE, A. M. RFC 454: File transfer protocol — meeting announcement and a new proposed document, Feb. 1973. Status: Unknown. Not online.

[124] MCKENZIE, A. M. RFC 495: Telnet Protocol specifications, May 1973. Obsoletes RFC0158 [151]. Status: Unknown. Not online.

[125] MCNEALY, S. The case against absolute privacy. Washington Post, May 2001. [online] http://www.washingtonpost.com/ac2/wp-dyn?pagename=article&node=&contentId=A89273-2001May28.

[126] MELISSA MACRO VIRUS. CERT Advisory CA-1999-04, March 1999. [online] http://www.cert.org/advisories/CA-1999-04.html.

[127] MERKLE, R., AND HELLMAN, M. On the security of multiple encryption. *Communications of the ACM 24*, 7 (1981), 465–467.

[128] MICROSOFT CORPORATION. Microsoft security bulletin (ms00-033). Tech. rep., Microsoft Corporation, 2000. [online] http://www.microsoft.com/technet/security/bulletin/ms00-033.asp.

[129] MICROSOFT CORPORATION. Microsoft security bulletin (ms00-055). Tech. rep., Microsoft Corporation, 2000. [online] http://www.microsoft.com/TechNet/security/bulletin/MS00-055.asp.

[130] MOATS, R. RFC 2141: URN syntax, May 1997. Status: Proposed Standard.

[131] MOCKAPETRIS, P. STD 13: Domain Name System, Nov. 1987. See also RFC1034, RFC1035 [135, 136].

[132] MOCKAPETRIS, P. V. RFC 882: Domain names: Concepts and facilities, Nov. 1983. Obsoleted by RFC1034, RFC1035 [135, 136]. Updated by RFC0973 [134]. Status: Unknown.

[133] MOCKAPETRIS, P. V. RFC 883: Domain names: Implementation specification, Nov. 1983. Obsoleted by RFC1034, RFC1035 [135, 136]. Updated by RFC0973 [134]. Status: Unknown.

[134] MOCKAPETRIS, P. V. RFC 973: Domain system changes and observations, Jan. 1986. Obsoleted by RFC1034, RFC1035 [135, 136]. Updates RFC0882, RFC0883 [132, 133]. Status: Unknown.

[135] MOCKAPETRIS, P. V. RFC 1034: Domain names — concepts and facilities, Nov. 1987. Obsoletes RFC0973, RFC0882, RFC0883 [134, 132, 133]. See also STD0013 [131]. Updated by RFC1101, RFC1183, RFC1348, RFC1876, RFC1982, RFC2065, RFC2181, RFC2308 [137, 60, 118, 49, 57, 55, 58, 3]. Status: Standard.

[136] MOCKAPETRIS, P. V. RFC 1035: Domain names — implementation and specification, Nov. 1987. Obsoletes RFC0973, RFC0882, RFC0883 [134, 132, 133].

See also STD0013 [131]. Updated by RFC1101, RFC1183, RFC1348, RFC1876, RFC1982, RFC1995, RFC1996, RFC2065, RFC2181, RFC2136, RFC2137, RFC2308 [137, 60, 118, 49, 57, 148, 187, 55, 58, 188, 54, 3]. Status: Standard.

[137] MOCKAPETRIS, P. V. RFC 1101: DNS encoding of network names and other types, Apr. 1989. Updates RFC1034, RFC1035 [135, 136]. Status: Unknown.

[138] MOORE, K., AND FREED, N. Use of HTTP state management. RFC 2964, October 2000. [online] http://www.ietf.org/rfc/rfc2964.txt.

[139] MORRIS, R. T. A weakness in the 4.2bsd unix tcp/ip software. Computing Science Technical Report 117, AT&T Bell Laboratories, Murray Hill, NJ, February 1985. [online] ftp://ftp.research.att.com/dist/internet_security/117.ps.Z.

[140] NATIONAL BUREAU OF STANDARDS. NBS FIP pub 46, "data encryption standard," U.S. Department of Commerce, January 1977.

[141] NATIONAL INFORMATION PROTECTION CENTER. [online] http://www.nipc.gov/.

[142] NEIGUS, N. RFC 542: File transfer protocol, July 1973. Obsoleted by RFC0765 [156]. Obsoletes RFC0354 [19]. Status: Unknown. Format: TXT=100666 bytes. See also RFC354 [19], RFC454 [123], RFC495 [124].

[143] NEMETH, A. G. RFC 43: Proposed meeting, Apr. 1970. Updates RFC0122 [193]. Status: Unknown.

[144] NETWORK ADVERTISING INITIATIVE. NAI Self-Regulatory Principles. [online] http://www.networkadvertising.org/press/overview.shtml.

[145] NEUMANN, P., BOYER, R., FEIERTAG, R., LEVITT, K., AND ROBINSON, L. A provably secure operating system: The system, its applications, and proofs, second edition. Tech. Rep. CSL-116, Computer Science Laboratory, SRI International, Menlo Park, California, May 1980.

[146] NEUMANN, P. G. *Computer Related Risks.* ACM Press, Addison-Wesley, NY, USA, 1994.

[147] NEWMAN, C. RFC 2192: IMAP URL scheme, Sept. 1997. Status: Proposed Standard.

[148] OHTA, M. RFC 1995: Incremental zone transfer in DNS, Aug. 1996. Updates RFC1035 [136]. Status: Proposed Standard.

[149] O'SULLIVAN, T. C. RFC 137: Telnet Protocol — a proposed document, Apr. 1971. Updated by RFC0139 [150]. Status: Unknown. Not online.

[150] O'SULLIVAN, T. C. RFC 139: Discussion of Telnet Protocol, May 1971. See also RFC0393 [197]. Updates RFC0137 [149]. Updated by RFC0158 [151]. Status: Unknown. Not online.

[151] O'SULLIVAN, T. C. RFC 158: Telnet Protocol: A proposed document, May 1971. See also RFC0393 [197]. Obsoleted by RFC0495 [124]. Updates RFC0139 [150]. Updated by RFC0318 [154]. Status: Unknown. Not online.

[152] PEW INTERNET PROJECT. Trust and privacy online: Why Americans want to rewrite the rules, August 2000. [online] http://www.pewinternet.org/reports/toc.asp?Report=19.

[153] POPPER, S. K. Lecture to British Academy, 20 Jan. 1960. In *Proceedings of the British Academy* (1960), **46**, 69.

[154] POSTEL, J. RFC 318: Telnet protocols, Apr. 1972. Updates RFC0158 [151]. Updated by RFC0435 [36]. Status: Unknown. Not online. See also RFC0139 [150], RFC0158 [151].

[155] POSTEL, J. RFC 328: Suggested Telnet Protocol changes, Apr. 1972. Status: Unknown.

[156] POSTEL, J. RFC 765: File transfer protocol specification, June 1980. Obsoleted by RFC0959 [161]. Obsoletes RFC0542 [142]. Status: Unknown. Not online.

[157] POSTEL, J. RFC 768: User datagram protocol, Aug. 1980. Status: Standard. See also STD0006 [158].

[158] POSTEL, J. STD 6: User Datagram Protocol, Aug. 1980. See also RFC0768 [157].

[159] POSTEL, J. RFC 788: Simple mail transfer protocol, Nov. 1981. Obsoleted by RFC0821 [160]. Obsoletes RFC0780 [178]. Status: Unknown. Not online.

[160] POSTEL, J. RFC 821: Simple mail transfer protocol, Aug. 1982. See also STD0010 [107]. Obsoletes RFC0788 [159]. Status: Standard.

[161] POSTEL, J., AND REYNOLDS, J. K. RFC 959: File transfer protocol, Oct. 1985. Obsoletes RFC0765 [156]. Updated by RFC2228 [89]. Status: Standard.

[162] RAGGETT, D., HORS, A. L., AND JACOBS, I. HTML 4.0 Specification, Apr. 1998.

[163] RAYMOND, E. S., Ed. *The New Hacker's Dictionary*, 3d ed. MIT Press, 1996.

[164] REKHTER, Y., MOSKOWITZ, B., KARRENBERG, D., AND DE GROOT, G. RFC 1597: Address allocation for private internets, Mar. 1994. Obsoleted by BCP0005, RFC1918 [165]. Status: Informational.

[165] REKHTER, Y., MOSKOWITZ, B., KARRENBERG, D., DE GROOT, G. J., AND LEAR, E. RFC 1918: Address allocation for private internets, Feb. 1996. See also BCP0005. Obsoletes RFC1627, RFC1597 [116, 164]. Status: Best Current Practice.

[166] RESOURCE DESCRIPTION FRAMEWORK (RDF) MODEL AND SYNTAX SPECIFICATION. W3C Recommendation, February 1999.

[167] RIVEST, R. RFC 1321: The MD5 message-digest algorithm, Apr. 1992. Status: Informational.

[168] SALTZER, J. H., AND SCHROEDER, M. D. The protection of information in computer systems. In *Proceedings of the IEEE* (September 1975) **63**, 1278–1308.

[169] SANS INSTITUTE. [online] http://www.sans.org/.

[170] SCHNEIER, B. *Applied Cryptography*, 2d ed. John Wiley & Sons, 1996.

[171] SCHNEIER, B. *Secrets and Lies*. John Wiley & Sons, 2000.

[172] SCHNEIER, B. Why digital signatures are not signatures. CRYPTO-GRAM, November 2000. [online] http://www.counterpane.com/crypto-gram-0011.html.

[173] SECURE HASH STANDARD, 1995.

[174] SEELEY, D. A tour of the worm. In *USENIX Conference Proceedings* (San Diego, CA, Winter 1989), USENIX, 287–304.

[175] SHOCH, J. F., AND HUPP, J. A. The worm programs—early experience with a distributed computation. *Communications of the ACM* **25**, 3 (March 1982), 172–180.

[176] SIMPLE MAIL TRANSFER PROTOCOL, 2001.

[177] SLUIZER, S., AND POSTEL, J. RFC 772: Mail transfer protocol, Sept. 1980. Obsoleted by RFC0780 [178]. Status: Unknown. Not online.

[178] SLUIZER, S., AND POSTEL, J. RFC 780: Mail transfer protocol, May 1981. Obsoleted by RFC0788 [159]. Obsoletes RFC0772 [177]. Status: Unknown. Not online.

[179] SMITH, R. M. Web bug FAQ. Tech. rep., Privacy Foundation, 2000. [online] http://www.privacyfoundation.org/education.html.

[180] SPAFFORD, E. H. The Internet worm incident. In *European Software Engineering Conference* (1989), no. 87 in Lecture Notes in Computer Science, Springer-Verlag.

[181] STOLFO, S., FAN, W., LEE, W., PRODROMIDIS, A., AND CHAN, P. Credit card fraud detection using meta-learning: Issues and initial results, 1997.

[182] THOMPSON, K. Reflections on trusting trust. *Communication of the ACM 27*, 8 (August 1984), 761–763. [online] http://www.acm.org/classics/sep95/.

[183] UNITED NATIONS. The universal declaration of human rights, December 1948. [online] http://www.privacy.org/pi/intl_orgs/un/intl-decl-human-rights.txt.

[184] UNITED NATIONS International covenant on civil and political rights, 1976. [online] http://www.privacy.org/pi/intl_orgs/un/international_covenant_civil_political _rights.txt.

[185] UPTON, J. U-M medical records end up on web. The Detroit News, February 1999.

[186] VBS/ONTHEFLY. (Anna Kournikova) malicious code. CERT Advisory CA-2001-03, February 2001. [online] http://www.cert.org/advisories/CA-2001-03.html.

[187] VIXIE, P. RFC 1996: A mechanism for prompt notification of zone changes (DNS NOTIFY), Aug. 1996. Updates RFC1035 [136]. Status: Proposed Standard.

[188] VIXIE, EDITOR, P., THOMSON, S., REKHTER, Y., AND BOUND, J. RFC 2136: Dynamic updates in the domain name system (DNS UPDATE), Apr. 1997. Updates RFC1035 [136]. Status: Proposed Standard.

[189] W3C. Platform for privacy preferences. [online] http://www.w3.org/P3P/.

[190] WARREN, S. D., AND BRANDEIS, L. D. The right to privacy. *Harvard Law Review* **IV**, 5 (December 1890).

[191] WHITE, J. E. RFC 74: Specifications for network use of the UCSB on-line system, Oct. 1970. Updated by RFC0217, RFC0225 [194, 84]. Status: Unknown. Not online.

[192] WHITE, J. E. RFC 105: Network specifications for remote job entry and remote job output retrieval at UCSB, Mar. 1971. Updated by RFC0217 [194]. Status: Unknown.

[193] WHITE, J. E. RFC 122: Network specifications for UCSB's simple-minded file system, Apr. 1971. Updated by RFC0217, RFC0269, RFC0399, RFC0043, RFC0431 [194, 27, 111, 143, 112]. Status: Unknown. Not online.

[194] WHITE, J. E. RFC 217: Specifications changes for OLS, RJE/RJOR, and SMFS, Sept. 1971. Updates RFC0074, RFC0105, RFC0122 [191, 192, 193]. Status: Unknown.

[195] WHITMORE, J., BENSOUSSAN, A., GREEN, P., HUNT, D., ROBZIAR, A., AND STERN, J. Design for multics security enhancements. Tech. Rep. ESD-TR-74-176, ESD/AFSC, Hanscom AFB, Bedford, MA 01731, December 1973.

[196] WINETT, J. M. RFC 109: Level III server protocol for the Lincoln Laboratory NIC 360/67 host, Mar. 1971. See also RFC0393 [197]. Status: Unknown. Not online.

[197] WINETT, J. M. RFC 393: Comments on Telnet Protocol changes, Oct. 1972. See also RFC0109, RFC0139, RFC0158, RFC0318, RFC0328 [196, 150, 151, 154, 155]. Status: Unknown.

[198] ZWICKY, E. D., COOPER, S., AND CHAPMAN, D. B. *Building Internet Firewalls*, 2nd ed. O'Reilly & Associates, June 2000.

Index

Apress Titles

ISBN	PRICE	AUTHOR	TITLE
1-893115-73-9	$34.95	Abbott	Voice Enabling Web Applications: VoiceXML and Beyond
1-893115-01-1	$39.95	Appleman	Appleman's Win32 API Puzzle Book and Tutorial for Visual Basic Programmers
1-893115-23-2	$29.95	Appleman	How Computer Programming Works
1-893115-97-6	$39.95	Appleman	Moving to VB. NET: Strategies, Concepts, and Code
1-893115-09-7	$29.95	Baum	Dave Baum's Definitive Guide to LEGO MINDSTORMS
1-893115-84-4	$29.95	Baum, Gasperi, Hempel, and Villa	Extreme MINDSTORMS
1-893115-82-8	$59.95	Ben-Gan/Moreau	Advanced Transact-SQL for SQL Server 2000
1-893115-48-8	$29.95	Bischof	The .NET Languages: A Quick Translation Guide
1-893115-67-4	$49.95	Borge	Managing Enterprise Systems with the Windows Script Host
1-893115-99-2	$39.95	Cornell/Morrison	Programming VB .NET: A Guide for Experienced Programmers
1-893115-72-0	$39.95	Curtin	Developing Trust: Online Privacy and Security
1-893115-71-2	$39.95	Ferguson	Mobile .NET
1-893115-90-9	$44.95	Finsel	The Handbook for Reluctant Database Administrators
1-893115-85-2	$34.95	Gilmore	A Programmer's Introduction to PHP 4.0
1-893115-36-4	$34.95	Goodwill	Apache Jakarta-Tomcat
1-893115-17-8	$59.95	Gross	A Programmer's Introduction to Windows DNA
1-893115-62-3	$39.95	Gunnerson	A Programmer's Introduction to C#, Second Edition
1-893115-10-0	$34.95	Holub	Taming Java Threads
1-893115-04-6	$34.95	Hyman/Vaddadi	Mike and Phani's Essential C++ Techniques
1-893115-96-8	$59.95	Jorelid	J2EE FrontEnd Technologies: A Programmer's Guide to Servlets, JavaServer Pages, and Enterprise JavaBeans
1-893115-50-X	$34.95	Knudsen	Wireless Java: Developing with Java 2, Micro Edition
1-893115-79-8	$49.95	Kofler	Definitive Guide to Excel VBA
1-893115-57-7	$39.95	Kofler	MySQL

ISBN	PRICE	AUTHOR	TITLE
1-893115-87-9	$39.95	Kurata	Doing Web Development: Client-Side Techniques
1-893115-75-5	$44.95	Kurniawan	Internet Programming with VB
1-893115-19-4	$49.95	Macdonald	Serious ADO: Universal Data Access with Visual Basic
1-893115-06-2	$39.95	Marquis/Smith	A Visual Basic 6.0 Programmer's Toolkit
1-893115-22-4	$27.95	McCarter	David McCarter's VB Tips and Techniques
1-893115-76-3	$49.95	Morrison	C++ For VB Programmers
1-893115-80-1	$39.95	Newmarch	A Programmer's Guide to Jini Technology
1-893115-58-5	$49.95	Oellermann	Architecting Web Services
1-893115-81-X	$39.95	Pike	SQL Server: Common Problems, Tested Solutions
1-893115-20-8	$34.95	Rischpater	Wireless Web Development
1-893115-93-3	$34.95	Rischpater	Wireless Web Development with PHP and WAP
1-893115-89-5	$59.95	Shemitz	Kylix: The Professional Developer's Guide and Reference
1-893115-40-2	$39.95	Sill	An Introduction to qmail
1-893115-24-0	$49.95	Sinclair	From Access to SQL Server
1-893115-94-1	$29.95	Spolsky	User Interface Design for Programmers
1-893115-53-4	$39.95	Sweeney	Visual Basic for Testers
1-893115-29-1	$44.95	Thomsen	Database Programming with Visual Basic .NET
1-893115-65-8	$39.95	Tiffany	Pocket PC Database Development with eMbedded Visual Basic
1-893115-59-3	$59.95	Troelsen	C# and the .NET Platform
1-893115-26-7	$59.95	Troelsen	Visual Basic .NET and the .NET Platform
1-893115-54-2	$49.95	Trueblood/Lovett	Data Mining and Statistical Analysis Using SQL
1-893115-16-X	$49.95	Vaughn	ADO Examples and Best Practices
1-893115-83-6	$44.95	Wells	Code Centric: T-SQL Programming with Stored Procedures and Triggers
1-893115-95-X	$49.95	Welschenbach	Cryptography in C and C++
1-893115-05-4	$39.95	Williamson	Writing Cross-Browser Dynamic HTML
1-893115-78-X	$49.95	Zukowski	Definitive Guide to Swing for Java 2, Second Edition
1-893115-92-5	$49.95	Zukowski	Java Collections

Available at bookstores nationwide or from Springer Verlag New York, Inc. at 1-800-777-4643; fax 1-212-533-3503. Contact us for more information at sales@apress.com.

Apress Titles Publishing SOON!

ISBN	AUTHOR	TITLE
1-893115-39-9	Chand	A Programmer's Guide to ADO.NET in C#
1-893115-44-5	Cook	Robot Building for Beginners
1-893115-42-9	Foo/Lee	XML Programming Using the Microsoft XML Parser
1-893115-55-0	Frenz	Visual Basic for Scientists
1-893115-30-5	Harkins/Reid	Access SQL to SQL Server Desktop Edition and Beyond
1-893115-49-6	Kilburn	Palm Programming in Basic
1-893115-38-0	Lafler	Power AOL: A Survival Guide
1-893115-28-3	Laksberg/Challa	Managed Extensions in C++ for .NET
1-893115-46-1	Lathrop	Linux in Small Business: A Practical Users' Guide
1-893115-43-7	Stephenson	Standard VB: An Enterprise Developer's Reference for VB 6 and VB .NET
1-59059-002-3	Symmonds	Internationalization and Localization Using Microsoft .NET
1-893115-68-2	Vaughn	ADO Examples and Best Practices, Second Edition
1-893115-98-4	Zukowski	Learn Java with JBuilder 6

Available at bookstores nationwide or from Springer Verlag New York, Inc. at 1-800-777-4643;
fax 1-212-533-3503. Contact us for more information at sales@apress.com.

books for professionals by professionals™

About Apress

Apress, located in Berkeley, CA, is an innovative publishing company devoted to meeting the needs of existing and potential programming professionals. Simply put, the "A" in Apress stands for the "Author's Press™." Apress' unique author-centric approach to publishing grew from conversations between Dan Appleman and Gary Cornell, authors of best-selling, highly regarded computer books. In 1998, they set out to create a publishing company that emphasized quality above all else, a company with books that would be considered the best in their market. Dan and Gary's vision has resulted in over 30 widely acclaimed titles by some of the industry's leading software professionals.

Do You Have What It Takes to Write for Apress?

Apress is rapidly expanding its publishing program. If you can write and refuse to compromise on the quality of your work, if you believe in doing more than rehashing existing documentation, and if you're looking for opportunities and rewards that go far beyond those offered by traditional publishing houses, we want to hear from you!

Consider these innovations that we offer all of our authors:

- **Top royalties with *no* hidden switch statements**
  Authors typically only receive half of their normal royalty rate on foreign sales. In contrast, Apress' royalty rate remains the same for both foreign and domestic sales.

- **A mechanism for authors to obtain equity in Apress**
  Unlike the software industry, where stock options are essential to motivate and retain software professionals, the publishing industry has adhered to an outdated compensation model based on royalties alone. In the spirit of most software companies, Apress reserves a significant portion of its equity for authors.

- **Serious treatment of the technical review process**
  Each Apress book has a technical reviewing team whose remuneration depends in part on the success of the book since they too receive royalties.

Moreover, through a partnership with Springer-Verlag, one of the world's major publishing houses, Apress has significant venture capital behind it. Thus, we have the resources to produce the highest quality books *and* market them aggressively.

If you fit the model of the Apress author who can write a book that gives the "professional what he or she needs to know™," then please contact one of our Editorial Directors, Gary Cornell (gary_cornell@apress.com), Dan Appleman (dan_appleman@apress.com), Karen Watterson (karen_watterson@apress.com) or Jason Gilmore (jason_gilmore@apress.com) for more information.